THE
SALTWATER
FISHERMAN'S
BIBLE

THE SALTWATER FISHERMAN'S BIBLE

THIRD EDITION

Erwin A. Bauer

Revised by Bob Stearns

DOUBLEDAY

NEW YORK   LONDON   TORONTO   SYDNEY   AUCKLAND

PUBLISHED BY DOUBLEDAY
a division of Bantam Doubleday Dell Publishing Group, Inc.
1540 Broadway, New York, New York 10036

DOUBLEDAY and the portrayal of an anchor
with a dolphin are trademarks of Doubleday, a division
of Bantam Doubleday Dell Publishing Group, Inc.

Library of Congress Cataloging-in-Publication Data

Bauer, Erwin A.
The saltwater fisherman's bible / Erwin A. Bauer. — 3rd ed. /
revised by Bob Stearns.
p.   cm.
1. Saltwater fishing.   I. Stearns, Bob.   II. Title.
SH457.B38   1991
799.1′6—dc20   91-7900
                                                          CIP

ISBN 0-385-26444-5

20 19 18 17 16 15 14 13 12 11

CONTENTS

PART I—SALTWATER GAMEFISH

1.	SHALLOW-WATER GAMEFISH	9
2.	TARPON IN DEEPER WATER	21
3.	SNOOK	29
4.	THE BILLFISHES	34
5.	THE MACKERELS	46
6.	THE TUNAS	50
7.	THE JACKS	58
8.	FISH OF THE SURF	62
9.	PACIFIC SALMON	74
10.	BOTTOM FISHES OF THE ATLANTIC AND GULF OF MEXICO	80
11.	BOTTOM FISHES OF THE PACIFIC COAST	90
12.	UNUSUAL GAMEFISH	99
13.	SHARKS, LARGE AND SMALL	106

PART II—SALTWATER TACKLE

14.	SPINNING AND BAITCASTING TACKLE	115
15.	SALTWATER FLY FISHING	119
16.	BIG-GAME TACKLE	127
17.	ARTIFICIAL LURES	132
18.	KNOTS, BAITS, AND RIGGING	142
19.	FISHING WITH LIVE BAIT	154
20.	CHUMMING AND CHUNKING	159
21.	HOOKING, LANDING, AND RELEASING GAMEFISH	165
	THE INTERNATIONAL GAMEFISH ASSOCIATION	171
	FOR FURTHER READING	172

ACKNOWLEDGMENTS

The authors would like to thank the following for their contributions to this book: Joel Arrington for information on red drum; the International Game Fish Association, and in particular Elwood Harry and Mike Leach, for photos and information on the IGFA; Don Mann for information on livebaiting billfish and high-speed trolling lures; Terry Rudnick for information on chinook salmon fishing; and Walt Stearns for the many line drawings that are a vital part of this book.

PART I

SALTWATER GAMEFISH

*As tarpon feed more at night than during daylight, it is easier to hook them
after the sun goes down.*

Chapter 1

SHALLOW-WATER GAMEFISH

Until about fifteen years ago, when a saltwater angler mentioned "fishing the flats" the images that immediately came to mind were the shimmering coraline shallows of the Florida Keys, Florida Bay, and the Bahamas. The only fish that were seriously considered to be "flats fish" were bonefish, tarpon, permit, sharks, barracuda, and small red drum (called "redfish" or simply "reds" along the Gulf Coast states).

But there are interesting shallows in other parts of the United States. The basic technique of flats fishing—stalking the fish by sight before making the cast—can be practiced in quite a few places in many other coastal states. There are lots of fishable flats in more northerly latitudes and, in fact, in all of the world's temperate and tropical oceans. Many fishable shallows are completely overlooked by anglers more inclined toward deepwater fishing.

Bluefish, for example, are not generally considered to be a flats fish. Yet they willingly seek forage in water that's less than three-feet deep, and if that water also happens to be clear enough to see them, then it truly becomes a flats fishing situation in every sense of the word. We have caught blues that would on occasion top 10 pounds on flats from Florida to Cape Cod. Many other anglers have reported similar experiences. There are also some areas of the northeastern coast where striped bass can be caught on the flats.

We have even fished some flats for several species of Pacific salmon, most notably chums, pinks, and silvers (cohos), usually on sandy bars in the tidewater mouths of those rivers where wave action is not a problem. This, too, has been reported by others in various locations from Oregon all the way up through Canada and southeastern Alaska.

Sometimes a flat is not very extensive, perhaps just shallow water over a sandbar at a particular stage of the tide, or the seaward shoaling extension of a point along a quiet beach. It may not even be as large as the floor plan of a small house, and catching fish there is often a matter of precise timing—and patience. The right stage of the tide, the right time of day, the right month(s) of the year, and the right weather conditions are all factors critical to success. But the results can most definitely be worth the wait.

Consider, for example, the first time we discovered flats fishing for salmon along the edge of a tiny, low-lying island at the mouth of a small Alaska river that empties into the Bering Sea. We were nearing the peak of an unusually high full-moon spring tide, which meant that this particular flooding water would peak at least three feet higher than the average high for the area, and even an extra foot or so above the height reached by the typical spring tide. We were there right at the peak of the chum salmon run, with thousands of ocean-bright fish entering the river on each high tide.

This unique combination of circumstances set up an exciting situation. There was a 10- to 15-foot-wide ribbon of almost white sand along the perimeter of the island that was much lighter and brighter than the typically dark, muddy bottom elsewhere. This flat was always dry land on all but spring tides, and without the unusual height of this particular tide still would never have sufficient water depth for big fish to navigate. But the extra foot of tide made the difference, and for over two hours we enjoyed Florida flatslike fishing for chum salmon that averaged 10 to 15 pounds. We would stand in one spot and let the fish come to us. We could see them from almost 100 yards away, looking like bonefish in the clear tidal water.

We would cast a fly or very light lure with spinning

A hen chum salmon, saltwater bright, taken on a fly in tidewater.

tackle, leading the fish and placing it in front of them in the same way one would cast to a bonefish. Invariably one or two fish would separate from the approaching school like wolves from a pack, stalk the lure, and attack with a short rush. It was every bit as exciting as fishing a Florida or Bahamas flat. We have repeated that same scenario a number of times since then, because of the predictability of those super-high tides and the exact time when the chum salmon arrive.

All shallow-water fish activity is governed by tide, weather, and season—even in the tropics, where day-to-day temperatures may vary very little. For some reason bonefish in such places as Christmas Island in the Pacific and Los Roques off Venezuela in the Caribbean have periods of the year when the fishing is better than others. Spring and fall, for example, are almost always more productive for bone-

fish—on the average—than winter or the peak heat of summer. But warm winter days (and some cold ones too) can also provide super bonefishing, while the hot midday periods of July and August are often a bust.

Big tarpon usually come into the Florida Keys flats in spring, starting in March as weather and water temperatures allow, and peaking in late May or early June. By July they have decreased in numbers very noticeably, and by August they're scarce. Yet along the northern coast of the Gulf of Mexico, July and August are the peak months for their appearance in the inshore shallows, and there are scattered flats along that coastline where, when conditions are just right, they can be sight-fished.

Tarpon occasionally show up on the Florida flats as early as January, usually briefly during really warm periods between cold fronts. The basic requirement for their appearance is water temperature. If it isn't at least 75 degrees F, don't waste your time looking in skinny water, even though they might be rolling energetically in a nearby deep channel where the temperature is as low as 70.

Bonefish can tolerate cooler water than tarpon. They've been caught on the seaward edges of flats with water temperatures as low as 56 degrees, often gathered in immense, sometimes hovering schools, apparently waiting for warmer times. On rare occasions we've seen them tailing when it was as low as 64 degrees, but they seem to become most active when the temperature is between 72 and 88. We've caught them in water of 92 degrees, although they seldom show the same amount of interest in food as they do at 75 to 85.

Permit, that giant member of the pompano family, have a preferred temperature range similar to the tarpon's. They begin to show at around 72 degrees and seem to be just as willing to eat at 92.

Tailing permit in clear water are very wary and must be approached quietly.

Redfish, the Gulf of Mexico angler's name for red drum (channel bass, spot-tail drum), seem to be most happy in water that's between 60 and 95 degrees. Sharks usually disappear if the water falls below 70 degrees, but seem quite content to look for food at 95 degrees. Barracuda move onto the flats readily at water temperatures in the high 50s or low 60s, but once it tops 90 the larger fish will usually be back in deeper water. Bluefish like it cooler, too, and show up most readily in the 50 to 70 range. Black drum like the flats, at least in some areas, and also parallel the red drum in their temperature preferences. Like the redfish, they also tend to be smaller on the flats than in the deeper channels, offshore, or in the surf. Anything over 10 pounds is big for either species in thin water.

Except in some places. A few red drum over 30 pounds have been caught on the flats in a few North Carolina sounds, in relatively clear water where sight casting was possible. It takes exactly the right conditions—summertime and light wind being the prime requisites.

Other fish that sometimes show up in the clear shallows include seatrout, grouper, jewfish, a few species of snapper, Spanish mackerel. The mutton snapper, which often grows to 15 pounds or more, is a frequent visitor to the flats in Florida and the Bahamas. Horseye and almaco jacks are frequently found on Bahamas flats, especially along the edges. And by the way, fishing the deeper edges of the flats is an art that we'll cover shortly.

Even blue-water species show up at very rare intervals. A school of small (less than 10 pounds) dorado (dolphin-fish) will invade the Florida Bay flats near Flamingo once or twice every decade, staying for several days and giving the small mullet fits. And a bonefish guide fishing the flats on the ocean side of North Key Largo once found a big blue marlin (estimated at 300 pounds or more) looking for something to eat in less than five feet of water. Another guide in Florida Bay found a small swordfish (under 100 lbs) cruising the flats.

Tides are everything to the flats fisherman. Basically, gamefish move onto the flats with the rising tide and work their way back to deeper water as the tide falls. Certain species show up on certain flats, or parts of a flat, at certain stages of the tide. That's because these fish also travel along the flat with the tide, rather than moving straight in from deeper water and then returning seaward by simply making a 180-degree turn. In fact, they often move onto the flat from one end and exit from the other.

The modern flats skiff is an advanced boat design with shallow draft and multiple capabilities.

Although most fish move into skinny water to feed with the tide, others simply use the shallows as a convenient highway. Tarpon most often use flats for the latter reason, and may only come onto certain flats from deep water when the tide is falling—in contrast to the movement of those species that come for food. Nevertheless, in spite of the fact that tarpon rarely feed on the flats during daylight hours, they will often hit a properly presented fly, lure, or bait if it's something they like.

No rule of fishing is ever cast in concrete. All species do the unexpected now and then. So don't be surprised if you find bonefish pushing up into very shallow water, tails, dorsals, and sometimes backs completely exposed, feeding with both abandon and an apparent total disregard for a rapidly falling tide. Reason? An unusual abundance of shrimp, crabs, sandworms, or other forage would be a reasonable guess. In spite of what would appear to be total absorption in their search for food, bonefish are not easy to catch at such times. Like all other fish in very shallow water during a falling tide, they usually are extra spooky, and even a perfect cast can cause a panicky exodus to deeper water.

As for tackle, what's needed for this type of fishing falls into three categories: ultralight, light, and medium, in spinning, baitcasting, and fly-fishing equipment. (See Part II, Tackle and Techniques, for a detailed explanation of all tackle discussed in this book.)

For the most part, the weight of the tackle you'll need is governed by two factors: the size of the fish you plan to catch, and the actual weight of the lure or bait you'll be casting.

Bonefish, redfish, permit, and even on occasion bluefish can be exceptionally spooky at times, especially during very calm conditions, and the only way to take them is to use a very light lure or bait. Heavy lines do not cast these well, so that means going to light or ultralight gear. A ¼-ounce skimmer jig, for example, doesn't cast well on lines heavier than 8- or 10-pound test. Since distance and accuracy count a great deal, experienced anglers typically choose 4- to 8-pound-test monofilament.

A good rule of thumb for open-water accuracy and distance casting is this: If the lure or bait weighs ¼ ounce or less, use 6-pound test or less. For ⅜ ounce or less, 8-pound mono or lighter is adequate. A ½ ounce lure or bait calls for 12-pound line maximum; 10 is better. For ¾ ounce or higher, you can get good results with 15. Anything over 15-pound test requires so much weight that it makes too much noise hitting

the water on all but very windy days. And under those conditions, an extra-heavy lure with 12 or 15 might be necessary just to cast accurately. Somehow lines testing much over 17-pound test prove to be counterproductive.

LURES AND BAITS

Barracuda

Usually big barracuda come up on the flats of the Florida Keys and the Bahamas in the winter months, although some are caught all year except when the weather is exceptionally hot. Surprisingly, live shrimp is not a particularly effective bait, but just about any small live fish is. Unquestionably the most exciting way to catch shallow-water 'cudas is on a tube lure. This is just a 12- to 18-inch-long piece of ¼-inch i.d. surgical tubing in natural or bright colors, with an inside wire running its length and a couple of 2/0 treble hooks (one at the end, the other near the middle). A small lead sinker (¼ to ½ ounce) is usually added to the front end for extra casting weight.

Barracuda of all sizes are common sights on tropical flats. Small baitfish and tube lures catch them.

This unlikely looking rig is cast out at least 12 to 20 feet in front of the cruising barracuda and retrieved as fast as possible. Spinning reels with high gear ratios are best for this, and it is almost impossible to retrieve the lure too fast. The skipping and sliding action and its long, skinny shape are more than all but the most educated 'cudas can resist. The fish often goes completely airborne in its torpedolike strike. Barracuda that top 50 pounds have been taken in just two to three feet of water this way, an extremely exciting and visually stimulating experience.

Bluefish

This unique and virtually omnipresent gamefish will be discussed in more detail in Chapter 12, but suffice it to say here that they are very much at home in shallow water. Look for them over sandbars, in inlets, and inside bays, cruising around looking for food just like they owned the place. Which, as far as anything smaller is concerned, they do. As aggressive as bluefish are in deeper water, now they suddenly become much more wary if approached too closely.

But a long cast with a surface lure, especially a slider, pencil popper, or floater diver that doesn't spook them by landing too close will certainly draw their attention, and they'll usually attack aggressively. It's pretty exciting to watch them dart after the lure and strike it savagely. Light tackle is the key here, just like the spinning, baitcasting, or fly tackle you would use for bonefish. The typical flats bluefish rarely exceeds 10 pounds; most are half that size.

Anglers wishing to catch them on fly tackle may find the required cast under those conditions is a bit too long. An easy solution is to have a companion cast a hookless lure and tease the blues to within fly range. A pod of frenzied fish competing for the lure will come closer to the boat. Brightly colored poppers and streamers seem to work, especially if they have a few strands of mylar added for flash.

A bonefish has a small mouth, so lures or baits must also be small. This ⅜-ounce flathead skimmer jig is just right.

Bonefish

Good baits are live or at least fresh shrimp and small live crabs. In the Bahamas, a piece of fresh conch is one of the best (harvesting live conchs in Florida is illegal). A whole shrimp is by far the most popular in the Florida Keys. A thumbnail-size piece of fresh shrimp added to the hook of a skimmer jig is also a deadly combination, as is a small piece of fresh squid or conch.

As for "pure" lures, a ¼- to ⅜-ounce skimmer jig is excellent. Popular colors are brown, yellow, white, pink, and various combinations. Another lure that is rapidly becoming very popular because of its lifelike motion in the water is a short freshwater curlytail plastic worm. The best length is around 4 inches, thus longer worms should be cut down to that size. Rootbeer seems to be the most effective color, although the others mentioned above for jigs will work too. Just as in bass fishing, it should be rigged weedless (see Part II, Tackle and Techniques) with just enough weight for accurate casting.

The most popular bonefish flies also follow the above color schemes. Good patterns include the Snapping Shrimp, Crazy Charlie, various epoxy flies, crab patterns, Chico's Bonefish Special. They should be small, 2 inches or less, and tied on size 1/0–#6 saltwater hooks. Some freshwater dry-fly patterns have also been used with great success during recent years, especially small Muddlers and Bombers in brown or green, tied on 2–#6 hooks.

Permit

Whole live crabs are the best, a little larger than a silver dollar. Skimmer jigs ⅜ to ½ ounce are also good, and the same colors for bonefish are good for permit too. Live shrimp will work often, but not as reliably as crabs. Tipping the jig helps, too. When permit are found in deep water around such structures as wrecks, they aren't nearly as selective as when on the flats and at times almost any lure or bait will work.

Fly fishing for permit is just coming out of its infancy. Not that anglers haven't been casting flies to these fish for decades, it's just that only during the past few years have effective patterns been developed. They still remain the flycaster's ultimate challenge on the flats. The most productive patterns so far seem to imitate crabs in one form or another. The bodies may be deer hair or molded epoxy, usually tied on 1/0 to 3/0 saltwater hooks.

Catching a permit on a fly is considered by many anglers to be the ultimate achievement in saltwater fishing.

Redfish

Considering their range, the red drum is very likely the most popular flats gamefish of all. In the United States, bonefish and permit are limited to the Florida Keys, tarpon to the Keys and a few widely scattered flats along the Gulf Coast. Redfish, on the other hand, are found on flats from Florida to Texas and even down into northeastern Mexico, plus scattered locations up the East Coast all the way to North Carolina, making the species readily available to more shallow-water anglers than any other.

So while a hooked red drum cannot run nearly as far as fast as a bonefish, it is a very thrilling sight-fishing challenge. And except in unusually clear water, it also isn't nearly as wary. It is also edible, perhaps not as naturally tasty as seatrout, snook, pompano, tripletail, or cobia, but with a little imaginative preparation, it can be a tasty dish. Witness the blackened redfish craze of the 1980s, almost the death knell of the species had commercial interests been allowed to go unchecked.

Intense pressure from the sportfishing sector eventually prompted tight conservation regulation and management in all coastal states except Mississippi (at this writing). The Fisheries Management Councils, largely because of pressure from the Houston-based Coastal Conservation Association

This 42-pound 5-ounce red drum is a fly-rod IGFA world record in the 12-pound-test tippet division. It was caught in 1981 on a flat near Oregon Inlet, North Carolina, by Chico Fernandez of Miami and is the largest of the species ever caught on fly tackle.

Either type of lure can also be sweetened with a piece of shrimp or fish, or even a piece of colorful plastic worm.

Plastic worms are also extremely effective. They should be rigged weedless, and kept fairly short (4 to 5 inches). Use just enough lead to allow accurate casting under the prevailing conditions. The same colors mentioned earlier are also good for plastic worms, but many anglers prefer rootbeer (a translucent brown) above all others. Work all lures slowly, just fast enough to skim along the tops of the wakes.

If there's not too much floating grass, surface plugs often get great results. The smaller variety, 3 to 4½ inches, are best. Don't make a lot of noise with them or you'll scare more redfish than you'll attract, and once you see a fish begin to chase the lure, cease any erratic motion and retrieve it in pretty much of a straight line at a slow but steady speed. Nature never really equipped this saltwater bass for striking at the surface, bestowing upon it the disadvantage of an underslung jaw. Nevertheless, redfish do seem willing to strike surface lures, often with real enthusiasm, and that certainly makes the effort very much worthwhile.

(which also has chapters in most coastal states), finally put a stop to unregulated netting in all federal waters inside the 200-mile limit. Texas declared the red drum a gamefish in the middle 1980s (along with many other species, also as a result of pressure from the CCA), prohibited all inshore netting, and established a saltwater hatchery that by the end of the decade was producing over ten million juveniles a year.

Florida, too, has added the species to its gamefish list. Almost completely gone from the flats of Florida Bay in the 1970s because of heavy fishing pressure and drought conditions, the red drum is now making an exciting comeback because of the protection it is receiving.

A wide variety of lures work very well on flats redfish. Weedless skimmer jigs, ¼ to ⅜ ounce, are excellent. Most colors seem to work, with white/blue and yellow/brown among the most popular. Small weedless spoons, ⅜ to ¾ ounce, are also extremely effective. Popular colors are gold, black, and silver.

A Florida redfish (red drum) tailing as it feeds in just inches of water—a good spot for a surface lure.

Most small baits, dead or alive, will get immediate attention, especially live shrimp. It is sadly too common along much of the Gulf Coast to use very small treble hooks with live bait, a very wasteful practice since most fish that get hooked this way will not survive if they break free or are released without removing the hook (which may not be possible). The treble usually lodges deep in the throat and blocks the passage of food, and the unfortunate fish is doomed to slow starvation. Florida has already outlawed this practice.

Conservation-minded anglers attuned to catch-and-release would do well to use barbless hooks. We have experimented with this method for years. Mashing the barb down with pliers leaves just enough of a hump to keep the hook firmly lodged, yet it can be very easily and quickly removed when it's time for the fish to be released. More fish are actually hooked with the barbless hook because it penetrates with less effort, and the percent of escapees is no greater than when using one with a barb.

Seatrout

A close relative of the redfish, the spotted seatrout (*Cynoscion nebulosus*) is one of *the* most popular saltwater gamefish in the southeastern U.S. It is also closely related to the weakfish, which is covered in Chapter 8, Fish of the Surf. While some books state that it ranges from New York south and throughout the Gulf of Mexico, its greatest stronghold is from the east coast of Florida to the northeast Yucatan Peninsula. It is also well established in various locations from Georgia northward through Virginia, and in fact the IGFA record books show that the all-tackle record, a 16-pounder, came from Mason's Beach Virginia, in 1977. All of the other line class records for the species come from Florida and Texas.

The average "speckled trout," the name by which this fish is so well known along the Gulf Coast, weighs between 1 and 2 pounds. Trout that weigh 3 to 4 pounds aren't uncommon, but anything over 5 is considered big. There are some areas that seem to produce more double-digit fish than others, among the most notable being the central east coast of Florida, near Cape Canaveral and the Indian River, and the Laguna Madre area of southern Texas.

Spawning takes place in the spring, summer, and early fall, primarily in bays and lagoons. Juvenile spotted seatrout stay close to shore, using the seagrasses, mangrove roots, and other available vegeta-

tion as a nursery. Even when adults they prefer shallow water, rarely wandering far offshore and are found away from the coast only where there are islands with extensive shorelines and surrounding shallows. The Chandeleur Islands, for example, fifty miles offshore and south of Gulfport, Mississippi, offer excellent fishing for both seatrout and red drum.

A spotted seatrout from Florida, one of the most popular gamefish in the southeastern U.S.

Big seatrout attack surprisingly large baitfish. One of the best places to take them is along the edges of those channels with broad seagrass margins at the beginning of the flooding tide, usually early in the morning or late in the evening when boat traffic is at a minimum. Use a floating or floater/diver plug, because one of the prime targets during the early flood is the finger mullet, and a 5-pound trout may eat a mullet that weighs almost a half-pound with an almost snooklike explosion. Very big trout often tend to eat just one big baitfish at widely spaced intervals, then quit feeding for a day or two while digesting the oversized meal. Thus it's possible to see them at times in very shallow water steadfastly refusing any bait or lure no matter how artfully presented.

In more open water, trout tend to gather in and around mullet muds, which appear as distinct light-gray clouds in water, sometimes quite large. The bottom may be muddy, sandy, or grassy; that seems to make little difference to the trout under these circumstances, because it is the abundance of food that attracted them to this turbidity in the first place. In the absence of patches of muddy water, fishing the deeper grass flats and channels is a good way to find them.

As a rule a hungry seatrout is not likely to be a selective feeder. Anything that vaguely resembles a small shrimp or baitfish will rarely be passed up. Prime baits are live shrimp or small live sardines, finger mullet, etc. Plugs that resemble small sardines or finger mullet also produce extremely well. So do jigs, which can be tipped with a piece of fish or shrimp for additional effectiveness.

Anglers along the Gulf Coast strongly favor a popping cork for live-bait fishing, because they feel that the loud pop produced by the cupped top of the cork when it is tugged sharply attracts these fish. The bait should be suspended far enough below the cork so that it is within a foot or two of the bottom. Most trout tend to stay close to the bottom, a fact that should also not be overlooked by lure fishermen as well.

Light tackle is by far the most productive. In fact more and more anglers find that ultralight gear, typically fishing lines that test between 4 and 6 pounds, will produce more fish. Some of the more adventuresome even use 2-pound test. Lighter lines allow the use of lighter and smaller lures, and there are many days when the smallest jig or plug will catch the most fish, especially when it's calm.

Inshore open-water shorelines produce a lot of trout, too. Fishing the light surf along the Gulf Coast is a popular pastime, with rewards that not only include many big trout, but also redfish and some pompano as well. In some areas the water may be clear enough to walk the beach and see big seatrout cruising very close to the water's edge, where they can be very carefully cast to like cruising bonefish. A particularly likely time to find them under these conditions is during the fall mullet run.

Sharks

There are several species that actively search the flats for food. The three most likely to be encountered are the blacktip, lemon, and bonnet. The blacktip is also known as the spinner shark because of its unusual acrobatic ability. The bonnet is a diminutive member of the hammerhead family. Some big hammerheads may invade the flats briefly now and then; also bull sharks, and in a few rare locations even tigersharks. But the blacktips and the lemons are the shallow-water angler's usual targets.

A big lemon shark can be as large as 200 pounds. Blacktips rarely exceed 100. The average is more likely to be 40 to 60 pounds for the majority that you can expect to find in less than 3 feet of water. In this environment they will readily eat just about any natural bait, dead or alive. But many anglers prefer to

Small sharks cruising in shallow water are a common sight along much of our southern coastline.

use artificial lures here. The most productive are large, bright, even flashy plugs, floater/divers or very slow-sinking types. Big is better, 5 inches or longer. Work any lure or fly slowly but enticingly right past the shark's nose; their eyesight isn't the best. And avoid loud, noisy plugs. A shark in shallow water is every bit as wary as a bonefish, regardless of its size.

For more information on sharks in general and shallow-water fishing for them in particular, see Chapter 13.

Tarpon

These fish show up on the flats in all sizes, from 5 to 150 pounds. The small tend to hang around mangrove shorelines, while those over 30 pounds are almost always in open water. The smaller fish will take the same lures and baits as bonefish. Also small plugs, surface and shallow running, fished slowly. As for flies, streamers 3 to 4 inches long, tied on 1/0 to 3/0 hooks, are best. Good color patterns are brown/grizzly (e.g. the popular Cockroach fly), green/white, blue/white, red/black.

Big tarpon on the flats like whole crabs and whole live shrimp—the bigger the shrimp the better. They also like the smaller floating/diving plugs, such as the Creek Chub Darter, Mirrolure models 88 or 99, and just about any other lure of similar action that's not too big. Slow-sinking lures also work at times, but the trick is to cast far enough ahead of the slowly cruising fish so that the lure or bait doesn't scare

them when it hits, and yet not so far that it sinks down into the bottom vegetation before they get to it.

Keep in mind that the various species of flats fish fall into two basic groups in terms of feeding habits: those that root in the bottom, and those that cruise. The bottom feeders, like bonefish, permit, and redfish will take a lure or bait even if it's lying still on the bottom and frequently when its moving slowly just above the bottom. The cruisers, which include tarpon, barracuda, sharks, and bluefish, require that the lure or bait be at or slightly above their swimming level or most likely they will ignore it.

Big tarpon on the flats are among the most thrilling gamefish in the world. That's why they are so eagerly sought throughout the Florida Keys and in a few small locations in Central America. And during the last decade, the popularity of fly fishing for them has zoomed. The same colors and patterns that work well on "baby" tarpon are also ideal for the big fish.

THE EDGE OF THE FLATS

A great deal of exciting angling awaits those willing to take some time and explore the deeper edges of the flats and the jade-green channels that crisscross some of them. The techniques that work here are also applicable to many other inshore fishing situations.

Many powerful and exciting species of gamefish live in this sparkling, mysterious, emerald-colored tropical world of deepening edges. This is the place to use baitcasting and spinning tackle, although certainly many of its inhabitants can be enticed by a properly presented streamer fly on a sinking line.

For the most part, what you can expect to hook in this deeper water depends largely upon the type of lure you use. Small jigs will produce the occasional bonefish or permit (or maybe even tarpon if there are any around), but the most common fare consists of several different species of snappers, blue runners, horseye jacks, bar jacks, jack crevalle, barracuda, almaco jacks, and mackerel. You'll need a short piece (6 to 12 inches) of light wire or heavy mono (40-pound test or more) to land any of the more toothy critters, but you'll hook more fish with the lightest leader your intestinal fortitude will allow you to use.

Some edges or channels are more prone to exceptionally large fish than others, even though they

A big tarpon is a tough adversary on fly tackle.

might be only a few hundreds yards apart. Mutton snappers in the 15- to 20-pound range (or larger) are almost as scarce as hen's teeth in the Florida Keys these days, but always a very real possibility throughout the Bahamas and much of the Caribbean Coast of Central America. However, most of the fish you'll hook in this deeper water will be under 10 pounds. One to 3 pounds is typical, most likely a member of the snapper family. This leaves the angler in somewhat of a quandary; lighter gear garners more strikes and adds measurably to the excitement of a hooked fish, but the risk of losing something really big is obviously greater.

Small jigs will typically produce better than most larger lures, but small underwater plugs should not be overlooked. Almost any color will work, although we've come to prefer white or yellow, perhaps with a touch of red, silver, or green. Those skimmer jigs with a horizontal flat head designed for bonefishing in skinny water are usually much less productive than others designed to sink rapidly, particularly if the depth is more than three feet. Allowing an extra second or two for the skimmer to reach bottom really doesn't help; it will still plane upward too quickly during even a slow retrieve, especially if there is any current, and usually no current means slow fishing. That means it won't stay down in the most productive strike zone, usually just a foot or two above the bottom. Stick with a faster-sinking lure, ¼ to ⅜ ounce, for best results.

Tipping any jig with a pinch of shrimp or very small strip of fresh fish increases the number of strikes. In some areas this seems to be more necessary than others. And often a little chumming is a big help. A 2- to 3-pound block of the ground variety will last several hours if you don't squander it too rapidly; a miserly dispersion is sufficient to attract most fish within casting range.

Good chumming locations include the upcurrent mouth of a channel if it bisects a flat. Or, if the other end terminates up on the flat with skinny water all around it, then the mouth is usually the most productive during incoming tide, and possibly near the upper end during the ebb. A channel doesn't have to be very wide or deep to hold a goodly number of fish or even some very large fish. You might have to hunt around a little until you find those channels that are the most productive.

Even though small jigs unquestionably catch greater numbers, medium-size (up to 4 to 6 inches) noisy surface lures often produce *larger* fish. For that reason it is often wise to use a little heavier gear for topwater angling. A stiff spinning or baitcasting rod and 12- to 20-pound-test line is usually just right. Expect to work a little harder for each strike, but those that come your way will certainly be exciting and more spectacular. One good way to fish a particular channel or flat edge is first to cover it with surface lures, then make another pass with jigs, and finally resort to chumming if all else fails. Almost any color surface lure will work, especially red and yellow or green and silver.

The *size* of the channel dictates technique more than anything else. If it's a narrow and/or shallow channel, fish it from a little way up on the flat if possible; otherwise stay very close to either side. Any channel you can cast almost all the way across is considered narrow for this purpose. If it's very light green and under 5 feet deep, then drifting up the middle might spook too many fish. One angler can maneuver the boat along the edge with the push-pole, staking with it to pause briefly and also to fish whenever a good spot is found.

Use longer and heavier leaders for surface plugs—up to 3 feet of 30- to 40-pound mono for big snappers and horseye jacks. Stick to lighter material for jigs, the thinner and shorter (2 feet or less) the better for both action and sink rate. It's better to try 12- or 15-pound first, and go to 20 only if absolutely necessary. If you're using ultralight (2- or 4-pound-test line), then perhaps adding a few feet of 8 or 10 above the leader is a good idea.

Chapter 2

TARPON IN DEEPER WATER

While sight-fishing for giant tarpon in water less than five feet deep might be considered the ultimate in light-tackle fishing, the fact is that by far the greatest numbers of silver kings are caught in deeper water. Within their range, which is extremely extensive, they may be found in a wide variety of fresh *and* salt water.

Although small numbers of this giant member of the herring family have somehow made it to the eastern Pacific, historically *Megalops atlanticus* is solely a fish of the tropical and warm temperate Atlantic. It is abundant along the western Atlantic and Caribbean, and the Gulf of Mexico shoreline all the way from Brazil northward to the Carolinas (summer only north of central Florida). Tarpon are also found in great numbers along the West African coast from at least Angola northward to Senegal. Since the completion of the Panama Canal, large tarpon have been appearing along the west coast of Panama in slowly increasing numbers. A 130-pounder was taken near Isla Coiba in the early 1980s, over 150 miles by water from the Pacific end of the Canal. Perhaps a significant population of silver kings will eventually evolve in the eastern Pacific, too.

There is only one other close member of the tarpon family, although the ladyfish is considered by biologists to be somewhat closely related, and therefore included in the family Elopidae. The "other" tarpon is a Pacific/Indian Ocean representative called the ox-eye or ox-eye herring (*Megalops cyprinoides*). The only major differences are the size of the eye (much larger on *cyprinoides*) and the weight—ox-eye seldom exceeds 15 to 20 pounds. While biological texts on that subject indicate they may grow to over 3 feet in length, we've caught many along the coast of Mozambique and in Australia's northern rivers, and have yet to see one that would top 10 pounds. The ox-eye is a superb fighter, if anything even stronger than its Atlantic cousin on a pound-for-pound basis.

A 6-pound ox-eye tarpon from the Indian Ocean. Note its exceptionally large eye. Its body is more stocky than an Atlantic tarpon's.

RANGE AND HABITS

The life history of the Atlantic tarpon is still not completely known. Some biologists believe that the species originated in Africa millions of years ago, possibly along with the bonefish and ladyfish, and because of its unique spawning habits its larvae drifted across the equatorial Atlantic to the northern shores of South America. Once there, Gulf Stream currents would certainly have assured its spread northward throughout the Caribbean, Central America, the Gulf of Mexico, the southeastern United States, and Bermuda, where a small population of tarpon also continues.

Tarpon don't spawn in rivers, as their lengthy upstream travels might seem to indicate. Instead the eggs are fertilized in open water, possibly from near shore to far out at sea. We once saw a school of silver

kings spawning several miles off the west coast of Florida, the milt from the males clearly backlit in the clear water by the late afternoon sun. Tarpon larvae have been collected in plankton nets many miles from shore, which indicates a big potential for very rapid and widespread current dispersion of the juveniles. If these young fish are thus carried to a habitat they find suitable for survival, a colony is likely to be established.

All of this suggests that very likely Florida's tarpon aren't born in Florida. They may be the result of spawning in Central America. And the younger fish that appear in Central America may have been hatched in Africa or South America, and so on. And there are other mysteries. Why are small tarpon, under 30 pounds, so scarce in Costa Rica, for example, when adults are so plentiful? Baby tarpon are common from Honduras northward, all the way to central Florida on both coasts.

A "baby" tarpon hooked near a mangrove shore.

Big tarpon have been taken on both sides of the Atlantic. A 325-pounder is reported to have been taken in a commercial net on the east coast of Florida many years ago. And when we visited Angola back in 1973, we heard many reports of 300 (or more) pounders taken from the mouth of the Congo River by natives with handlines. While fishing the rivers of Angola, especially the Cuanza, we saw some fish we estimated to possibly exceed 200 pounds, but the largest we caught during our brief visit was 125 pounds. The current all-tackle IGFA world record of 283 pounds was caught in Venezuela in 1956.

Tarpon exceeding 200 pounds have been taken on sporting tackle in both Angola and the United States. The magic 200-pound mark has also been approached closely on fly tackle by a 188-pounder from Florida's west coast in 1982. Much larger have been hooked on fly, and other light tackle as well, and fought for many hours until something failed. Any tarpon bigger than the "baby" class (50 pounds or larger) are tough, long-lasting fish on any light tackle.

Although it has been definitely established that tarpon do *not* spawn in freshwater (that is, they are not anadramous), they willingly ascend tropical freshwater rivers for hundreds of miles. Whether this is in search of food, or at least a special kind of food, or simply a primal instinct that somehow lingers from their prehistoric origins, no one knows. But they can show up in some of the strangest places, like deep in the freshwater area of the Florida Everglades, where their backs and upper sides turn almost black. Every so often some largemouth bass angler has an unexpected tackle-destroying encounter with one that would, if landed, easily weigh over 50 pounds.

Most of the freshwater rivers along the Caribbean coast of Central America and the northeast coast of South America have tarpon at least part of the year. For example, they ascend the San Juan River that separates Costa Rica from Nicaragua, all the way to Lake Nicaragua. Perhaps they even descend from that same lake down the river that flows to the Pacific Coast. And thus they are routinely caught up and down these rivers by anglers who manage to find access, usually via fishing camps established just for that purpose.

Most of the fresh and brackish canals in south Florida have small- to medium-sized tarpon during the warmer months. They offer great sport for the angler who fishes for them with light tackle and small lures or flies right after dawn or at dusk.

Catching a big tarpon on light spinning tackle is exciting. The fish was released as soon as the photo was taken.

During the brighter time of the day, unless it's overcast and maybe rainy, they can be maddeningly uncooperative.

In many ways a latter-day dinosaur of the fish family, the tarpon is even a partial air breather with the ability to absorb atmospheric oxygen directly through a network of blood vessels along the walls of its swim bladder. Thus it has survival capabilities that almost rival other primitives like the lungfish, allowing it to live happily in water so warm and dirty that there is almost no dissolved oxygen present. It has, for example, been observed rolling in oily Tampa Bay dockyard water where the midsummer temperature is around 100 degrees.

Rolling, or porpoising as it is sometimes called, is how the tarpon gulps air into its swim bladder. The warmer the water, the less dissolved oxygen it will hold, and the more supplemental oxygen from the atmosphere will be required. Like any other animal, exertion increases its oxygen requirements. But rolling is also a big advantage to the angler, because if you see the fish, you know for sure they are there. Even though it isn't always possible to catch them.

Tarpon will rise to the surface for a gulp of air from depths that exceed a hundred feet. And even the manner in which they roll offers useful informa-

*Tarpon usually reveal their presence by rolling on the surface to gulp air
into their swim bladder.*

tion. Natives along the Caribbean coast of Central America claim that if the tarpon are slapping their tails hard against the surface of the water when they roll, there will be strong wind within the next twenty-four hours. Perhaps, although we've never observed any direct correlation.

However, when tarpon travel to the surface from great depths and return immediately to the same depth, they roll rapidly with a high, arching motion. Tarpon that move little and tend to stay close to the surface are just the opposite. They roll slowly in a horizontal direction with a soft, almost lazy sigh, sometimes sinking just a foot or two below the surface afterwards. Slow traveling fish roll slowly, whether singly or in schools. Fast movers roll rapidly, but still mostly horizontally, in the direction they are traveling.

Then there's the classic "daisy chain," a group of fish swimming nose-to-tail in an almost perfect circle, thought by some biologists to be part of the spawning ritual. They may roll when they do this if close enough to the surface.

Tarpon in a hurry to be somewhere else very rarely eat any sort of bait or lure. It's with the slow rollers that your best chances lie. And if fishing in deep water where the high, arching roll is prevalent, confine your fishing efforts to the zone that extends from halfway to the bottom all the way down to the bottom. That's where the greatest number will be holding.

Water temperature is every bit as important to tarpon in deeper water as it is on the flats. As a rule, in deeper water it usually doesn't pay to look for big tarpon (over 50 pounds) unless the water is at least 70 degrees or higher. This confines reasonably dependable winter fishing to extreme south Florida, the Keys, and Central America. The deeper channels from Ft. Lauderdale to Key West are the last locations they disappear from in the face of falling water temperatures brought in by a cold front, but as long as it is over 70 degrees look for them in such places. Key West harbor is historically one of the great winter and early spring hotspots.

The late spring and summer months are the migratory times for tarpon. As the water warms, they move along both Florida coasts, following the general northward progression of the 70–72-degree isotherms. By late August they are well distributed along the gulf of Mexico and the Atlantic coastline to the northernmost extent of their range. A few of these fish have even appeared as far north as Nova Scotia during exceptionally warm summers, but for fishing purposes the small group of silver kings that sometimes reaches the Virginia shoreline of Chesapeake Bay are as far north as they are ever likely to be caught with any regularity. Northeastern North Carolina, especially the Pamlico Sound area, seems to hold a fairly good population of big fish during August.

When the first rush of chilly Arctic air reaches the Middle Atlantic coastline, usually in September, all of the silver kings present in that area immediately head for deeper water and begin a fast trip southward. They then reappear in great numbers along the southeast Florida coast, following the southward fall run of mullet and gorging themselves upon those oily baitfish. It's fast action: just find a big school of mullet along the beaches or in any of the inlets, and the tarpon will surely be there.

Tarpon eagerly take a wide variety of lures and baits. The best fishing is usually in late afternoon, at night, and early morning. As a rule, the brighter the daylight, the more difficult it is to get them to bite, although there are many times when midday action is everything anyone could want. Cloudy and/or rainy days often prolong the morning action for many hours or start the late afternoon activity early.

Flycasters and live-bait anglers often do well through the brightest daylight periods, even though the silver kings may have stopped striking other artificial lures entirely. Then there are times when *nothing* works, but that's tarpon fishing.

Lures that work especially well on tarpon of all sizes include flashy plugs, both surface and sinking types, such as the Mirrolure. We found the tarpon in Africa ate a model 65M18 Mirrolure, which looks like a small mullet, just as quickly as the Florida silver kings. And spoons, especially when trolled very slowly. Also effective are jigs, from ¼ ounce through 1½ ounces. White, yellow, yellow/red, silver/green, rootbeer, chartreuse, and hot pink are colors that seem to do the job especially well. Plastic worms 6 to 9 inches long, rigged on 2/0 to 5/0 hooks with just enough weight in front to sink at the desired rate, are deadly. Especially the kind with the curlytail swimming action.

Excellent live baits include mullet (finger to corncob size), pinfish (also known as sailor's choice),

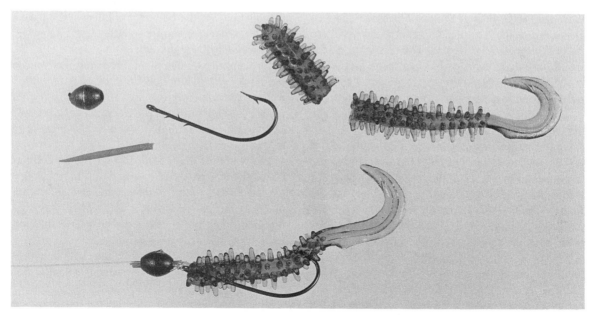

Rigging a plastic worm for tarpon, small red drum, or bonefish. The length is reduced for smaller fish, as shown here, or used in full for big fish. The toothpick section keeps the sinker from sliding.

shrimp (the bigger the better), crabs, and the more brightly colored smaller members of the snapper family. At times, just about any small fish will do. Unless the situation indicates these baits should be fished deep, as a rule it is better to use as little weight as possible. Both drifting and anchoring work. If the fish are moving around a lot, drifting is the better choice.

LIVEBAITING FALL TARPON

Although we tend to think of spring and summer as the principal tarpon seasons, there is some really excellent fishing for them in south Florida in the fall and sometimes in early winter. The prime area, to be even more specific, is most of the east coast and the southwest section from Charlotte Harbor southward. Included, of course, are all of the Florida Keys.

In most of these areas, silver king action begins to slack off toward the middle of July and may continue to decline until middle or late August when the fall mullet run begins. This annual southward baitfish migration usually reaches the Keys by mid to late September, but the action can start further up the line several weeks earlier.

The first sign of activity is the arrival of the first small schools of mullet and the explosive attacks on these baitfish by hungry tarpon of all sizes. The best places for this to happen seem to be areas where there is a good flow of tidal current, such as the mouths of canals, rivers and creeks, inlets, and under bridges. Occasionally there is a temporary concentration of action along open stretches of beaches, but as a rule this is somewhat less predictable than the places mentioned above.

Once the action starts, it's likely to continue, off and on, until cold weather chills the water below the tarpon's tolerance level. If the fall is warm, it can last through the end of December in Florida Bay and the Keys.

The outgoing tide is best in most places, although if the action is unusually good because of high baitfish concentrations, it may last into the first hour of the flood. Night fishing is often the best time, especially when the tide is right, but when there are plenty of silver kings and lots of hysterical mullet around, it can be super in the middle of the day, too, particularly in September and October.

Live mullet are by far the best bait, although sometimes other small baitfish (e.g. pinfish, small lane snappers, de-barbed catfish) or even live shrimp or live blue crabs will work. And artificial lures, particularly the darting-type plugs in mullet coloration, are often very effective.

Most livebait anglers prefer mullet from finger size to no bigger than a corn cob. Very large mullet *can* be eaten by very large tarpon, but often the fish can range anywhere from 10 to 150 pounds. A 150-pounder will eat a 6-ounce mullet just as quickly as a 16-ounce mullet, but anything under 30 probably cannot, so you'll miss some strikes that way. Unless, of course, you only want to catch the bigger fish.

As long as you have a boat to follow the hooked fish, heavy tackle isn't needed even for the bigger silver kings. A light but stiff graphite rod designed for 12- to 20-pound-test line is sufficient.

A good float on the end of the anchor line is a must. If you hook a fish that decides to go out to sea in a hurry, you won't have time to pull the anchor. Particularly if the current is running strong, because you can bet it will be very solidly hung in the bottom. It's also a good idea to use a waterproof felt-tip marker to print your boat's numbers on the float, just so someone else won't assume that spot is open for grabs while you're busy elsewhere.

It doesn't take a big hook to land a big tarpon. A short-shank 3/0 to 4/0 is quite sufficient. If the hook is too big, you'll miss a lot of strikes. However, you *must* keep it sharp enough to scratch your thumbnail, if you want the best shot at burying the barb in that fish's concrete-mixer mouth. That's true with any lure or bait, by the way.

Hooking the mullet is simple. Bring the point of the hook upward through the roof of its mouth, ¼ inch or so back from the lips. If you'll also use the point of a sharp knife to split the mullet's lower lip, it can breathe better and will stay frisky quite a bit longer.

You won't need any lead. Just let the mullet back 40 to 60 feet behind the boat, and wait for the action. The bait should swim right on the surface, even in muddy water, clearly visible if it's daylight. Very often it will become quite obviously nervous just before the strike occurs.

And while you're waiting for something to happen to your live baits, you might try casting a floater/diver surface plug. If it's the same size and coloration as a mullet (dark green back, silver sides), sooner or later some tarpon will assume it is a mullet. Especially if you can quickly cast it to the spot where a mullet has just been ambushed. As a rule the tarpon responsible won't wander very far, and your chances of getting a strike on the artificial are very good.

Tarpon, both large and small, take live bait in a variety of ways. Sometimes there's a big explosion that knocks the bait right out of the water, with the silver king actually inhaling the mullet in midair. And sporadically the strike is a complete miss, the fierce rush actually blowing the mullet into the air. On other occasions there's barely any disturbance at all, just a slight eddy as the bait is sucked under. Those are the best strikes, the ones that hook the most fish. And don't be surprised if 6 feet of silver explodes after gently sipping the bait; there's just no way to tell the size from a strike like that.

A long drop-back isn't needed, and in fact if you overdo it you run the risk of gut-hooking the fish. Some anglers strike as soon as the line comes tight and they feel the weight of the fish. Others let just a few feet of line slip from the reel, or better yet just drop the rod tip to the horizontal position and wait just long enough for the line to come really tight.

Unless you have a source of good live mullet at a friendly price, you'll need a cast net. If you're using a small boat, you can idle along a sandy stretch of beach near the spot you'll be fishing and let the shadow of the boat spook some of the frightened baitfish into water shallow enough to throw the net. If the boat is too big and the water too shallow, go ashore and walk the beach. Pay careful attention to small sloughs and tiny creek outlets; these are prime locations for right size mullet.

Other baitfish can be caught with a light spinning rod and small pieces of shrimp or squid for bait. Chumming helps speed things up, and usually a can of fish-flavored catfood or oily sardines with holes punched in the side is just fine for that job. Like the mullet, stick to the smaller sizes.

Remember, however, that the fall mullet run is almost always the catalyst needed to concentrate the silver kings; if the baitfish aren't in abundance, the odds are the tarpon won't be either and you'll be better served to look elsewhere. But, when it's right it is really *right*, and the action can be as good as it gets.

SETTING THE HOOK

Perhaps the greatest thrill of all is to watch six feet of silver king take a lure, bait, or fly on or just below the surface. Despite tales of arm-jerking strikes, even a 100-pounder frequently takes your offering with surprising softness. It almost appears to happen in slow motion, and without a doubt the angler who tries to set the hook quickly will miss most of the strikes. The best pathway to a solid hookup with a silver king is patient self-restraint, until the rod is sharply bent and the full weight of the fish is felt. At that point the angler should sweep the rod sharply sideways, until maximum pressure for the tackle is brought to bear.

The silver king's mouth is as hard as concrete. Trying to set the hook by jerking back on the rod many times in rapid succession is more likely to pull the hooks free than to bury them past the barb. A steady, strong pull on the rod keeps constant pressure on the hook point as it slides around inside the tough mouth until that point finds a spot soft enough to penetrate. Just be sure to ease the pressure a bit when the fish starts to jump, otherwise it can break the line.

And while the strike may appear to be slow, the events that follow the sting of the hook are certainly anything but that. The most immediate response is either a wild series of jumps, or a long run, or both. More like missile than fish, the silver king will explode from the water, at times clearing the horizon by more than its own body length—a spectacular sight that will never lose its razor edge of gut-wrenching excitement, no matter how many times you're fortunate enough to witness it.

The leader and how it is rigged is extremely important. (See the section on leaders in Part II: Tackle and Techniques). A special "shock" leader 12 to 20 inches long is tied directly to the hook or lure. Monofilament is best, because it doesn't kink and will usually draw more strikes than wire, but if large toothy critters (i.e. king mackerel or barracuda) are likely to be a problem, coffee-colored leader wire will work in most instances. For tarpon 50 pounds and up, 100-pound-test mono is the most popular. For smaller fish, use 30- to 60-pound test. Even a 5-pounder can fray through 20-pound mono, because even though they have no teeth, they do have lips like very rough sandpaper.

Many serious tarpon anglers seeking large fish use a secondary leader (actually a leader extension) between the heavy shock leader and the line. I've found that at least 5 feet of 30- to 40-pound test mono are needed to keep the lighter line from rubbing along the scaly body, and it will zip through the guides easily during the cast.

Once you hook one of these wonderful gamefish, if it's not overgunned for its size with too heavy tackle, be prepared for a fight that can last from twenty minutes to several hours. These fish are both very strong and exceedingly stubborn, so to land a big one you'll certainly have to pay your dues.

Florida has a no-kill law for tarpon, the only exception being the prior purchase of a special Tarpon Stamp at $50 per fish. But there really is no need to kill one of these grand gamefish for any reason. It can be photographed and released alive. And you don't need a dead tarpon to have one mounted. One of the nice things about modern taxidermy is that the best mounts are fiberglass anyway, produced from precision molds with all of the artistry that goes into the best skin mounts. Even the scales are dupli-cated in exact detail. Unlike skin mounts, a fiberglass replica won't turn yellow and crack with age, the large scales won't curl and lift off. And the cost is exactly the same as a skin mount. You only have to provide the length of the fish to get an extremely close reproduction.

If you'd like to know what your trophy weighs, you don't even have to bring it back to the scales. Just measure the length and girth; a piece of string can be converted to inches back ashore. Multiply the square of the girth by the length (all in inches) and divide the result by 800. This formula is so accurate that you won't be off by more than a few percent. It's good for most other fish, too.

Chapter 3

SNOOK

One of the most unusual fish families is the Centropomidae, found only in the tropical portions of North, Central, and South America. There are at least seven known species of snook, all under the genus *Centropomus*, of which only two gain any real size. *C. undecimalis* is the largest species on the Atlantic and Caribbean coasts, while on the Pacific side it is *C. nigrescens* (known as the black snook). Both reach weights in excess of 50 pounds. There are even rumors that black snook have been taken commercially in excess of 75 pounds.

RANGE

Interestingly, the only other parts of the world where the snook has any close relatives are in freshwater Africa (the Nile perch, *Lates niloticus*, which may exceed 300 pounds), and the barramundi of Australia and New Guinea (*Lates calcarifer*), which grows to a weight of at least 120 pounds. Except for the convex tail of both, and the more rotund shape of the Nile perch, they closely resemble the American snook in profile but lack the snook's distinctive head-to-tail black lateral-line stripe.

Why the snook is not found in other tropical parts of the world is a mystery. When we fished the west coast of Africa during the early 1970s, we found tarpon and bonefish abundant, as well as jack crevalle and many other species common to the U.S. side of the Atlantic Ocean. We saw miles and miles of jungle river-mouth and estuarine mangrove habitat, identical to the most prolific areas of Central and northern South America. But no snook, nor even a saltwater version of the Nile perch. The snook is completely unknown throughout Africa.

When an angler in Florida, Texas, the Caribbean coast of Costa Rica, Belize, or the Yucatan Peninsula mentions "snook," he or she is really talking about

C. undecimalis. The lesser members of the family are called by their specific given names, such as the fat snook, swordspine snook, or tarpon snook. The last is in no way related to tarpon, by the way. These others are much smaller, some never exceeding 18 inches in length. Only the fat snook might be of some angling interest on very light tackle, because it may now and then reach 24 inches and weigh as much as 4 or 5 pounds.

In Florida the best snook fishing extends from Cape Canaveral on the east coast southward to the Florida Keys and up to the west coast to Tarpon Springs. Within this range fish that exceed 30 pounds are not uncommon and several 40-pounders are caught each year, although the average snook is more like 8 pounds. In Texas snook are not in great abundance nowadays, although twenty years ago they were both large *and* abundant. A few are caught in the extreme southwest corner of the state near the Mexican border. From there south throughout the Gulf Coast of Mexico and around the Yucatan they are more numerous.

Florida is enjoying an upsurge in its snook population, a dramatic turnaround from sharp declines observed in the 1970s. Hardest hit was the West Coast, from Florida Bay northward, estimated to have dropped to less than 30 percent of what it should have been. For some reason the snook population from Miami to Ft. Pierce wasn't hit quite as hard. During the 1980s Florida took several bold steps, which included two annual closed seasons (January–February and June–August) to protect them through winter cold weather and the spring spawning period. The bag limit was also reduced from four to two per angler per day, and a slot length of 24 to 34 inches. The minimum size prior to that had been 18 inches. Now each angler can keep only one per day over 34 inches in length. Snook also enjoy protected gamefish status in Florida, and cannot be sold commercially, regardless of how caught.

A barramundi, the snook's only close saltwater relative. The freshwater Nile perch of Africa is identical in appearance to the barramundi, suggesting common ancestry.

Most anglers at all interested in saltwater view the snook as a very special fish, ranked right up there with bonefish and tarpon in popularity. And there is probably no saltwater fish that appeals quite as much to freshwater anglers as well. Especially to bass fisherman, because the snook's basic behavior pattern is quite similar to both species of black bass. The major difference, of course, is that the snook is both stronger and much larger. The current IGFA all-tackle world record for snook is 53 pounds 10 ounces, caught in 1978 near Parismina, Costa Rica (Caribbean Coast). In fact, Costa Rica from the mouth of the Rio Colorado all the way down to Parismina has produced outstanding numbers of giant snook through the various fishing camps that operate there. Undoubtedly the rest of that shoreline all the way down through Panama could do the same if there were facilities for the sporting angler.

Because the snook has basslike habits, it is obviously susceptible to bass-type lures, tackle, and techniques. That's why thousands of inland freshwater anglers have made regular trips to tropical saltwater areas to fish for this grand gamefish. But you don't

have to be an expert bass fisherman to beat a snook at its own game.

Even though the snook is a saltwater fish, it is also very much freshwater oriented. It likes brackish creeks and rivers, and will even ascend some streams many miles inland from saltwater. But it is also content following the shoreline of open, completely saltwater beaches. And yet rarely is it very far from some fresh or brackish-water source. Snook spawn in saltwater, usually along beaches near passes or inlets, but in between spawning sessions they are entirely food motivated. Find the greatest abundance of forage fish, and that's where you'll usually find snook.

This is why most of the best snook fishing in tropical America is located in and near the many rivers, creeks, and canals that empty into saltwater. Mangrove shorelines are especially attractive to them, since they are also structure-oriented.

But for some reason, on the Caribbean coast of Central America, the largest snook seem to be more likely encountered in the greatest numbers in the surf along the beaches near the various river mouths, or in the lower few miles of the major river systems.

They travel up and down the coastline in schools, some of which can be quite large. When a school passes a spot where several anglers are fishing, almost everyone hooks up at the same time.

In Costa Rica, the biggest snook show up in the surf and river mouths during September and October, and again in late April and May. The best run is in the fall months, and that's when the average fish can weigh almost 20 pounds. At times large numbers are taken in a single day, but as a rule it's a matter of persistence if you really want that trophy snook. There are frequently a lot of casts between fish, but if you stick with it, the results are usually well worth the effort.

There are a number of camps on the Caribbean coast of Costa Rica that offer excellent trophy snook fishing. There are several in the northeast corner near the mouth of the Rio Colorado, including such notables as Casa Mar, Isla De Pesca, and Rio Colorado Lodge. Further south, about 40 miles, there's a lodge at the mouth of the Rio Tortugaro, and about the same distance even further south is Parismina Tarpon Rancho at the mouth of the Parismina River.

Spring and fall are for the most part the best times to catch the biggest snook anywhere in its range. Most experienced snook anglers would probably choose fall as the best of all.

A big snook from Florida's mangrove backcountry.

Bill Barnes, owner/manager of Casa Mar fishing camp on the Caribbean Coast of Costa Rica, lands a 40-pound snook in the surf.

Medium sinking plugs, like the Mirrolure series, also work well. At times floating/diving plugs such as the Darter or the jointed Pikie Minnow will score, mostly in protected, quiet water. But if there is a breeze, these lures are tough to cast any distance upwind. On an open beach, when there's wind there is often floating debris in the surf, which means lures with treble hooks tend to get fouled far more frequently than a single-hook jig, especially since that hook is to some extent protected by the bucktail skirt.

Fly fishing for big snook calls for special conditions. It rarely works where there is a lot of current and the fish are deep. Protected inside water is best. Many man-made canals in south Florida have produced a lot of snook over the years. Typical of these is the canal that parallels the Tamiami Trail (U.S. 41) between Miami and Naples. At times it is even possible to see snook swimming just under the surface (cruising), and it takes a 3-inch streamer fly placed quietly just a few inches in front of the fish's nose to get a strike.

Sometimes the fly cannot be large and bright. Often a small, dark Muddler Minnow will hook more fish than a 3- to 4-inch brightly colored streamer. Snook in freshwater canals feed heavily on small, dark minnows and the Muddler is an excellent imitation of these. Other small, dark streamers of similar

LURES FOR SNOOK

The same lures that work for big tarpon are excellent for big snook. When fishing the surf where you might have to spend most of your time making long casts into a fairly strong wind, a ⅝- to 1¼-ounce bucktail jig is tough to beat. Popular colors are white or yellow, and adding a brightly colored curlytail plastic worm to the hook improves the lure's action. A 7- to 9-inch worm is best. Productive colors are bright yellow, hot pink, fluorescent orange, chartreuse, and black.

Heavy jigs are often best when fishing from a drifting boat in a river mouth where there is a lot of current. The idea is to get to the bottom quickly and stay there, because that's where the fish will be, so figure on using ¾ to 1¼ ounces. In especially fast current, we've found that jigs weighing 2 to 3 ounces might be needed to hit bottom. Snook definitely respond best under these conditions to lures that constantly bump along the bottom while being retrieved with short sweeps of the rod.

Chico Fernandez of Miami lands a big snook on fly tackle. Protected waters are best for fly fishing.

size also work well. They should be tied on hooks appropriate to their size; even though at times they may seem a bit small, they will still catch surprisingly big fish.

Although even a very large snook might be only half the weight of a typical tarpon, the snook's lips are even more abrasive. Plus there's that sharp cutter on each gillplate that can slice through thinner mono in short order. Most anglers use 12 to 18 inches of 80- to 100-pound-test mono as a shock leader directly in front of the lure or fly when fishing for big fish. Or you might also use mono coated wire, 60-pound test or heavier, but the mono seems to get more strikes.

Some circumstances require lighter shock leaders. Clear, calm conditions dictate a shock leader of 50-, 40-, or even 30-pound test. Especially when you're forced to go to small flies to get strikes. To be sure, some fish will be lost because of the light mono, but if that's what it takes to get strikes, you really have no other choice.

BAITFISHING

Live baits that produce especially well on snook include the pinfish (sailor's choice), small mullet, various small grunts, large live shrimp, and just about any larger (3 to 4 inches) member of the sardine family.

Success with live bait on snook requires the same presentation techniques as for any other gamefish. Get the bait to the zone or level where the fish are holding, and let nature take its course. Use a weight if needed, and definitely *do not* if one isn't required. A float may even be necessary to suspend the bait in a productive zone. In the final analysis, however, no lure beats live bait when it comes to catching snook. So if you fish an area with lures and fail to get even the first strike, don't assume there are no snook there until live bait has been tried. You might be in for a big surprise.

Chapter 4

THE BILLFISHES

There are nine major species of billfishes worldwide, plus a few minors. Included in the exalted first group are unquestionably the world's most prized blue-water gamefish. There are, for example, two sailfish: the Atlantic sailfish and the Pacific sailfish. There are five marlin: Atlantic blue, Pacific blue, white, striped, and black. Then there is the swordfish, a single species found globally in just about all offshore tropical and subtropical waters. Finally, there's the spearfish, of which at least two species actually exist, the longbill (*Tetrapturus pfluegeri*, in the Atlantic), and the shortbill (*T. angustirostris*, only in the Pacific and possibly the Indian oceans). Both are so rare that they are for angling purposes considered as one: simply, spearfish. And not too many years ago marine biologists have labeled a seldom found variation of the white marlin as a new species called the hatchet marlin (*Tetrapturus sp.*). It so closely resembles a white that the only visible difference is in the slightly flattened tip of the forward part of the dorsal; thus very possibly if caught it is almost never recognized as a separate species by anglers.

The blue marlin is the same species worldwide, *Makiara nigricans*. And so is the sailfish, *Istiophorus platypterus*, in spite of its much larger size in some areas than others. The white marlin (*Tetrapturus albidus*) is entirely an Atlantic species, while its close cousin the striped marlin (*Tetrapturus audax*) is found only in the Pacific. Most anglers also consider the black marlin (*Makaira indica*) to be found only in the Pacific and Indian oceans, yet every year a few are captured, almost always by longliners, in the South Atlantic. Apparently they somehow manage to make the journey through the chilly waters off the Cape of Good Hope.

Which billfish reaches the greatest size? That contest is solely between the black and blue marlins. Even the swordfish (*Xiphias gladius*) have never been known to approach the ton mark, while both blues and blacks have been taken commercially well in excess of 2,000 pounds. At present the evidence seems to point toward the blue as the largest billfish, primarily because there are even some reports of a Pacific blue caught on a commercial longline that supposedly weighed almost 3,000 pounds. Also at this writing the largest billfish ever taken on rod and reel is a Pacific blue, a huge 1,805-pounder caught near Honolulu, Hawaii, in 1972. It never made the record book because more than one angler fought the fish. Next in size, behind the blue and black, comes the striped marlin, then the Pacific sailfish, followed by the white marlin. The Atlantic sailfish is the smallest of the commonly caught billfishes, and the uncommon spearfish is apparently the runt of the entire family (the IGFA all-tackle record is just 90 pounds 13 ounces).

Why is the spearfish the rarest of the billfishes? Is this a matter of population dynamics, or possibly habitat? Unlike the marlins and swordfish, which tend to congregate along the deeper edges of the continental shelves, and the sailfish, which shows a decided preference for the blue water edges of some surprisingly shallow reefs, the spearfish confines its range in all oceans to very deep water and rarely strays even close to the outer limits of the continental shelf. Perhaps the best known "concentration" of these slender billfish, if you can call it that, is near Hawaii where extremely deep water comes very close to shore.

For many decades, going back to the adventuresome angling days of Zane Grey just after the turn of the century, the most prized billfish has been the swordfish. Catching a large one—over 250 pounds—is considered by many to be the ultimate angling achievement.

The most commonly encountered billfish is the sailfish, and this goes for just about everywhere they are found. Next are likely the white marlin in those particular areas where they are abundant. In some sections of the Atlantic, Pacific, and Indian oceans blue marlin are also surprisingly plentiful, and the same can certainly be said for blacks. Striped marlin

The largest billfish ever landed on rod and reel. This 1,805-pound Pacific blue marlin didn't make the IGFA record books because it was fought by more than one angler.

A 13-pound baby swordfish. The species has been so overfished by longliners that much of the population has been stunted and many undersized fish are hooked.

also have their own very specific areas of especially high abundance, often appearing in numbers that rival sailfish.

ATLANTIC SAILFISH

We'll start with the Atlantic sailfish first, since it is the most available species of billfish to anglers in the United States. It ranges abundantly from the Texas–Mexico border all the way around the Gulf of Mexico to the tip of Florida, and commonly up the east coast as far as Cape Hatteras. Some even wander as far north as Delaware, and a rare few even beyond the New York/New Jersey area.

Sailfish are commonly found off southeast Florida and the Keys all year, but prime time is November through April. The greatest peak of all occurs between Ft. Pierce and Palm Beach, where great numbers are driven south from Cape Canaveral (or just north of there) by strong cold fronts. Warm winters in south Florida mean far fewer sails than cold, windy winters.

In addition, there is a major northward migration from the Caribbean up the coast of the Yucatan Peninsula that begins in March and lasts through May. These fish follow the Gulf Stream currents into the Gulf of Mexico and reach the northern Gulf by June, where they remain until the first strong cold fronts of fall push them south again. On the east coast the

A sailfish shows its stuff. It is a superb aerialist, and one of the fastest gamefish in the world.

fish that winter along southeast Florida begin to spread northward during April and May, reaching the Carolinas by June or July. Their fall southward movement is also dictated by cold front activity.

As for the rest of the Atlantic, they're common from Brazil northward and westward through the Caribbean, especially along the coasts of South and Central America. Particularly productive hotspots include Brazil, Venezuela, and the Yucatan Coast near Cozumel and Isla Mujures. In the eastern Atlantic, sailfish are commonly found along the west coast of Africa from Angola northward.

For some reason, most likely food availability, both Atlantic and Pacific sailfish average much larger along the eastern sides of their respective ocean basins. The Atlantics are much bigger off Angola than Florida, where they average close to 80 pounds, compared to around 40 in the sunshine state. Pacific sails typically run close to 100 pounds along the west coasts of South and Central America, yet records of the same species we examined from the Indian Ocean coast of Africa revealed an average size no larger than the Florida fish. Sailfish off Japan in the western Pacific are also about the same size as the Florida fish.

The largest Atlantic sailfish in the record books came from Luanda, Angola, in 1974 and weighed 128 pounds 1 ounce. In fact, every Atlantic sail in the books over the 100-pound mark except two came from Africa. These came from Florida: a 105-pounder from Key Largo and a 106 from Ft. Lauderdale. So a few giants of the species do appear in the western Atlantic now and then, but for the most part any sail over 60 pounds in that part of the ocean is considered very big.

Along those coasts with deep water close to shore and lots of coral reefs, sailfish frequently come into very shallow water. We've seen them shortly after sunrise swimming over clear white sand patches between the reefs of the Florida Keys, and also Yucatan, where the water was less than 20 feet deep, obviously searching for food. As a rule the best depth range in which to fish for them is 60 to 300 feet. Although they prefer clear, clean water, they will sometimes venture into "green" water if there's a lot of food. But as a rule, if inshore water isn't clean, move offshore until some sort of distinct color change or current edge is found. Don't waste time fishing in anything but clean water unless you see visual evidence that there are sails feeding in closer.

Sailfishing in the Gulf of Mexico is mostly a matter of long offshore runs since deep water is rarely closer than twenty miles, and often much farther. The bottom is mostly sand, and slopes slowly. Thus clean blue water, mostly a product of the Loop Current of the Gulf Stream that eddies around the perimeter of the Gulf of Mexico, is never very close to shore. Some years there is a weak Loop Current and billfishing is slow, but most often it can be quite good if the boat has the speed and range to get to good water—which may be as much as sixty (or more) miles offshore along some parts of the coast.

Sailfish can be fished in a wide variety of ways, with both artificial and natural baits (see Part II, Tackle and Techniques). Live baits produce best by far, either fished with a kite, a breakaway float, or trolled very slowly. Especially productive baits are balao, blue runners, mullet, goggle eyes, pinfish, and menhaden. These are about the size of an adult hand.

Next come rigged natural baits, of which balao and small mullet are excellent when used whole, or larger fish cut into 6- to 8-inch strips and used in conjunction with trolling artificials.

As for artificial lures, among the best seem to be the soft plastic variety, especially plastic squid in 6- to 10-inch lengths. Most colors seem to work, but among the most popular are white, orange, blue, and a sort of yellowish "natural."

Increasing in popularity is fly fishing for sails, where rigged hookless dead baits and lures are trolled to raise the fish, which is then teased to within casting range. The bait is then suddenly yanked out of the water and a large streamer fly is substituted in its place.

As for tackle, whereas twenty years ago it was common for charter boats to use heavy rods and big reels loaded with 50-pound-test line, today the almost universal choice is 12- to 20-pound gear. Many advanced anglers even go as light as 6. Reels should never be loaded with less than 200 yards. A smooth drag is important, since these are among the fastest gamefish in the world and always provide a breathtaking aerial display.

PACIFIC SAILFISH

Compared to the Atlantic variety, Pacific sailfish grow quite a bit larger. The IGFA all-tackle record is 221 pounds from the Galapagos, but they've been taken in excess of 150 pounds throughout their mid- and eastern Pacific range. Included are such diverse

*Playing a sailfish on fly tackle. A hookless bait or lure is first trolled to
raise the fish, then replaced by a large streamer.*

locations as Panama, Costa Rica, Equador, Mexico, Australia, and Fiji. Sails in excess of 100 pounds are quite common in those waters, while it's rare to catch one under 50 pounds.

Sailfish in any ocean are not commonly an island fish, with some notable exceptions. There are a few islands, large and small, with extensive fringing reefs that attract them in some numbers. They're very scarce around even the largest islands like Hawaii, for example, where the reefs are narrow and very limited. Nor do they occur in fishable numbers around Bermuda in the mid-Atlantic, even though those islands do have extensive reefs. But on the other hand, during a 1980s trip to Cocos Island, Costa Rica, a tiny dot over three hundred miles off-

shore in an otherwise huge expanse of empty tropical Pacific Ocean, we found lots of big sailfish. In three days we raised well over a hundred, fishing with just two boats. And Cozumel, in the western Caribbean just fifteen miles east of the Yucatan Peninsula doesn't have anywhere near as many sailfish as the mainland edge, clearly visible from there on a clear day.

Pacific sailfish are found in the eastern Pacific from southern California all the way down to at least northern Peru. Noted hotspots for these fish include the southern tip of the Baja Peninsula, Mazatlan, Acapulco, and just about any other seaport along the Mexican coast. There is also excellent sailfishing to be had in various locations along the coasts of Guatemala, Salvador, and Nicaragua, should the politics of those countries ever permit serious sportfishing exploration. Costa Rica and Panama are noted for exceptionally good sailfishing, and there are many places where boats are available.

Then there is Columbia, with the potential for outstanding billfishing of all types, if the internal situation there ever becomes safe for foreign visitors again. Salinas, Equador, had super fishing for exceptionally large sailfish up until the late 1970s, when they were commercially netted to extreme scarcity. A few more fish have been showing up every year since the late 1980s, so possibly one day that area might become a prime producer again.

The same fishing techniques that work so well for Atlantic sailfish do exactly the same in the Pacific, although as a rule the Pacific species is both more aggressive and more tenacious, making them significantly easier to catch with artificial lures. Of all billfish they are the most responsive to teasing with a hookless lure or bait, thus making them the prime bluewater target for the flyrodder. Because of their much larger average size, many anglers prefer somewhat heavier tackle than that typically used for Atlantics.

While some might choose to go as high as 30-pound-test gear, especially if fishing in an area where one of the larger species of marlin might appear, 12 to 20 is still the most popular range. Spinning, baitcasting, light trolling, and more recently stand-up tackle (*which see* in Part II) are the gear of choice.

high enough temperature, during August. And the northern Gulf of Mexico also sees good fishing during the summer and early fall. Topnotch white marlin fishing can also be found at Chub Cay in the Bahamas, Cozumel (Mexico), Venezuela, and Brazil. Vitoria, Brazil, may well be the best spot of all in terms of both quantity and size.

Whites are the smallest as marlin go, actually not much larger than western Atlantic sailfish on the average (about 45 pounds), but they are exceptionally popular as a light-tackle gamefish because of their incredible serial demonstrations (many rate them as the best jumpers in the entire billfish family) and energetic fight. And surprisingly, the IGFA all-tackle record was a fish of 181 pounds 14 ounces taken off Brazil in 1979. Fish over 100 pounds have also been caught in the Bahamas, Nantucket, and Florida. A few large white marlin have also been caught along the eastern side of the Atlantic, but that is apparently rare.

White marlin tend to prefer somewhat deeper water than sailfish as a rule, but it is not uncommon to find the two species intermixed. They feed primarily along the edge of the continental shelf, often somewhat closer inshore than blue marlin seem to like. Still, it is not uncommon to find white and blue marlin mixed in any given area.

Sailfish tackle and techniques are just the ticket for white marlin. With the possible exception that most experienced white marlin fishermen prefer a very short drop-back for these fish.

WHITE MARLIN

White marlin are found along the same range as Atlantic sailfish, and appear in good numbers almost every year in certain areas. In U.S. waters the mid-Atlantic seaboard has historically produced some outstanding fishing, particularly from Cape Hatteras to Montauk Point in the late summer and early fall. Cape Hatteras and the Baltimore Canyon, when the conditions are right in August and September, become overrun by vast numbers of whites. They are attracted by huge concentrations of baitfish, and it is not unusual to see many white marlin feeding on the surface in a relatively small area. Catches of up to twenty or more per boat have been recorded—almost all of them released, by the way.

Cape Cod also has brief but intense runs most years, if the weather is good and the water reaches a

ATLANTIC BLUE MARLIN

Atlantic blue marlin range very widely in size, but probably the overall average is close to 200 pounds. In some locations, like the Cayman Islands and Jamaica, a 200-pounder is big and the average is barely over 100, but they are unusually plentiful. In the Virgin Islands the story is just the opposite. The average is closer to 300 pounds, and fish over the half-ton mark are taken almost every year. Here, and in Puerto Rico as well, big blues are exceptionally abundant. And while commercial longlining efforts in the Atlantic thus far haven't matched the maximum size recorded from the Pacific, a blue estimated to weigh close to the ton mark was caught in the Gulf of Mexico during the 1950s by a fisheries research vessel. Why not the same size fish in both oceans, since they are the same species?

Atlantic blue marlin are found throughout the Gulf of Mexico and along the Atlantic coast from Florida to Long Island. In U.S. waters there are some locations that seem to produce better than others, although none will consistently approach the better Caribbean hotspots. The "wall," a sharp drop-off in 600 feet of water 20 miles south of the lower Florida Keys, has been the scene of some excellent marlin fishing during the summer and fall, and even at times during the winter and spring if the winds are not too stiff.

The entire East Coast all the way to Cape Hatteras has periods of fairly good blue marlin fishing during the warm months. At times Hatteras can be one of the top hotspots, both in size and numbers, but that varies from summer to summer. When it's right there, it is really right.

Atlantic blues are found from Brazil (very good there) northward. Primarily a true deep-water species, they rarely roam inshore of the 100 fathom (600 feet) line. Thus it is common to find them in completely open ocean, hundreds of miles from land, as

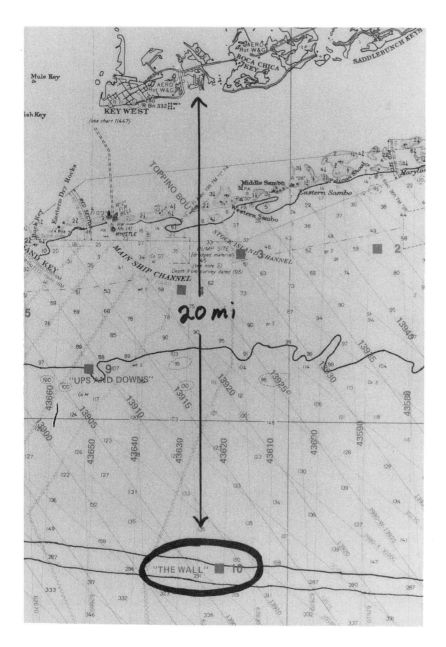

The "Wall," twenty miles south of Key West, is one of the more productive blue marlin hotspots in the continental U.S.

well as around islands, even those with little or no reefs, as long as deep water is close at hand. Bermuda, for example, has during recent years been "discovered" to have a much larger fishable population of blue marlin than previously suspected. It was just a matter of using the right techniques.

Blue marlin fishing is fair to good around most of the Caribbean. Other particularly productive areas not mentioned earlier include Venezuela and Cozumel, and the north coast of Cuba. Also the Bahamas, especially Walker's Cay, Chub Cay, Bimini, Cat Cay, and San Salvador, to name a few. And during recent years an outstanding fishery for very large blues has been developed around both the Azores and the Cape Verde Islands.

Dedicated blue marlin anglers seem to be sharply divided into two groups when it comes to technique. On one side are those who favor such live natural baits as small bonito and other tunas (up to 15 or 20 pounds when fishing for very large fish), dolphin (fish), or very large mullet. On the other are the high-speed lure aficionados. Rigged dead baits like mullet, mackerels, and small tunas are still used extensively.

Live bait is by far the most productive if two conditions are met: The area cannot have too many sharks or you'll spend most of your time dealing with them: it must be an area with an above normal concentration of blues. Live bait is especially deadly around deepwater banks and points when there is a good concentration of baitfish.

High-speed artificials are possibly the best choice where the fish are likely to be scattered, and they also help locate areas of unsuspected concentration. Trolled at 10 to 16 mph, they allow the boat to cover a much larger area in a day's fishing than possible by any other method. These artificials come in a wide variety of shapes, sizes, and colors, and they offer a particular advantage. They never need refrigeration, and if you don't loose a lure it will last almost forever. Or at least through a lot of fish. See Chapter 18 in Part II for more details on rigging and using these and other forms of bait.

See Chapter 17 for details on high-speed lure fishing, and Chapter 19 for more information on live bait.

Big billfish require big-game tackle in tiptop shape. The late Capt. Tommy Gifford, a real giant billfish pioneer, maintained that any marlin could be caught on 50-pound gear if it was in proper shape and the angler experienced enough to use it effectively. Blues over the half-ton mark *have* been

Landing a big blue marlin off the "Wall" near Key West.

caught on 50, by the way. Most fishermen, particularly newcomers to this type of fishing, prefer the cushion of heavier tackle and choose 80 or 130 for the really big billfish.

In recent years there has been a growing trend away from the traditional big-game fighting chair and heavy rod toward much lighter stand-up tackle, and some very big fish have been taken on it (see Chapter 16).

BLACK MARLIN

Black marlin are extremely rare in continental U.S. waters, and then confined to extreme Southern California during periods of unusual ocean warming when an El Nino occurs. A few have been caught in Hawaii over the years, although not in enough numbers for a seriously directed sportfishing effort for them. Mostly it's a matter of accidental catch by anglers seeking Pacific blue marlin.

Considered a grand gamefish by a vast number of big-game anglers, it is abundant along the Central and South American coastline from the lower Baja Peninsula all the way to northern Peru. Cabo Blanco, Peru, was *the* hotspot for giant blacks during the 1950s, when the all-tackle IGFA record fish of 1,560

A big black marlin comes aboard off Panama.

pounds was caught. Several others in excess of 1,400 pounds were also caught there during those halcyon days, and many over 1,000. So far not even the fabled black marlin fishery of Cairns, Australia, has been able to put a black over 1,323 pounds in the record books, although more "half-tonners" have been caught there than anywhere else in the world.

Today the Cabo Blanco black marlin fishery is nothing like its glory days, the result of commercial overfishing of the baitfish that brought these fish into that area. The 1990s angler looking for a half-ton black marlin has his or her best chance in Australia, although a few spots in Central and South American have produced a few such fish. Manta, Equador is one. Longliners bring them into port from time to time. Ditto the tip of Baja California. And at least one black estimated at well over 1,000 was hooked and fought for several hours off the northwest tip of Costa Rica back in the 1970s. But the odds truly are, if you are ever fortunate enough to hook a 1,000-pound marlin in the eastern Pacific, it will be a blue.

The average black marlin off the west coast of Central or South America runs close to 300 pounds. Fish over 700 have been taken in Panama, Costa Rica, and Equador. Pinas Bay, Panama, is an exceptionally productive spot for blacks.

PACIFIC BLUE MARLIN

Pacific blue marlin are also very rare in the continental U.S. but abundant around Hawaii, where at least two in excess of 1,600 pounds have been caught on rod and reel. By comparison, the largest blue in the record books from the Atlantic weighed 1,282 pounds (Virgin Islands, 1977), and the IGFA all-tackle Pacific blue record is 1,376 pounds (Hawaii, 1982).

For angling purposes the Pacific and Atlantic blues are the same. They prefer the same habitats, regardless of the oceans in which they are found. Other good fishing locations around the globe include Panama and Costa Rica, the tip of the Baja Peninsula, Equador (Salinas and Manta), Columbia, Australia, Fiji, and most of the tropical Indian Ocean.

Baits, tackle, and fishing techniques are the same, too.

STRIPED MARLIN

If you want the largest members of this species available, the place to go is New Zealand, where all but one of the record fish over 250 pounds have been taken. The largest is currently 494 pounds (1986), but seven of the eight over 300 pounds also came from that country. The eighth came from Australia. Striped marlin from down under are big, but not found in the large numbers common to some parts of Central and South America, where the average size is more like 125 pounds.

Striped marlin commonly range as far north as Southern California, where they have been successfully fished for decades. For pure numbers, until recently Salinas, Equador, was the place to go. Commercial pressure has reduced that fishery somewhat, but they are still plentiful in Equador (all year, September through April best) and northern Peru. Another hotspot with outstanding stripe fishing is the tip of Baja and the lower Sea of Cortez, where during the peak of the season (November through March) a single boat may present baits to twenty or more per day.

For some reason there are big gaps in that fishery between the Baja Peninsula and Columbia. Nowhere in Costa Rica, for example, are striped marlin commonly found. Nor in Panama, until you get close to its common border with Columbia (e.g. Piñas Bay). But if you do catch a stripe in Costa Rica or northern

This big Pacific striped marlin is being handled carefully at boatside so that it can be released when the hook's removed.

Panama, usually it's well above average in size. Hawaii records a few striped marlin every year, also usually above average in size.

Due to its relatively small average size, tackle for striped marlin is the same as that used for Pacific sailfish. Many anglers still use 50-pound-class gear for these fish because they frequent areas where big blues and blacks are common, but the trend today is more toward 30, especially 30-pound-class stand-up tackle.

Unlike all other marlins, the stripe exhibits one characteristic that allows some interesting variations in fishing technique. More often than not it is first spotted cruising on the surface, the tall upper lobe of its caudal (tail) fin clearly visible. They often travel in pairs or small groups, and not all are necessarily on the surface. Sometimes only one or two out of five or six are visible, the rest remaining slightly submerged.

The standard procedure is to place the boat in a position to drag rigged baits (large balao are especially effective) across the path of travel of the swimming fish, placing the baits just far enough in front to be clearly visible but not so close that their sudden appearance might startle the fish. Obviously the boat must also be kept well clear of the fish during this maneuver.

Another variation is to use a rod suitable for casting small bonito or mackerel of 1 to 2 pounds. The boat is positioned well in front of the fish and slightly to one side of their path of travel. The angler uses a 20- or 30-pound-class outfit to cast the bait so that it lands 30 to 40 feet in front of the lead fish, then waits for the pickup.

A hungry striped marlin is not a timid eater. It usually takes the bait with a swift rush. The drop back from an outrigger is all that's needed, sometimes less. Especially with live bait if you wish to avoid gut-hooking the fish.

When overpowered with 50-pound tackle, the average-size striped marlin is unable to demonstrate all of its aerial capabilities. The fight is short and frequently disappointing. On lighter tackle it is a marvelous gamefish capable of exciting jumps and long, powerful rushes.

SWORDFISH

This unique billfish is found from the tropics all the way through temperate waters on both sides of the equator and probably in all oceans except the Arctic and Antarctic. In fact scientists estimate this is by far the most widely distributed billfish of all. In U.S. waters it is found along the Pacific Coast along the lower half of California, and on rare instances as far north as Oregon. On the Atlantic side its range covers the entire Gulf of Mexico and the East Coast as far as Massachusetts (summer months), and not infrequently all the way to Maine.

Rarely venturing inshore of the 100-fathom (600-foot) curve, it is most likely to be found where the water is 200 fathoms or deeper.

The body shape of the swordfish is different from other billfishes. All of the others are oval in cross-section; the swordfish is almost cylindrical. This allows much more weight per unit length, the reason why a swordfish whose body length is the same as a 300-pound blue marlin (length of bill excluded in both cases) will weigh between 400 and 500 pounds. This heavily muscled body shape also produces tremendous power and is the prime reason for the swordfish's exceptional endurance. The current all-tackle IGFA world record, by the way, is 1,182 pounds, a swordfish caught in Chile in 1953. The mounted fish today hangs in the dining room of the Miami Beach Rod & Reel Club on Hibiscus Island, a truly impressive sight.

Until the early 1970s the traditional way to catch a swordfish on rod and reel was by trolling a bait by it on the surface. But, it is extremely rare indeed that a swordfish will actually feed on the surface. They usually look for food in very deep water and at night. Squid is their favorite. Nature has equipped this species with the largest eye for its size of any billfish, enabling it to locate food hundreds of feet below the surface on a moonless night. This same zone, by the way, is also the preferred habitat of many species of squid.

Fisheries scientists believe that because the swordfish eats its food in very cold water at great depths, it must then come to the surface to allow the warmer temperatures to aid its digestion. This would certainly explain the extremely low response rate to baits, alive or dead, no matter how skillfully presented to surfaced swordfish.

In the early 1960s it was discovered that swordfish could be taken in greatest numbers by fishing rigged baits very deep with longlines. Typical depths ranged from 100 feet on the dark nights to 600 feet or more if the moon is more than half full. When we were attending a marlin tournament in Havana, Cuba, in 1979, a fisheries scientist from that country suggested the biggest swordfish would be caught on baits as far down as 1,000 feet or more.

Eventually the longlining technique was refined to include chemical lights, such as Cylumes, because swordfish are apparently attracted to weak lights. Then Jerry and Jesse Webb of Miami proved that this same procedure could also be adapted to rod-and-reel fishing. As a result, during a few years in the middle 1970s *more* swordfish were caught this way by sportfishermen than *all* of the others previously landed by any other rod-and-reel technique. The prime time seemed to be the week before the full moon, and the least productive from a day or two before the full moon to a week or so afterward. Fishing was done by rigging large (2- to 4-pound) squid on one or two 14/0 hooks, and attaching the Cyalume lightstick 20 feet above the bait. Lead weights are used only as necessary to get the bait to the desired depth.

Some boats were hooking as many as five swordfish per night during the peak summer months of May through August. That's more than all of the boats in many historically productive New England ports were hooking in a summer season of baiting them on the surface.

Unfortunately this fishery has since diminished to a point where it has almost disappeared. Completely uncontrolled overfishing by commercial longliners has reduced swordfish stocks in U.S. waters to a very small percentage of its former size. Sadly, the very agencies charged with protecting the species, the regional Fisheries Management Councils created under the 200-mile limit law of the 1970s (PL 94–265), have failed to take *any* steps to manage the swordfishery. Most of the vessels longlining U.S. waters are out of the swordfish catching business today—not enough fish were caught to keep the boats going. A few others have moved to the Caribbean, where they continue to overfish those stocks.

As late as 1989, swordfish were successfully being taken by sportfishermen night fishing off Venezuela and to some extent the Mexican island of Cozumel, but at least for the time being the future of even those fisheries remains uncertain.

U.S. BILLFISH LAWS

In 1988 the Fisheries Management Councils for the East and Gulf Coasts of the U.S. passed minimum possession sizes for billfish caught inside federal waters of the Atlantic and Gulf of Mexico. They are:

BLUE MARLIN: 200 pounds, or 110 inches total length, or 86 inches as measured from the tip of the lower jaw to the fork of the tail, or 75 inches as measured from the eye to the fork of the tail.

WHITE MARLIN: 50 pounds, or 81 inches total length, or 62 inches as measured from the tip of the lower jaw to the fork of the tail, or 53 inches as measured from the eye to the fork of the tail.

SAILFISH: 30 pounds or 76 inches total length, or 57 inches as measured from the tip of the lower jaw to the fork of the tail, 49 inches as measured from the eye to the fork of the tail.

SPEARFISH: no minimum size limit.

SWORDFISH: No size restrictions as of May, 1990. The swordfish is *not* considered a billfish by the Management Councils.

In the Pacific Ocean, the only billfish commonly found in U.S. waters is the striped marlin off southern California. At present there are no size restrictions.

In addition, many coastal states now have limits on the number of billfish that can be retained. See Chapter 25 for these and other saltwater fishing laws.

MOUNTING BILLFISH

Outside of tournaments that require dead fish on the dock, which incidentally seem to be slowly declining in numbers, billfish have traditionally been killed so that they can be mounted and proudly displayed on the wall. But modern technology no longer requires the body of the fish to mount it. Major marine taxidermists now have molds of just about all popular saltwater gamefish species in a wide range of sizes. All that's needed is the name of the species and its approximate length, and they can reproduce it in long-lasting fiberglass replica. The results have the same detail and appearance of the traditional skin mount, only now you have the pleasure of knowing that the fish it represents is still alive because you released it.

Chapter 5

THE MACKERELS

Both the mackerels and the tunas belong to a broad family of fishes called Scombridae. The essential differences between the two branches are that the tunas (with a few exceptions) have no large cutting teeth, and mackerels do. Tunas are also much heavier for their length than the more slender mackerels. Both branches, however, range around the globe in tropic and some temperate waters, inshore and far out in blue water.

By far the most widely distributed mackerel is the wahoo. A tropical fish, it will follow warm currents into more temperate areas, but it is found in all tropical oceans worldwide. It is also the largest, but it has several close cousins of almost equal size. Perhaps most familiar of these to East Coast anglers is the king mackerel. Australia and nearby portions of the Indo-Pacific have the greatest number of different species of large mackerels, which include the narrow-barred Spanish mackerel (also called a kingfish, which grows to 130 pounds), the spotted mackerel (to 18 pounds), and the shark mackerel (has larger than average scales for a mackerel, grows to 25 pounds). Along the Atlantic and Pacific coasts of Central and northern South America there is a close cousin of the Spanish mackerel called the sierra mackerel, which reaches a weight of at least 12 to 15 pounds.

Then there are many smaller mackerel/tuna species that go unnoticed except by anglers who prize them as bait.

The four major species of mackerel found in U.S. waters are confined to the Gulf of Mexico and East Coast. They are, in terms of size from largest to smallest, the wahoo, king mackerel, cero, and Spanish mackerel. There is also a smaller species, the Atlantic mackerel (found from Cape Hatteras to the Gulf of St. Lawrence), which does reach panfish size (average about 15 inches, max perhaps 25). And the smallest mackerels, often used for bait, include the chub and frigates.

One of the many species of mackerel common to Australian waters, this barred mackerel is very much like the king mackerel of the southeastern U.S. and Caribbean.

WAHOO

This largest of mackerel is entirely an offshore fish, rarely venturing near shore except where deep water is very close. For this reason it is most often encountered by anglers seeking billfish or tuna in blue water, although along the tropical Pacific Coast of Central and South America it may be found around rock reefs in quite shallow water—because deep water is very close at hand. In that part of the world it is often known as the "wet fish," because its arrival in greatest numbers coincides with the start of the summer rainy season.

In U.S. waters it is found throughout the Gulf of Mexico and up the East Coast as far as Cape Cod. Cape Hatteras is a good wahoo spot during the summer months. It is also in the Bahamas, Bermuda, and just about any other spot in the world where the water is warm enough for its liking.

Averaging around 30 pounds, it reaches a length of more than 6 feet. The IGFA all-tackle record is 149 pounds (Cat Cay, Bahamas, 1962), and there are rumors of a 180-pounder caught near Freeport in the Bahamas. A very strong fighter, it can make incredibly long and fast runs against surprisingly heavy tackle. It occasionally jumps, too, both when taking the bait and after hookup.

Except for schooling around some Pacific reefs when small (under 20 pounds), wahoo are seldom encountered in large quantities. Most are loners, or occasionally travel in pairs.

Wahoo will attack just about any bait or lure that moves, the faster the better. Deep-diving plugs trolled around deep reefs work wonders in some areas, while in others the action is on the surface where the strike—if you're quick enough to see it—can be spectacular. We have often watched these speedsters streak many yards just under the surface, visible only as a silvery blur, to strike a bait with unerring accuracy. As for lure colors, just about anything works, but purple, dark red, and black are very high on most experienced anglers' list.

Anglers deliberately seeking big wahoo on light

The wahoo is the largest and fastest member of the mackerel family. It strikes almost any bait or lure with incredible speed.

tackle should use reels with enough capacity for 300 or more yards of line. Otherwise that first run may result in just a bare spool.

The wahoo certainly has something for everyone. It is uncommon enough that simply catching one puts it in the prize category. It is a superb gamefish unless hopelessly overgunned with tackle that's far too heavy. And wahoo steaks are some of the finest white fish meat you'll ever eat.

KING MACKEREL

Also called kingfish, this species is found in U.S. waters from the Mexican border around the entire perimeter of the Gulf of Mexico and up the East Coast as far north as Cape Hatteras. Occasionally it even strays to Cape Cod. Its range also extends down through the Caribbean, and from there southward to Brazil.

The kingfish reaches a weight of almost 100 pounds (the IGFA all-tackle record is 90 pounds from Key West in 1976), but it is most likely to be caught in the 5- to 25-pound range. Anything over 40 pounds is called a "smoker." They range from far offshore to very close to the beaches, moving in concert with the schools of baitfish they are feeding upon. Some may be encountered throughout the warmer months, but the basic pattern for Gulf of Mexico king mackerel is to be in the northern Gulf during the summer months and in the more southerly waters during the winter. There are definite migrations, northward during the spring and southward during the fall.

The same behavior is exhibited by Atlantic coast kingfish. They are commonly caught in winter months south of Cape Canaveral, and from spring through summer they range well north through the Carolinas. They remain in those more northerly waters until late fall when declining water temperatures send them southward again.

Biologists consider the Gulf of Mexico kingfish stocks to be essentially separate from the southeastern Atlantic group. There is thought to be some possible slight intermixing in the waters off Key West, but if so the exchange is apparently so small that it is of little consequence. During the 1980s both stocks took a sharp nosedive, the results of heavy overfishing by both commercial and recreational anglers. As a consequence, most coastal states have bag, size, and seasonal limits (often federally im-

This youngster is justifiably proud of his large king mackerel. The kingfish always strikes the bait on the way up, often jumping ten feet in the air.

posed) that apply to both commercial and sport fishermen.

A king mackerel will willingly strike live and dead baits, as well as artificial lures. Live bait is considered to be the best way of all to take the biggest fish. A 60-pounder will readily attack a 3-pound live blue runner, mullet, or other similar size bait. They infrequently jump when hooked, but they will take a trolled bait with such a rush from below that they catapult high into the air in the process. Unlike wahoo, which often leap high into the air and strike a trolled bait on the way down, king mackerel almost always strike on the way up. A big king at the peak of its jump may be ten feet above the surface. It is indeed a wild sight to be looking *up* from the cockpit of the boat to see this fish eating your bait in midair!

King mackerel, like others of their family, seem to possess extremely sharp eyesight. They can, with surgical precision, cut off the rear portion of a live or trolled dead bait just a millimeter behind the hook. That's why many experienced anglers and charter skippers rig a second (and sometimes smaller) hook farther back in the bait, often hidden just under the skin.

Drifting or very slow trolling with live bait is extremely effective. And where live bait keeping facilities might not be available, such as on some head boats, anglers do extremely well with a dead balao or strip of mullet rigged on a ¾- to 1½-ounce jig. Usually one or even two more hooks are added to the jig for the reasons mentioned above.

During recent years flycasters have been taking big king mackerel with great regularity by anchoring in productive spots, particularly near wrecks or reefs, and chumming with "trash fish" from commercial shrimp nets or blocks of ground-up frozen fish. Sinking lines and large streamer flies, 5 to 6 inches long, are very productive. Popular colors seem to be blue/white, green/white, or anything else that resembles baitfish common to the area. Many charter boat captains in the Key West area have made a specialty of taking big kingfish this way, and on other forms of light tackle too.

An effective Florida west-coast kingfishing technique calls for using a net to catch large quantities of live sardines, which are transported to the fishing grounds in a well-circulated bait tank. Each rod is fitted with a short piece of light (e.g. no. 7) coffee-colored wire, and a 3/0 to 5/0 hook. The sardine or other small baitfish is hooked through the nose and slowly trolled. As soon as the first strike occurs, the boat is put into a tight circle at idle speed and a handful or two of live sardines are thrown into the middle of the circle. This chumming with live bait can at times bring the kingfish boiling to the surface, and the action can certainly be fast.

CERO MACKEREL

This third largest mackerel in U.S. waters has a range that's identical with the king mackerel, except it is far more common along the Atlantic coast of southern Florida, especially the Keys, and throughout the Bahamas. It may reach a top weight of around 25 pounds, although the IGFA all-tackle record is 17 pounds 2 ounces (Islamorada, 1986). Nowhere is it found in great abundance.

As a gamefish it behaves much like a king mackerel, and is even at times confused with that fish because of its very similar appearance. It is also susceptible to the same techniques as king mackerel, and large live shrimp should be added to the list of live baits it prefers. As table fare it is, like the king

mackerel, far less oily than the Spanish mackerel, and it has a pleasant taste.

SPANISH MACKEREL

This mackerel grows almost as large as the cero. The current IGFA all-tackle record is 13 pounds (North Carolina, 1987), but it has been caught commercially to almost 20 pounds. Its range is the greatest of all Atlantic mackerels, from Brazil northward to New Jersey, and occasionally as far north as Cape Cod. Like the king mackerel, it follows warming water north during the spring and summer, returning to the southeast coast of Florida for the winter. Primarily a coastal fish, it can wander into the nearshore edge of blue water in areas where there are reefs.

Also popular as a commercial species, Spanish mackerel have been subjected to steadily increasing fishing pressure by both user groups, the net result of which was a sharp decline in their numbers during the 1980s. During some years the netting pressure was so heavy off Ft. Pierce, Florida, that very few fish made it even as far south as Palm Beach. Since that time state and federal regulations have imposed bag limits and seasons. At this writing there seems to be some improvement in their numbers.

Spanish mackerel often enter inlets and bays, making them available to small-boat anglers, pier and bridge fishermen, and sometimes surfcasters. Like all other mackerels they are often willing to strike just about any lure or bait that moves, but there are times when they can be terribly picky. Live bait scores best when strikes are hard to come by with artificials. Small baitfish, like sardines, or medium to large live shrimp are excellent.

Stick to light tackle for this species. And while their sharp teeth might always seem to dictate at least a few inches of light wire as a leader, don't eliminate heavy monofilament too. Many experienced anglers prefer the mono because it almost always gets more strikes than wire, even though a fish is lost now and then. They use 40- to 50-pound test and cut it back as often as necessary to retie the hook before it gets cut through.

Mackerel may feed anywhere from the surface to the bottom, so if possible it is always a good idea to fish lures and baits at many different levels until fish are located. Lures that sink are a must for casting, and fly fishermen should have at least one or two sinking lines in their tacklebox.

Chapter 6

THE TUNAS

Long before man ever had a chance to experience the thrill of angling for billfish, he was already well acquainted with some members of the tuna tribe. Perhaps the main reason is because the undisputed giant of the family, the bluefin, is so willing to leave the safety of the open sea to search for food close to shore, even to enter shallow bays and estuaries. Thus the opportunity presented itself to fabricate traps for these behemoths, allowing early man in his primitive, frail watercraft to capture them successfully and regularly.

It was only natural that as saltwater sportfishing evolved in the U.S. around the beginning of this century, bluefin tuna would become the first of the giant big-game fish (other than sharks) the angler could challenge. In those early encounters, most of the time the tuna won. But as tackle and technique improved, the size of the bluefin landed steadily went up.

And as man ventured farther and farther out to sea he came to realize that the bluefin wasn't the only tuna. Possibly he had already caught some of the smaller members of the family, because several of them venture close to shore. But bluefins aren't the only giants among tunas. In some parts of the world there is a species called the bigeye, which may top 500 pounds. Then there is the yellowfin tuna, which undoubtedly exceeds 400. And another large tuna, found only in the western Pacific, is called the dogtooth (*Gymnosarda unicolor*). The IGFA all-tackle record for the dogtooth tuna is 288 pounds 12 ounces (Korea, 1982). The species, like the mackerels, has big teeth; most tuna have small teeth.

The somewhat rare southern bluefin tuna of Australia and New Zealand waters is a close relative of the Atlantic bluefin, but doesn't grow as large. The current IGFA all-tackle record is 348 pounds 5 ounces (New Zealand, 1981). Both Atlantic and pacific bigeye tuna run larger than that. Moving down in size, there's the albacore, and then the longtail tuna (*Thunnus tonggol*) of Australia. Neither of these probably exceed the 100-pound mark by very much, if at all. The rest of the tuna family is made up of little tunny, bonitos, kawakawa, skipjacks, and the ever-popular blackfin tuna. The tunas belong to the Scombridae family of fishes, which also includes the mackerels.

BLUEFIN TUNA

Although bluefin tuna are technically considered to be worldwide in distribution, only in the Atlantic and (rarely) in the eastern Pacific is it possible to capture the giant *Thunnus thynnus*. The current IGFA all-tackle record is 1,496 pounds (eastern Canada, 1979), but there are rumors of commercially captured Atlantic bluefins that came close to the ton mark. Giant Pacific bluefins are rarely caught by sportfishermen these days, but some are caught by longline each year that reach or exceed 750 pounds. Regardless, the bluefin's immense bulk places it only behind several species of sharks and the black and blue marlins in terms of ultimate fish size.

Bluefin tuna are very wide ranging. In Europe it is found from Norway to the Mediterranean Sea. It is also reported off the African coast southward from Gibraltar to the Cape of Good Hope, but there is a possibility that some of those reports may have confused it with the look-alike bigeye tuna. On the Atlantic Coast of America its general range is from the central Caribbean northward to Newfoundland. In 1958 a bluefin weighing 30 pounds was tagged at Guadalupe Island, Mexico. Five years later, and 6,000 miles away, it turned up in Japan weighing over 240 pounds.

After a grueling fight, a large bluefin tuna is gaffed in warm waters off Bimini, Bahama.

All of the tuna are efficient, relentless beasts of prey, with enormous food requirements. Since the bluefin is by far the largest of the tunas, it is also the most voracious eating machine of all.

A schooling fish that feeds principally on smaller schooling fish, the tuna is one of the chief enemies of its own relative, the mackerel, as well as of menhaden and herring. Tuna will even attack dogfish sharks; in fact, whole dogfish weighing as much as 8 pounds have been found in the stomachs of bluefins. In addition to almost any kind of schooling fish smaller than itself, the tuna consumes vast quantities of squid as well. There is no doubt that its appearance in any local waters and its movements across the ocean are governed by the abundance or absence of fish on which it depends.

But as terrible as tuna surely seem to smaller fish, even the largest bluefins are preyed upon by killer whales. The killers are known to seize them by the back, near the head, thereby cutting the spinal cord for an instant kill. At other times, bluefins have been found stranded in shallow water from which they could not escape. Apparently they reach this predic-ament by pursuing smaller fishes or perhaps while fleeing from killer whales.

Although fishermen have hunted tuna for food for at least twenty centuries, it was only in the past fifty years that anglers sought tuna for sport. The records are most obscure on the first angler to catch a blue-fin on hook and line, but one of the first was a Wedgeport schoolmaster named Thomas Pattilo, who ventured out into Liverpool Bay, Nova Scotia, in 1871.

This pioneer had only 32 fathoms of ordinary cod line wound on a swivel reel of unreliable design. He used a steel hook ⅜ inch thick, 8 inches long, and with a 3-inch shank. Then with a single companion to do the rowing he went fishing.

Pattilo quickly hooked a monster tuna, which towed his boat across the harbor much faster than his friend could row in the other direction—until it hurtled head on into a fleet of herring netters. One netter was swamped and the rest were scattered in confusion. One of the angry herring fishermen finally cut Pattilo's line, thus enabling his first tuna to escape.

But on the next attempt there were no herring fishermen nearby, and at the cost of blistered hands and an aching back Pattilo achieved complete success. Somehow, in spite of his crude tackle, he boated a tuna weighing over 600 pounds.

For reasons which bluefin fishermen know better than anyone else, tuna fishing can become a pure addiction, though it usually is more hard work than it is a lively sport. Because of their streamlined body proportions and ample dimensions, bluefins have been aptly called the torpedoes of the sea. Among the speediest of fish, bluefins have been observed keeping pace with a ship logging 8 knots.

Their bullet-shaped heads and oblong bodies seem to cut through the water with a minimum of drag. Their dorsal and pelvic fins fit into grooves as the fish propel themselves forward with a quick motion of powerful, crescent-shaped tails. A taut, mucus-covered skin with minute scales slides easily through the water.

One indication of the bluefin's extraordinary speed is its manner of pursuing the unique and graceful flying fish, a staple of its diet. When chasing a flying fish, a tuna seems to estimate its trajectory and then captures it when it reenters the sea. That means that a tuna would have to be moving far faster than the 8 knots mentioned before.

The bluefin's weakness for flying fish inspired a curious method of angling dubbed the tunalane or the kite-fishing technique, first devised by Captain George Farnsworth of Avalon, California, and it since has been adapted to fishing elsewhere.

Just after World War II, Harlan Major, a fishing writer, learned about the kite-fishing technique and introduced it to the East. He passed the method on to Tommy Gifford, a gamefish guide from Montauk, New York, who, before long, had boated the first white marlin, the first tuna, and the first broadbill swordfish ever taken on kites along the Atlantic coast. Since then he has flown his kite successfully for sailfish as well as these other species in almost all eastern U.S. waters, as well as those of Nova Scotia, Bimini, Cat Cay, Cuba, Puerto Rico, and Jamaica.

As you can guess, the angler's line is fastened by a clothespin to the kite string and the bait skips over the surface of the water in a manner tantalizing to many of the big gamefish. The technique can be used when trolling or—if there is a wind—when still-fishing.

An average angler's best chance to catch a big bluefin is to intercept one of its annual migrations at one of the regular fishing ports along our coast. On chartered boats, the method most universally used to catch bluefins is to chum for them. Menhaden, herring, or mackerel are ground up into an oily "liquor" and slowly spilled over the transom of the boat into the sea. As this chum dissolves into the tide, it lures the big tuna close to the stern of the boat where a bait is waiting for them.

Baits are usually 6 to 10 1-pound herring (usually with their backbones removed), spaced about a foot apart and tied to a piece of tarred cord. The cord is attached to a light string about 15 feet long which in turn is tied to a 15-foot bamboo pole. The angler's hook, buried inside one of the herring near the end of the string, can be any size from 6/0 to 12/0.

A deckhand or first mate stands in the stern of the boat, alternately raising and lowering the long pole, thereby causing the herring to skip along the tops of the waves as the tuna come near. This is to simulate an actual school of herring in flight.

If all goes well, a striking tuna will swirl up behind the teaser and grab it. He may gulp only one of the herring or he may take all of them. If the angler is lucky, the gulp will include the herring which has his hook embedded in it.

When the tuna makes the first run, it usually sounds, breaking the light cord which attaches the string of herring to the bamboo pole. That is the moment when an angler sets his hook. It's an exciting moment which he had better enjoy to the fullest because from that point on it is nothing but pure, back-breaking drudgery.

When a giant bluefin is solidly hooked, it will make one terrific run after another trying to free itself. It'll shake and shudder and frequently tow even a heavy boat for many miles. And if not handled skillfully, it can snap the line with apparent ease.

Charter-boat captains resort to another technique that is very effective at slack tide with the boat completely adrift. A 1-pound herring is hooked through the back and dropped astern. Just above the wire leader a toy balloon is attached with a light piece of string and small safety-pin swivel. Occasionally the balloon can be moved up or down on the line to change the depth of the bait. If and when the tuna strikes, the balloon simply disintegrates and the long hard fight is on.

The proper line size for giant bluefins is 80- to 130-pound test, but since other fish (white marlin, sailfish, wahoo) are often taken in the same water, a boat captain may recommend that his more experienced customers use 30 or 50.

In 1935, Michael Lerner, a big-game fishing pioneer with experience around the globe, went to Nova Scotia for a whirl at the fabled swordfishing. On his way back to Yarmouth to catch the Boston ferryboat, he stopped for gas near Wedgeport. He happened to have his big-game fishing gear in the car and that led to fishing talk with the gas station attendant and a group of cronies gathered there.

Lerner's ears almost popped when he heard about the 1,000-pound bluefin tuna that the native said were regularly harpooned at the mouth of the Tusket River and at Soldier's Rip, a tidal channel so named because a troop transport once foundered there off Wedgeport.

Without further conversation, Mike canceled his reservation on the Boston boat, rigged a crude fighting chair in the stern of a lobster boat, and went tuna fishing.

That first day out he caught two tuna. Two days later he caught another bluefin, but business called him back to New York. The business transacted, he was back in Wedgeport a week later and in eight days of fishing boated 21 large tuna weighing a total of 3,677 pounds! As a result of this effort, Lerner convinced several commercial fishermen and lobstermen to rig their boats for sportfishing. And a number of years later the International Tuna Cup match was organized in the tiny lobster town of Wedgeport.

Like moths to flame, big-game anglers came from all four corners of the globe to match their skills and muscles with giant bluefin tuna every September. And the action was definitely worth the trip. Even though the matches do not exist anymore (because in recent years the bluefins wouldn't cooperate and wouldn't guarantee to arrive at Soldier's Rip at the same time as the fishermen who traveled from as far away as Havana, Cape Town, and Lisbon), they were among the most colorful events in saltwater fishing history, and no chapter on tuna fishing would be complete without mentioning them.

The giant bluefin is found at various times of the year all along the Atlantic coast of North America, from the Bahamas and Cuba northward to Newfoundland. They cruise in a roughly circular migration that begins in their spawning grounds somewhere in the Gulf of Mexico, that vast, deep blue "meadow" area between Florida and Mexico. Traveling northward from there the 500-pound bluefin tuna usually pass Cat Cay and Bimini in the Bahamas in May and June. They reach Montauk Point, Long Island, and Rhode Island in late June and early July. Of all tuna summering grounds (including Cape Cod Bay), Wedgeport, Nova Scotia, has always had the biggest concentration of tuna from August through September. Occasionally, large concentrations are found as far north as Newfoundland. As the winter months arrive, the bluefins begin their southward migration, which carries them past Bermuda and on to the Lesser Antilles.

The winter migration continues in a westerly direction off the Venezuelan coast and by February the fish are running past Jamaica. A possible spawning ground may be in the Windward Passage between Cuba and Haiti. Scientists believe that some tuna head north through the passage and also up the Old Bahama Channel and Mona Passage, between the Dominican Republic and Puerto Rico, northward toward Cat Cay and Bimini. Others head northward past Cozumel and enter the central Gulf of Mexico to spawn.

Bluefins are fished in a variety of ways, including trolling and "stationary trolling" (anchored in a strong current), often with some chumming. Preferred baits include artificials, rigged whole baits (mackerel and squid are especially popular), and more recently a spreader rig. The spreader consists of a V-shaped piece of 3/16-inch stainless-steel wire with a 90-degree angle between the two 24-inch arms. It is attached to the leader at the apex of the "V". Five or six whole rigged *hookless* mackerel are attached directly to the arms with light twine or clips, so that they are easily pulled off at the strike, and spread evenly from one end to the other. Two more are also attached in tandem at body-length intervals to a longer line extending back from the apex of the "V"; only the very last bait in that line is the one with the hook. As the rig is dragged through the water, it creates the appearance of a small school of mackerel swimming in tight formation, visible to a tuna at great distance. Although only the last bait in the "school" has the hook, even if the tuna misses it on the first try, rarely will it fail to come back and keep striking until it finally gets hooked.

It is sad to note that during the last twenty-five years the bluefin tuna stocks have steadily decreased, some years at an alarming rate. Longliners intercept them in the open sea, often taking giant females in spawning condition by the hundreds. And the rocketing price for bluefin tuna meat during the 1980s, because of the insatiable appetite for it in Japan, has sadly turned the fishery into an almost completely commercial one. Even those caught on rod and reel are instantly purchased by wholesale buyers as soon as they hit the dock, and within twenty-four hours transported by jet to the Tokyo market.

Will this lead to the demise of the largest of tunas? Let us hope that some sort of sanity (with proper management practices) prevails during the 1990s, so that the bluefin tuna won't become just another item in the history books to show our grandchildren.

BIGEYE TUNA

The International Game Fish Association maintains records on this tuna separately for the Atlantic and Pacific, but like the blue marlin and sailfish, fisheries scientists consider it the same species (*Thunnus obesus*) worldwide. It is the second largest of the tunas, and the IGFA Pacific all-tackle record for it is 436 pounds (Peru, 1957). In the Atlantic the record is 375 pounds (Maryland, 1977).

Bigeye tuna are entirely a deepwater fish, seldom venturing inshore of the 50-fathom (300-foot) curve. More likely they are to be found far seaward of that depth. Several years ago we encountered a huge school of bigeyes approximately 25 miles west of Salinas, Equador. They were busy feeding on flying fish and showed no interest whatsoever in anything we had to offer. But it was a grand sight to see them hurl their 400-pound bodies skyward as they crashed through schools of frantic flying fish.

Bigeyes look very much like a bluefin, or perhaps what a blackfin tuna would look like if it grew that large. They have much greater girth for their length than the more slender yellowfin tuna and albacore. And although they will at times strike the same lures and baits that work for billfish or yellowfin tuna, experienced anglers have found that usually the best time to catch them is at dawn or dusk. Their large eye size suggests that unless there's considerable bait to attract them to the surface during daylight, they're more likely to stay deep and/or feed at night.

Along the U.S. Atlantic seaboard they are most commonly found from Cape Hatteras to New York, and boats venturing out to prime spots forty or so miles offshore to the Hudson and Baltimore canyons are enjoying a real bonanza. Part of this tuna bonus comes from fishing for another species. When big sportfishing boats started staying far offshore through the night to fish for swordfish in those waters, the catch rate for bigeyes rose considerably because the best times for this species to feed on or near the surface are around dawn and dusk, especially the first hour or so of daylight.

A 300-pound Pacific bigeye tuna landed off Ecuador.

YELLOWFIN TUNA

This grand gamefish, also known as the allison tuna in its larger sizes, is truly one of the most exciting light to medium tackle prizes in the world. Fortunately *Thunnus ablacares* is distributed worldwide in all tropical seas all year, and as waters warm outside of the tropics during the summer months, their range extends far into temperate latitudes as well.

It is the third largest tuna in U.S. waters. The

current IGFA all-tackle record is 388 pounds 12 ounces (Mexico, 1977), but fish in excess of 150 pounds have been taken throughout most of its ranges. At present the largest yellowfins are being caught off the west coast of Mexico, mostly by big long-range party boats fishing for eight to twenty-one days out of San Diego, California.

Big yellowfins are commonly encountered along the Atlantic Coast of the U.S. from Florida and the Bahamas northward to New York. They stay almost entirely out in blue water, but occasionally foray near the outer edges of the deeper reefs when food is abundant there. Heavy chumming along the edge of a reef near blue water will often draw them into surprisingly shallow depths. Such a situation occurs at times along the reefs of the Florida Keys when there are a lot of boats in a relatively small area chumming for yellowtail snappers. Because of the high concentrations of this chum, quite a long slick is developed and if the wind and current conditions are right, it will extend out into blue water where it may be encountered by passing yellowfins.

Yellowfins are also deliberately brought close to anchored or drifting boats by chumming and chunking (see Chapter 20 for more details). There are spots off the east coast of the U.S. where this is extremely effective during the summer months. And perhaps the whole thing really got its start many years ago by boats anchored along the edges of the deepwater banks in Bermuda. Chumming for yellowfins has also been done successfully in the Bahamas and around various islands in the Caribbean, including the Caymans.

In Australia and South Africa they have even been caught by anglers fishing from the shore, perched high on slippery rocks dangerously washed by huge waves where deep water runs right against the shoreline. A big yellowfin hooked from shore requires a *lot* of line on the reel, and a strong back to successfully bring it within reach of a gaff. Yellowfin tuna over 80 pounds have been caught "from the rocks" this way.

Although often hooked on lures and baits trolled for marlin, yellowfin tuna will take cut bait in a chumline quite readily. They also respond very well to lures retrieved with casting tackle, especially noisy surface lures of the chugger variety (e.g. the 99M series Mirrolures, or the Arbogast Scudder). Most of the yellowfins taken in a Bermuda chumline range from 30 to 100 pounds, but occasionally one over 150 is caught. The prime time for this is June through August.

Big yellowfins are common to Hawaii, mostly during the summer months, although some are caught there all year. As yet none have topped 300 pounds in those waters, but over 200 isn't all that rare. There are several in the IGFA record books from there that exceed 240.

Catching yellowfins in the open sea by trolling is mostly a matter of luck if no fish signs are present. As a rule if they're actively feeding on or near the surface, you'll see birds hovering overhead. Often the largest fish aren't in the biggest, most obvious schools, but rather under small groups of birds flying at high speed to keep up with the rapidly moving fish. It can take some topnotch boat handling to get a bait in front of these erratic fish, but the strike of a big yellowfin tuna under those circumstances is a sight forever etched in your memory.

Yellowfin tuna often travel in the company of porpoises, a fact not lost on commercial tuna netters that has sadly resulted in the demise of many thousands of those intelligent mammals. We have also taken advantage of that relationship, by drifting the boat through an active school of porpoises and dropping ½- to 3-ounce jigs straight down to depths of up

The most streamlined of the big tunas, the yellowfin is found worldwide in all tropical seas.

to 150 feet before jigging them rapidly back to the surface. Most of the fish we've hooked that way have ranged from 10 to 30 pounds, but every so often one would exceed 50, a *big* handful on light tackle.

ALBACORE

Also sometimes called longfin tuna (not to be confused with the longtail tuna of Australian waters), *Thunnus alalunga* is a single species worldwide. The IGFA all-tackle record is 88 pounds 2 ounces (Canary Islands, 1977), and it possibly might reach 100. They share essentially the same distribution worldwide as the yellowfin tuna, but rarely are they as abundant. Some are caught off the East Coast of the U.S. each year, but by far the most productive sportfishery is July through October from Southern California southward along the northern Baja Peninsula. Entirely a blue-water fish, it is often necessary to travel a hundred miles offshore to find them. The best action is usually to be had aboard the long-range party boats out of San Diego, on three- to eight-day trips.

Unlike most other tunas, albacore seem to have a rather narrow preferred temperature range of 60 to 66 degrees F. Anything warmer or colder is likely to push them out of reach of even long-range boats. The standard angling procedure is to locate a school by fast-trolling lures, then stop and fish with live bait. Anchovies, sardines, and herring are the most popular choices. Of all the tunas, they have the whitest meat, which makes them highly prized table fare.

BLACKFIN TUNA

This species, *Thunnus atlanticus*, is found only in the western Atlantic from Brazil to Cape Cod. Primarily tropical by nature, it reaches the northern end of its migratory pattern only during the summer months. While not reaching even close to the maximum size attained by albacore (the IGFA all-tackle record is 42 pounds, Bermuda, 1978), it is far more abundant in the Atlantic within its prime range.

For many years caught primarily by accident while trolling baits for billfish on heavy tackle, over the past three decades it has attracted a rapidly growing

Rarely exceeding 40 pounds, the blackfin tuna is ideal for light tackle. This tuna often feeds in the shallows.

legion of light-tackle devotees. Many rate it pound for pound above the yellowfin in terms of strength and stubbornness, an observation considered heretic by those who arguably feel the yellowfin is stronger. Nevertheless, on light tackle it is unquestionably one of the world's great gamefish.

Unlike the yellowfin, blackfins invade shallow water in search of food. They often appear along the shallow edge of a reef as a large school of widely scattered fish, their feeding activity visible in the form of whitewater explosions here and there as they chase balao under a loose canopy of diving pelicans. December through March along the Florida Keys is a prime time for this. If you can get close enough quickly enough, they can be caught by casting plugs or jigs and working them rapidly on or just under the surface. Most anglers choose lures that are heavy enough to be cast great distances on long spinning or baitcasting rods.

Blackfins eagerly respond to chumming. One popular way in the Gulf of Mexico north of Key West is to use trash fish from a commercial shrimper's net. Because these shrimp boats trawl at night and anchor through the day, it is often possible to anchor near the boat the trash fish came from, since cleaning the nets from the previous night's dragging will likely already have attracted many fish, including blackfins, bonitos, mackerel, and so forth.

THE OTHER TUNAS

Bonitos, skipjack tuna, and many others of that family are found throughout all of the tropical and much of the temperate seas. Some reach blackfin size, or larger. Some years ago in a Honolulu fish market we saw many baskets of huge skipjack tuna that averaged over 50 pounds each, taken apparently from the mid-Pacific between Hawaii and Midway. All of these are excellent gamefish if caught on appropriate tackle. Most will take trolled or cast artificial lures readily, lures tipped with bait, or live bait. Many are caught each year, for example, by flycasters in the surf around the Cape Cod area. And by anglers in boats of all sizes near shore in southern California. As a rule these are mostly dark-meat tunas, more sought after by sportfishermen for bait than for the table.

A little tunny, also called a bonito in some areas.

Chapter 7

THE JACKS

There are many members of the jack family (Carangidae), and they are found in all tropical and warm temperate waters of the world. Most of those that are of particular interest to the sportfisherman fall into one of three distinct branches: the pompanos (*Trachinotus*), which also includes the giant of that group, the permit; the well-known amberjacks and Pacific yellowtails (*Seriola*); plus the Atlantic and Pacific jack crevalles, the ulua of Hawaii, and the trevallies of Australia and the Indo-Pacific, which fall under the genus *Caranx*. Then there are a few loners, represented by just a few different species, like the African pompano of the tropical Atlantic that actually isn't a pompano at all. Or the rainbow runner, very common in both Atlantic and Pacific, which doesn't even remotely look like a jack.

And in addition to those jacks large enough to be gamefish, there are others, like the blue runner and goggle-eye, that are highly prized as live bait. Goggle-eyes, for instance, are held in such great esteem as sailfish bait that during some Palm Beach tournaments they have been known to sell for over $200 a dozen!

One of the nice features about the jacks is that they are almost always willing to accommodate. In fact it is rare to meet a jack that isn't hungry. And while some are good to eat and others are not, they all share another characteristic: power. Nature has equipped each and every one with a wide body and large, high-speed tail fins. They are capable of making long, very powerful runs, and also a dogged fight that seems almost without end. Some species will strike lures readily on the surface, too.

All species of jacks are essentially schooling fish. Once in a while an exceptionally large jack (for its particular species) will be a loner, but usually if you see one you can rest assured there are more nearby. Jack crevalles in particular like to stay in tightly packed schools, and usually almost every fish in that school is the same size.

In U.S. waters the various species of jacks commonly range on the East Coast from Cape Hatteras southward and throughout the entire Gulf of Mexico, with some stragglers as far north as Massachusetts during the summer months. On the Pacific Coast they're found from the Gulf of Santa Catalina southward. Some are more wide-ranging than others, but the movements and availability of all members of the family are entirely temperature-related. They are warm-water fish, and move into the northern limits of their respective ranges only when the temperature is to their liking. An exceptionally warm spring and summer might see jacks as far north as the New York bight, and possibly even Cape Cod. Jacks are all-year residents of south Florida and the southern Gulf of Mexico, as well as the Caribbean and other tropical areas.

THE POMPANOS

As a group these are among the finest fish to eat in the world. The most common species is the Florida pompano, perhaps also the most sought after as an epicure's delight. It is an inshore fish, preferring sloughs along sandy beaches, inlets, and other similar coastal habitat. Very often it betrays its presence when frightened by leaping clear of the surface and skipping like a flat rock on its side for some distance. A big Florida pompano would be 5 pounds or more. Most are under 3. Surf fisherman catch them with small crustacea as bait, especially shrimp and sand fleas. Anglers casting with light tackle prefer small (¼ to ⅜ ounce) lead-headed nylon or bucktail jigs, usually white or yellow. The jig should be bounced along the bottom in slow, deliberate hops.

There are many other pompanos almost as good on the table. The palometa, the gafftopsail pompano and paloma pompano (the last two are Pacific spe-

The permit, found in both deep and shallow water, is a member of the jack family that can go 50 pounds.

cies), and permit (Atlantic or Pacific) under 6 or 7 pounds certainly qualify as exceptionally good to eat. Large permit may be eaten, but those over 15 pounds or so don't have quite as good flavor. Besides, permit are not as plentiful and most anglers prefer to catch and release them.

Permit grow to well over 50 pounds, although in other respects except for the large, fairly visible dark spot on each side of those over 10 pounds, it looks very much like the Florida pompano. The current IGFA all-tackle world record is 51 pounds 8 ounces (Florida, 1978), but during the 1970s one that had been in captivity at the Miami Seaquarium for many years died and was found to weigh 81 pounds. Permit frequently feed on the tropical flats of Florida and the Bahamas, but far greater numbers are to be found around certain reefs, wrecks, and other structures in deep water where they apparently spawn. They have been taken in the surf on rare occasions as far north as Morehead City, North Carolina.

Most anglers consider flats fishing for permit as one of the ultimate challenges. In shallow water they are extremely wary, and their eyesight is so good that they can under very calm conditions be difficult to approach within casting range. So is their sense of smell, which makes a properly placed live crab tough for them to pass up. Most shallow-water permit are hooked on bonefish tackle, and because of their greater size and endurance this makes them a diffi-

cult fish to subdue. See Chapter 1 for more details on flats fishing for them.

OFFSHORE JACKS

By far the largest members of the jack family are the amberjacks. There are two real heavyweights in this group, both very similar. In the Atlantic, it's the greater amberjack; the other is the Pacific amberjack. Both attain weights well over 100 pounds. The IGFA all-tackle record for the Atlantic species is 155 pounds 10 ounces (Bermuda, 1981), and from the Pacific it is 104 pounds (Mexico, 1984). The habits and fighting characteristics of both are identical.

The amberjacks are primarily reef and structure fish. They have been taken in just a few feet of water along the edge of the reefs where deep water is not too far away. And they have also been caught near the bottom around wrecks in up to 300 feet of water. Usually, if there is high structure present, they will be schooled most heavily in mid-water. While they will almost always strike any small live baitfish, many anglers prefer the extra fun of catching them with light tackle and artificial lures. Even tarpon-size (12- or 13-weight) fly rods have been used to catch amberjacks of just over 100 pounds.

Amberjacks in deep water, up to around 200 feet, can be taken by deep jigging (see Chapter 17) with stiff spinning and baitcasting rods and lines testing 10 to 20 pounds. The most popular jigs are white, 1 to 3 ounces, often with a plastic worm added to the hook for extra action.

Amberjacks can often be teased to the surface, where they can be caught with surface lures or large fly-rod streamers. Live bait is the key here, usually fished without a hook if teasing is the objective. Sewn onto a large swivel with heavy Dacron fishing line, the bait is lowered just far enough for the always hungry amberjacks to see and give chase. Then it is brought back to the surface where it can be lifted clear of the water the instant before it is eaten. The big jacks have no fear of boats, and will stay close by as long as they feel there is a chance to eat something. A noisy surface plug or a big fly can be substituted for the teaser as soon as the feeding reaches a frenzy.

If nature ever wanted a mule with fins, the result would have been a amberjack. Tough and stubborn when hooked, if this fish can make it back to any form of structure, the line will soon be frayed

Amberjack are found in tropical waters through the Atlantic and Pacific.

through. We once hooked a big amberjack on 6-pound-test line and spinning tackle after luring it over half a mile away from its home wreck with a live-bait teaser. We never even slowed it down; it made a quick trip back to its lair with our boat in hot pursuit, and the fight was over before it hardly began. Even on a stiff baitcasting outfit and 15-pound-test line you can figure a minute of fighting time for every pound of weight on that fish; it's likely to require a brutal hour of hard work to subdue a 60-pounder.

The California yellowtail is only slightly smaller than the two biggest amberjacks it is so closely related to. The IGFA all-tackle record is 78 pounds (Mexico, 1987), and there are also at least two others that include the southern yellowtail common to Australia and New Zealand, and the Asian yellowtail of Southeast Asia.

There are also several smaller members of the amberjacks. The lesser amberjack is one, and the almaco jack another (in the Atlantic; the Pacific almaco, which is the same species, is in the record books at 132 pounds). Both take artificial lures readily, and often feed at the surface along the outer edges of deep reefs where they can be found attacking small baitfish that are trying to hide in floating rafts of sargassum weed. A plug or fly tossed right into the middle of the vegetation when they are feeding there will usually draw a quick strike, no matter how badly the hooks are clogged with weeds.

THE CREVALLES

The *Caranx* side of the jack family has the greatest number of different species. The tree extends from the giant ulua of the Central Pacific to the turrum of Australia. A deep-bodied fish, its single most identifiable characteristic is a ridge of triangular bony plates called scutes on each side of the caudal peduncle. The amberjacks and pompanos do not have scutes.

Perhaps the best known is the jack crevalle, an Atlantic species with a very close cousin in the Pacific. The largest is the ulua (giant trevally), and the IGFA all-tackle world record for that fish is 117 pounds 9 ounces (Hawaii, 1983). The largest jack crevalle on the record books is 54 pounds 7 ounces (Gabon, 1982), although when we were in Angola in 1973 we heard tales of crevalles that weighed 80 pounds or more.

While it certainly can be said there is almost no such thing as a finicky eater among the jacks, the crevalles are the true gluttons. Anything that moves is considered fair game, and if the fish misses on the first pass it will be right back for another. And another, until it finally gets hooked if the target is a lure. Yellow, often with red, are colors they seem to find particularly attractive. Floater/diver surface plugs in those colors are sure to get a lot of attention, and the strike can be a spectacular explosion of white water. The fight is typical of all jacks, stubborn and protracted.

The trevally side of the crevalle family has much whiter and finer tasting meat than the others. Most trevallies have a darker skin than the jack crevalles; many have beautiful, brightly flecked markings. Entirely an Indo-Pacific species, they are quite common in Hawaii all year.

Another large member of this group is the horse-eye jack, found in both Atlantic and Pacific oceans. The IGFA all-tackle record is just 24 pounds 8 ounces (Miami, 1982), but we have observed larger specimens in Bermuda and once caught a 28-pounder in Costa Rica a few years before IGFA recognized the species. Then there is also the black jack, also found in both Atlantic and Pacific oceans, a rare species that might possibly reach 30 pounds.

AFRICAN POMPANO

This jack (*Alectis crinitus*) is perhaps the most unusual of all. It is not a true pompano, and has the hard body scutes along both sides of its caudal peduncle, as well as the body shape that is deeper than an amberjack and even most other Atlantic jacks. It looks a lot like a permit, except for the more angular forehead. In profile it is perhaps closest to a Pacific trevally. There is also a somewhat smaller Pacific version of the African pompano. We caught them in Panama, Costa Rica, and 300 miles offshore around Costa Rica's Cocos Island. The IGFA all tackle record for the African pompano is 49 pounds (Florida, 1977), but anything over 40 is considered exceptionally large. The most common size is 15 to 25 pounds.

Like all other members of the jack family it is extremely structure-oriented. Steep reefs, ledges, drop-offs, and wrecks are the most likely places to find Africans. They'll take the same live baits as other large jacks, as well as artificials. Deep jigging is a very productive method for hooking them in deep water on light tackle, but since they often congregate around the same structures as amberjack, if you're really intent on catching an African, keep your lure or bait near the bottom since that's where they are most likely to be.

Many fishermen like to eat smoked African pompano, but this can be a somewhat risky practice, as there have been several reported cases of very severe fish poisoning (ciguatera) involving this species. It is not a particularly abundant fish anywhere in its range, and for this reason it should probably be released as often as possible.

Jack crevalle are very aggressive and willing to take a wide variety of artificial lures.

Chapter 8

FISH OF THE SURF

We've grouped the striped bass and the red drum (also known as the channel bass, redfish, or spottail bass) together in this chapter because of their overlapping habitat and somewhat similar behavior patterns. We've also included the black drum, which though not accorded the gamefish status of the other two, does grow large and shares a lot of the same habitat. And, of course, the weakfish, a close cousin to the red and black drums, because it too is an important surf fish.

As a group, the basses discussed in this chapter are in no way related to the sea basses of the grouper or blackfish families. The striper is in a class by itself, with its closest relative probably the freshwater white bass (*Morone chrysops*) of similar appearance, although in saltwater it is considered a member of the temperate bass family (Percichthyidae) and thus related to the giant seabass of California and the wreckfish of the eastern Atlantic. The red and black drum belong to the drum family (Sciaenidae), which also includes the croakers, northern kingfish, spotted seatrout, weakfish, the spot, the corvinas, and the white seabasses. The seatrout and weakfish are legendary in their popularity along the East and Golf Coasts of the U.S., while the corvina and white seabasses extend from Central America up through Southern California. Some of the corvinas and white seabasses grow quite large. During the early 1970s, while fishing the Angola shoreline in Africa, at the month of the Cuanza River, we caught many corvina-like seabass that exceeded 20 pounds, and they are said to top 100 pounds in some areas.

STRIPED BASS

Also called the rockfish in some parts of its range, *Morone saxatilis* is the only major member of the saltwater basses that is truly anadromous, leaving the sea to spawn in freshwater rivers and creeks throughout its range every spring. It has been known to ascend some streams more than 100 miles above tidewater, and even lay its eggs in whitewater rapids. All of this suggests that the striped bass may have had its origin as a species in freshwater, eventually migrating to the sea like the steelhead (a seagoing rainbow trout) because of the ocean's greater food abundance. We've caught them in whitewater rapids on the Umpqua River in Oregon; under those conditions a 10-pounder fights like a 30-pounder in tidewater.

Unfortunately, because it is a freshwater spawner, it is more sensitive to pollution and habitat degradation than most other marine species. Thus the striper stocks of the middle Atlantic states from Virginia to Massachusetts (their prime area of concentration) have been severely depleted in the past twenty years owing to pollution of many major spawning streams.

Finally, during the latter half of the 1980s, legislation was passed in several states that severely restricted their harvest, both commercially and by sportfisherman. Efforts have been made in some critical areas to improve spawning conditions through improved water quality. And now this wonderful gamefish is beginning to show slow signs of recovery along the Atlantic Coast.

The striped bass reaches a weight of 80 or more pounds. There have been reports of commercially netted stripers that have greatly exceeded 100 pounds (including a 125-pounder), but the current IGFA all-tackle record is 78 pounds 8 ounces (New Jersey, 1982). Any striped bass over 50 pounds is certainly bragging size, and the average today is more like 10 to 20 pounds.

Incidentally, the striped bass has been successfully introduced to the Pacific Northwest (more on that shortly), as well as to many freshwater lakes throughout the southern half of the U.S., where it grows to large size (over 50 pounds). Along the Atlantic coast it is today found from Maine to northeastern Flor-

Dick Kotis and friend admire a 36-pound striper he caught spinning in the surf with a scudder surface plug.

ida, and also entirely in freshwater in a few northern Gulf of Mexico rivers where it was introduced many years ago. On the Pacific coast it now ranges from central California (e.g. San Francisco) to southwestern Washington State, although north of California it has not been particularly welcome as a gamefish because it is (incorrectly, according to biologists) thought to prey on precious salmon and steelhead juveniles.

Striper addicts take their fishing seriously. They're willing to trudge miles and miles along sandy shorelines to reach a bit of booming surf, just on mere rumor that striped bass have gathered there. It also causes them to creep and crawl over barnacle-encrusted rocks without regard for life or limb. Many will fish day and night until fatigue alone causes them to doze for an hour or so before returning to the beaches. It causes the faithful to mire and slide on muddy riverbanks or precarious jetties and to spend long hours on the slippery deck of a boat tossed by high seas.

It is easy to pinpoint the reasons for a striper's tremendous appeal to fishermen. There are other fish which grow bigger and still others which fight harder. A few are more handsome, and some are more difficult to catch. A very, very few are better on the table, but not many species rate so high in all these categories. A striped bass is a great gamefish which has almost everything.

You can take stripers from the beach or by trolling for them offshore. You can catch them in protected tidal waters and inlets, and on all types of lures from tiny flies to thick hunks of crab. If the striper has one outstanding characteristic, it's the vast number of ways you can fish for it and the great variety of tackle you can use.

Say you're a heavy-tackle fisherman trolling offshore. Usually a big spoon or plug will tie you into a big fish. If you like light tackle—if you are a flycaster or spinning fan—the inshore bays, channels, and estuaries of many coastal rivers will give you all the action you need. In addition, it's even possible to still-fish for stripers from an anchored boat, from a beach or pier, using anything for bait from shedder crabs, squid, and eels to sandworms, shrimp, or clams. The striper will eat anything it can swallow.

But no method of catching stripers packs all the high adventure and excitement of casting for them in the wild, wind-whipped surf. This can mean fishing with nature baits or with such counterfeits as metal squid, wobbling spoons, eel-skin jigs, or an assortment of plugs too numerous to list. It's true enough that surfcasting for stripers can be a heartbreaking proposition because it's so uncertain. The stripers have little regard for time and tides and a fisherman's convictions. Still, one of the greatest thrills which saltwater angling has to offer is the hooking, playing, and landing of a large striped bass while chest-deep in surf.

As long ago as colonial times the striper was held in highest esteem. In 1634, William Wood set a rough pattern for modern outdoor scribes when he wrote: "The basse is one of the best fishes in the countrye and although men are soon wearied with other fish yet they are never with the basse. It is a delicate, fine, fat, fast fish having a bone in its head which contains a saucer full of marrow, sweet and good, pleasant to the pallat and wholesome to the stomach."

One of the most dramatic incidents in the history of American fish management involved the striped bass, and it occurred as long ago as 1879. Details are somewhat sketchy today, but it is known that a number of small striped bass were seined from the Navesink River in New Jersey and transported across the continent to San Francisco Bay. Only 435 fish survived the transcontinental trip. Twenty years later the Pacific commercial catch of stripers alone reached 1,234,000 pounds. In 1915, some 1,785,000 pounds were marketed from waters where stripers had never existed before!

Such an interocean transfer seems almost impossible to modern biologists, who now have the equipment to do such a thing easily. But in 1879 there were no aerated tank cars and so the fish were transported in anything available. Water in milk cans and makeshift aquariums had to be changed frequently and manually. It was also agitated by hand to keep the fish alive. And when the shipment passed the Mississippi, a few of the stripers were tossed in that river, according to an old account, "just for luck."

There isn't any way to estimate the number of stripers in Pacific coast waters today because commercial netting has been forbidden since 1935, and

the striper has been considered a game species ever since. But the original planting has extended over a major part of the West Coast from San Diego northward as far as the Columbia River in Washington.

Scientific studies have revealed that young fish spawned in the Hudson River rarely travel farther than Long Island Sound. In Chesapeake Bay, which is the largest hatching area for stripers, there are "groups" of fish which appear to remain or to circulate in the bay area throughout the year. But strangest of all the nonmigratory stripers are those who live in the Santee-Cooper drainage area of South Carolina. Stripers have always lived in these rivers, but until recently—after two giant dams were built to form Lakes Moultrie and Marion—they were able to return each year to saltwater. Now that the stripers are landlocked, they are spawning successfully and reproducing in vast numbers in an entirely freshwater environment.

The most mysterious and perhaps the biggest striped bass of all are those which migrate long distances up and down the coast. No one has been able accurately to predict their movements. What marine biologists suspect, though, is that schools swimming out from Chesapeake Bay, Delaware Bay, and from the Virginia Capes region join together with other passing, northbound schools. Probably they spend the summer in New England or even as far north as the Maritime Provinces only to return south again as autumn comes.

Generally, it can be said that stripers follow the sun. They go northward as water temperatures increase and then they return south again as water temperatures fall. Most fisherman, however, do not care where stripers come from. They are far more interested in where to find them on the days they spend fishing.

Because stripers can be taken in so many varied situations, a fisherman must choose from a bewildering array of tackle. Of course everything depends upon the type of fishing he plans to do. For surf-fishing, a good rod should have a 30-inch butt and a 7-foot tip of from 10 to 16 ounces. The reel should be able to hold 200 yards of from 12- to 30-pound-test line. It can be either a large saltwater spinning reel or a casting reel with a star drag.

For boat fishing, use a regular boat rod with an 18-inch butt, or 5- to 6-foot tip of from 5 to 10 ounces, a reel which can hold 150 to 200 yards of 12- to 30-pound-test line, 5/0 to 7/0 hooks on 24-inch wire or heavy nylon leaders. In addition, an angler should have a supply of 1- to 6-ounce sinkers, plus any of a wide variety of baits, including sandworms, bloodworms, softshell crabs, squid, menhaden, or plugs.

Since these fish seem to enjoy a turbulent environment—white water smashing against solid ground—a good spot to look for them is along rocky cliffs, breakwaters, or at any similar places where the wave action is violent. Here a light-tackle fan can have plenty of action spinning or flycasting from the shore. The ideal spinning outfit includes a rod from 6 to 8 feet long, a reel that can hold about 200 yards of 10- to 12-pound monofilament, and for artificial lures, a supply of small feathers, plugs, eel skins, and spinners. The spinners can be used with worms and other live bait. For live bait, a 2/0 to 6/0 hook is just about right. Of course, this same spinning tackle can also be used for trolling or casting from a boat.

It's fortunate for fishermen that striped bass will attack or eat anything that swims, creeps, or crawls in saltwater. While artificial lures can incite a bass into striking either through anger or through curiosity, the success of natural bait depends upon one thing—a striper's hunger. If the striper happens to be feeding, some natural live bait will probably work out best of all. If it is not actively feeding it's entirely possible that it will most often strike an artificial lure. Of course, there are times when it doesn't make any difference which is presented because everything from sooty terns to cigarette lighters have been found in their stomachs.

SURFCASTING

There aren't really any shortcuts to successful fishing in the surf, except perhaps to imitate exactly the technique of an expert striper fisherman and/or to study the beach at an extreme low tide. At this time an ideal observation point is from the top of a car or beach buggy, or high on a sand dune. Then while the sea is at its lowest ebb and the ripping currents are still, it's possible to examine the conformation of the bottom in order to determine the probable haunts of feeding stripers. It's good to note any sudden dropoffs, holes, offshore bars, gullies, or cuts. It's also well to make a mental note (or even to draw a simple map) of eelgrass beds and mussel-studded bottoms. Also keep in mind any mud flats (where sea worms are likely to be plentiful) and all points where tide rips will develop as soon as the tide begins to flood again.

Striped bass are indeed partial to so-called "live" water. They are powerful, robust, and quite at home in swirling ocean currents or in a breaking surf. Perhaps it's because these turbulent areas hold masses of smaller fish in a kind of suspension. Although there are exceptions to the rule, the smaller stripers generally come closer inshore to forage. Either the larger bass wait until night falls, or they approach the shore via gullies or cuts, which an angler is fortunate to have located before the flood tide begins.

Pockets of white water or any obvious depressions in the surf line are apt to hold the largest bass of all. It's worth repeating that stripers do not like still water and it's a clever fisherman who looks for such turbulent areas as those scoured by strong currents, or choppy because of the most violent tide rips.

There are a number of unmistakable signs that striped bass are feeding in a given vicinity. Some old-time surfcasters insist that they can locate feeding bass by smelling them. Maybe they can. Anyway, it's believed that the fresh and pleasant scent that is given off when a striper is first landed is the same odor that can be distinguished simply by walking along a beach.

On other occasions, feeding bass are betrayed by telltale bulges on the surface and the sudden skittering of small baitfishes. The appearance of a slick in otherwise choppy waters is also worthy of investigation, and no fisherman ever fails to keep an eye on schools of menhaden as they drift along, even though apparently unmolested by larger fish.

The most dramatic evidence of feeding bass is the sudden gathering of such seabirds as terns and gulls. Occasionally, it's possible to find them circling and diving like interceptors locked in combat. And chances are that, underneath them, squid are squirting nervously all about. Somewhere beneath all this activity is a school of striped bass.

Of course, birds gather when other fishes besides stripers are attacking the baitfish but few other species feed so noisily. Big bass splash and boil on the surface, sometimes swapping ends and slapping the water with strong, broad tails. Usually it's possible to see clearly the barred flanks of the feeding fish, but waste no time watching them. Get to the spot as quickly as you can and cast right into the center of the feeding. In such a situation, the odds are greatly in favor of the angler no matter what lure he casts.

There are about as many opinions on the best time of day or night to go striper fishing as there are striper fishermen, but the truth is that it's a twenty-four-hour proposition and the bass are likely to arrive on the scene at any time. At certain seasons, especially in spring and fall, daylight casting tends to be more productive than it is in midsummer. Along most of the Atlantic seaboard it doesn't pay to spend much time fishing at midday during most of July and throughout August. Quite a number of veteran surfcasters regard a flood tide, no matter what the month, either very early in the morning or at dusk, as the ideal period.

Not too many striper fishermen will agree on which bait is consistently the best. Generally, blocktin squid, bullhead jigs, and small plugs work best for fish in the 2- to 10-pound class (at least according to a consensus of Cape Cod fishermen). But where the stripers are running larger than 10 pounds, much larger squid and the largest size in surf plugs or large rigged eels or eel skins are usually preferred.

When casting at night many anglers use large jointed plugs that operate just on or under the surface. Some prefer the noisy poppers, darters, and splashing-type plugs.

One of the greatest striped bass killers of all, for day or night along the Atlantic seaboard, is an aromatic but hard-to-cast combination of artificial and natural baits called the rigged eel or eel skin. There are all sorts of ways to prepare this bait, but the most common is to rig an eel skin onto a lead-head jig or some other casting weight. Either way, it should be retrieved slowly along the bottom. The best way to give an exciting and undulating motion to the eel skin is simply to raise and lower the rod tip during the retrieve. The rig actually should be made to bounce and crawl along the bottom.

One variation of the eel bait is simplicity itself: String a length of leader completely through the eel, attaching two, three, or four hooks at intervals, and then wrap a strip of lead around the eel's head to make it sink and to give it casting weight. An eel rigged in this way should be retrieved in the same manner as the eel skin and jig combination.

Landing a good striper in a heavy surf is not an easy or uncomplicated matter. Beginners too often make the mistake of trying to drag a fish through the inshore breakers. This usually results in a broken line or straightened hooks.

It's always important to let the surf work for you instead of against you. Pump the bass shoreward on each crest of a wave but allow it to slide back with the undertow. Then if your timing is correct you will find that it's possible to keep the fish coming on a wave that will eventually leave it high and dry on the beach. Now get there as fast as possible, grab the leader and pull the fish to a safe location far back from the water's edge.

But surf fishing involves dangers other than removing the hook from a big striped bass. If you have ever watched sandpipers, those tiny shorebirds that scamper lightly along the edges of every beach, you may have noticed that even these tiny birds occasionally are caught unawares by towering, incoming breakers. Since no surfcaster on earth is as agile as a sandpiper, it's evident that everyone who fishes from the surf is likely to get ducked someday. It's not always a pleasant experience.

No matter how practiced they are, surfcasters seem unable to resist the desire to wade in the surf and, once wading, they can't resist wading too deep. And no wonder, because often the best fishing lies near the outer extremity of the breaking surf. But great care must be taken not to be knocked down by the waves.

Never turn your back to an incoming wave and never let a wave catch you in the stomach. Keep a constant eye on incoming waves and meet them sideways with the legs braced to prevent being swept off your feet.

If you are knocked down by a wave, remember that the water tends to lift your feet and submerge your head. And this is true despite the fact that you may be wearing heavy waders, because the upper part of the body is heavier than the legs. But above all, in such an event, stay calm, paddle hard with your hands until you are able to regain your feet.

It isn't wise to wear hip boots because, no matter how cautious the angler, the waves will eventually reach over the tops and, except in the middle of the summer when the water is fairly warm, wet feet and legs in the Atlantic will soon make any fisherman uncomfortable. The best outfit for surf fishing is a good pair of waders and a waterproof jacket with a belt that will tighten about the waist and hold both waders and jacket snugly. Waders with felt soles are probably best for slippery rocks since the felt affords a better grip than rubber. But better even than felt is a pair of cleats, such as ice fisherman use, worn on the outside of the wader shoe.

Besides his terminal tackle, a surfer should always carry a sharp knife, pliers, headlight for fishing early or late in the day or at night, sunglasses, chapstick, sunscreen, creepers for movement over slippery rock, a gaff, a surf belt, a sand spike, and a billy.

BOAT FISHING

Surfcasting is far more thrilling and a far more adventuresome method to catch striped bass than fishing from a boat. But still it probably isn't as effective in most places along the Atlantic seaboard. The boat fisherman is not limited by how far he can cast. When a boat fisherman finds a school of fish, he can stay right with it casting into the school and following it as it moves along. When no striped bass are in evidence, he can keep exploring and probing by bottom-fishing, drifting, or trolling. And nowadays with the outboard motor so handy and so portable, trolling for striped bass in a variety of situations is a very easy matter.

Trolling is especially effective. An experienced charter-boat captain or guide needs only to troll across known gravel bars, past tide rips, and wherever the current clashes with underwater boulders, rocks, old wrecks and piers. Shellfish beds are also extremely good striper grounds. In the Chesapeake Bay area, particularly, striper captains know all these locations as intimately as they know the backs of their hands. The best trolling lures are spoons, bullhead-type feathers, nylon and bucktail jig perhaps with a strip of pork rind added. But no matter what tackle or what technique he decides to use, a trophy-hunting striper fisherman's best bet for a really big fish is in the vicinity of Cape Cod or such Massachusetts inlands as Cuttyhunk, Martha's Vineyard, and Nantucket. The Narraganset, Charlestown, and Newport Beach sections of Rhode Island, Montauk Point area on Long Island, and the vicinity of Sandy Hook, New Jersey, are also good spots for stripers.

Here follows a state-by-state schedule of striped bass movements along the Atlantic seaboard:

In Massachusetts the high season usually lasts from early May to late November, sometimes later when weather conditions permit. The largest stripers, called "bulls" even though they invariably are female, arrive in the largest numbers about July 1 on the mainland coast and about June 1 off Cuttyhunk and Martha's Vineyard. The cream of Massachusetts fishing usually occurs from mid to late fall in the offshore tide rips and reefs near Cuttyhunk and Martha's Vineyard.

The season for casting and trolling for school fish around Cape Cod begins on May 1 and lasts until it is too cold or too uncomfortable to go out any longer. Ordinarily the first catches are made around Buzzards Bay and Falmouth. However, the best fishing doesn't begin until June or the first part of July and then it slacks off during midsummer only to improve again by mid-September.

In Rhode Island school stripers begin to arrive at such spots as Watch Hill, Weekapaug, Quonochontaug, and Point Judith about mid-April and remain until November. At Narraganset Bay, fishing begins about May 1 when the smaller school stripers arrive in great abundance. Later on, the trophy fish show up in such celebrated locations as Beavertail, Brenton Point, Newport, and Sakonnet Point, all of which have produced many huge bass only a few pounds off the world's sport-fishing record. Block Island, though not as well explored by striper fishermen as the Massachusetts islands, nonetheless has great potential.

On the northwest shore of Long Island Sound, Connecticut does not catch some of the best runs of large bass. However, it does have extremely good fishing for school stripers. As early as March some of them appear in the Thames River near Norwich and New London. A little later, bass begin to run in the Niantic estuary. Other Connecticut hotspots where fishing beings from mid-April to early May are around Greenwich, Cos Cob, Norwalk, Darien, Southport, the mouth of the Housatonic and Connecticut rivers at Mystic, and at Stonington.

The Hudson River was shamefully polluted in the past, but massive efforts have resulted in vast improvement in water quality. It is now an important spawning ground for many of the school striped bass that are taken around Long Island and elsewhere along the New England coast. There is some light-tackle casting and trolling in the Hudson River itself as early as April 1. New York City anglers have much sport with school-size fish beginning at Flushing, Little Neck and Manhasset bays, and at Glencoe, near New Rochelle and Mamaroneck. Fishing off the south shore of Long Island at Jamaica Bay and at the Rockaways is good in May and in some years remains good until November.

Montauk Point at the extreme tip of Long Island is one of the greatest striped bass fishing areas in the world. Here it is possible to catch them by surf-casting or from one of the charter boats specially designed for use close to the wild and rocky surf. The biggest bull bass arrive here late in May and remain until mid-December.

Although Sandy Hook, New Jersey, ordinarily accounts for the largest striped bass taken in New Jersey coastal waters, there are a number of extremely good areas nearby. Fishing begins along the north shore of Delaware Bay about April 1. At the same time school stripers are available around Cape May and near Atlantic City, New Jersey. Barnegat Bay also has school stripers—sometimes throughout the summer and early fall months. The Manasquan River is a popular spot for night fishermen. Some extremely fine bull bass are taken in this area early in the summer and late in September. Other New Jersey striper areas extend from Sea Girt to Long Branch around Sea Bright, off Monmouth Beach, and in the vicinity of the Raritan River mouth.

Striped bass fishing in Delaware waters isn't what it might be because of heavy pollution. Still, some fine bass are taken in Delaware Bay from (occasionally) as early as March 15 to late December. There is good fishing in Rehoboth Bay and Indian River Bay from April through December and in the Indian River inlet. This is the state's best-known striper area, and surf-casting for school fish gets under way on both sides of the inlet early in April. Here fishermen can continue to catch fish if they can stand the weather through January and February.

A list of the best bass fishing areas in Maryland and the District of Columbia would include Chesapeake Bay and all the rivers that drain into it, such as the Susquehanna, Elk, Sassafras, Back, and Patapsco. There are also excellent trolling grounds around such well-known places as Rock Hall, Bloody Point, Poplar Island, Herring Bay, Tilghman Island, Sharps Island, Solomons Island, the Cedar Point area, and the Patuxent River.

In Virginia, where striper fishing begins in March, the Rappahannock and York river areas are good. So is the vicinity of Norfolk and the James River estuary.

From Virginia southward the striped bass becomes more and more a river fish, taken either in the streams themselves or in their mouths. Trolling is the most popular method, while surfcasting, the preferred method in the New England area, is not practiced here to any extent. Some scattered catches are made by surfcasters in spring and late fall, but it really isn't a developed technique.

Stripers are found in most of the Carolina rivers and in Pamlico and Albermarle sounds. In Maine there is a certain amount of fishing in Casco Bay, Penobscot Bay, and near Kennebunkport. Ordinarily the fishing does not begin here until mid-June and is all over by the tag end of September.

On the Pacific coast the best striper fishing is available in San Francisco Bay and in the San Joaquin delta area. There the fish are found during the summer months off sandy beaches and rocky shorelines, sometimes within casting distances of the shore. The beaches immediately adjacent to the

Golden Gate are the best, year in and year out, but occasional runs are encountered as far south as Monterey and as far north as Bodega Bay. The shoreline near Candlestick Park is also very productive. Stripers along the Pacific coast do not strike as great a variety of live and artificial bait as they do in the Atlantic. Or so it seems to anglers who have sampled both oceans. Off California they seem to prefer shrimp and anchovies to all other live baits and on occasion will take a variety of jointed wooden plugs fished fairly near to the surface after dark. Also fly-rod poppers.

Stripers up to 78 pounds have been netted off the California coast, but anything over 30 pounds is an extremely fine fish.

Unfortunately, today the entire West Coast striper fishery is in a severely depressed state for a variety of complex reasons that primarily include habitat degradation, poor reproduction, and (for the limited stocks remaining) overharvesting. There may be some hope for California stripers, however, since several rehabilitation programs are now active or in the making. And anglers who know where to fish can still score well.

Oregon's striped bass population may never have a chance to regain lost ground unless anglers in that area undergo an attitude change. The majority of them consider the striped bass a trash fish, rejecting programs that could significantly improve the fishery there. It's their sad loss, because a healthy striper population could take some of the sportfishing pressure away from a somewhat overstressed salmon fishery by offering an excellent alternate gamefish.

RED DRUM

For years most surfcasters in the Carolinas called *Scianops ocellata* the channel bass, but only more recently has the name red drum begun to become the prominent title for this fish, at least north of Florida. Smaller sizes of this very popular gamefish are also called spottail bass and puppy drum in the Carolinas, while Florida and the Gulf states prefer the name redfish, regardless of size.

By far the largest red drum come from the outer banks of North Carolina. The current IGFA all-tackle record fish of 94 pounds 2 ounces came from that area in 1984. Red drum up to 40 pounds or more are caught every year from the Virginia Capes southward to Cape Canaveral, Florida. Also occasionally

A happy Ken Lauer with a 35-pound red drum from the Hatteras Island surf. (Photo by Joel Arrington.)

in a few spots along the northern coastline of the Gulf of Mexico.

For many years, the big drum, sometimes over 50 pounds in size, that inhabited the offshore waters of the Gulf of Mexico from Florida to Texas were considered far too coarse to be good table fare. Then a New Orleans chef came up with a recipe for cooking them in a special "blackening" coating that was so spicy it even made the low quality meat of the big red drum taste good. Commercial netters, long somewhat familiar with the deepwater spawning habits of red drum in the Gulf of Mexico, immediately saw a burgeoning market for heretofore worthless "trash" fish, and the annual harvest quickly zoomed into the millions of pounds. It didn't take long for the future of this popular gamefish to become seriously clouded.

Fortunately, a then fledgling organization in Houston, Texas, called the Gulf Coast Conservation Association (now also called the Coastal Conservation Association, or CCA) took the plight of the redfish in their state waters to heart, along with other

gamefish they felt to be threatened, and successfully lobbied the Texas legislature to pass laws protecting inland waters from commercial overharvest. The momentum thus gained quickly expanded beyond the borders of the Lone Star State across the entire Gulf of Mexico. Other states soon passed laws to protect red drum, and consequently pressured the federal fishery management council responsible for that area to bring a halt to offshore netting of red drum. The now far more protected status of this fish has fostered strong comeback in many areas.

Fishing for the big red drum in the surf is best in spring (primarily April/May), summer (in some areas), and fall (October/November, but even into December if the weather is unusually warm). Fall (especially November) is the best time of all for the largest fish, and the prime spot of all for them is the Cape Hatteras area, because the largest fish consistently come from the northernmost extent of their range. But it also takes a certain amount of luck to be in just the right location when a big school hits the beach.

At one time red drum were abundant all the way north to New Jersey's Barnegate Light, but since WW II that population has been steadily declining to its current point of rare occurrence. Today they are in greatest abundance from Chesapeake Bay southward to the northeastern part of Mexico, possibly as far down as the Bay of Campeche. And a few are also found now and then around the northern tip of the Yucatan Peninsula and from there southward toward Belize.

Beside in the surf, red drum are an excellent flats or shallow-water fish all along the Gulf of Mexico shoreline, where they average under 10 pounds and rarely exceed 20 nowadays. See Chapter 1 for more details on that fishing.

Wind direction plays a major role in the availability of big red drum to the surfcaster. Offshore winds blow the warm surface water away from shore and cause upwelling of cooler, more nutritious water from off the edge of the continent. Onshore winds, conversely, blow warm surface water to the beach. Since the shoreline runs northeast from Georgia to Cape Hatteras and then takes a sharp turn to the north, and the prevailing winds here blow from the southwest much of the year, the result is an onshore wind south of the cape and offshore north of it.

Therefore, north of Cape Hatteras from spring through fall the prevailing southwest wind pushes warm water away from shore, causing nutrient-rich water to upwell from the cool depth. And thus creat-

A typical Florida Bay redfish (red drum).

ing an ideal environment for the giants of the red drum family.

That's why the ten largest in the current IGFA record books all came from north of Cape Hatteras. Also, from 1984 through 1989, anglers have registered an average of 168 red drum weighing over 30 pounds in the North Carolina and Virginia state-sponsored fishing tournaments. All were caught north of the Cape.

Small red drum are fun to catch, too, and as mentioned earlier also much better to eat than the very biggest members of the species. Anglers catch them in spring and fall, for the most part, as fish migrate between offshore wintering locations, along the beaches and into the estuaries. Fishing is likely to be good from Florida to South Carolina from October well into December and again from March until May. Virginia has its best fishing in September and October. The most productive locations are along the beaches, at inlets where fish tend to school tightly and where they often remain for weeks or months, feeding on the rich array of bait migrating through, and at one exceptional deep-water location in Virginia. In a general sense, red drum on the East

Coast live in the estuaries in summer and spend the winter in the ocean. South of Cape Hatteras, however, where winter temperatures do not normally drop so low, many (if not most) red drum remain in estuarine waters all year except during extreme cold spells. Unlike speckled trout, drum are not highly susceptible to mortality from near-freezing water temperatures.

While red drum move into the sounds and river mouths during the summer months, they are not caught there in great numbers. At one time schools of giant reds used to be seen with regularity in western Pamlico Sound, but increasing boat traffic in recent years now keeps them in deep water, where they are seldom seen and even less frequently caught. Biologists tell us that red drums are especially sensitive to boat noise in shallow water.

The best spots to catch red drum are most often in the shallow, turbulent water of inlet bars, along the beaches, and on the shoals around the capes. They are found less frequently on flats inside inlets and in relatively shallow inlet channels. In Chesapeake Bay, big red drum are caught in water from 30 to 50 feet deep.

Many states now have strict red drum bag and size limits. North Carolina, for example, limits anglers to 5 fish per day, minimum size 14 inches. Only 1 per day can be 32 inches or longer. Some biologists in that state (and a North Carolina conservation lobby) want the minimum increased to 18 inches. South Carolina and Georgia also impose catch restrictions, and Florida has taken the redfish off the commercial market altogether and imposed strict limitations on anglers.

A surfcaster fishes for red drum in the same manner that he would fish for stripers; the only difference being that redfish prefer calmer waters. They feed close to shore in a quiet environment, where they can search at leisure for crabs and other bottom food. They move so slowly and conspicuously while feeding that often they can be seen by a cautious fisherman. They give the impression of being sluggish until they're off in a tremendous surge of power which can melt a hundred or more yards of line from a reel.

Surfcasting for the red drum can be done with either conventional gear or heavy spinning tackle. Since metal squid are very effective when casting to a feeding school, any baitcasting or wide-spool surf reel which can handle squid from 2½ to 4 ounces is suitable. Line testing 20 to 30 pounds recommended, although an expert fisherman doesn't need it quite so heavy. When there is ample room to play a fish without fouling up anyone else, spinning tackle is excellent for this type of redfishing. Line of 10- to 12-pound test is stout enough, and lures from 2 to 2½ ounces are excellent.

Surfing for red drum is mostly a matter of bottom-fishing, for which any angler needs a supply of patience. For this he'll also need the same gear as for casting squid—a wide-spool surfcasting reel or spinning tackle. On the wide-spool use 20- to 30-pound-test line and a 4-ounce pyramid sinker to keep the bait from rolling and traveling in the surf. Use an 18-inch steel leader and several ounces of cut mullet, sand crabs, or shrimp.

The ideal spinning outfit includes a saltwater reel with 150 to 200 yards of 12- to 15-pound-test line, a 2-ounce pyramid sinker and a wire leader. Size 6/0 or 8/0 O'Shaughnessy hooks are fine during the April and November season because the fish run larger during these periods. Too often, smaller hooks fail to hold in the fish's mouth and a trophy is lost. This happens most frequently when the point of the hook becomes buried inside the bait. The best rods for redfish should be from 8 to 10 feet long, for normal surfcasting and spinning.

It's wise to remember the red drum habit of grubbing on the bottom, perhaps even of scavenging a meal that can be any kind of readily available fish, clams, crabs, or shrimp. Their jaws are made to crush shellfish easily, to eat the meat and spit out the shell. Many old time surf-fishermen believe they can hear these fish "drum" as they crunch shellfish close to the beach (hence the name).

Red drum fishing anywhere is a feast or famine proposition, and it's possible that a fisherman can wind up skunked even after a whole week of hard effort. On the other hand, you could strike it hot from the first cast and proceed to enjoy uninterrupted good fishing through an entire weekend holiday. But more often than not there will be a series of three or four very poor days followed by a day or two of the fastest sport.

Most of the drum taken when trolling from boats run extremely large, from 40 to 60 pounds during the spring and fall months. A large plug or spoon is excellent for trolling and has landed as many bass as any other artificial lure.

Farther south the Florida Bay area and the entire Ten Thousand Islands sector is one large redfish nursery. Here the fish feed along the edges of banks and shell bars where small fishes, shrimp, and assorted crustaceans are very plentiful. But even where natural "baits" are abundant, the redfish in Florida can be taken in numbers on jigs, and nylon lures or trolled spoons. We have also taken them on small plugs cast and retrieved near the bottom.

It's true that many redfish are taken more or less accidentally while light-tackle fishing for other fish, but they can also be taken deliberately. One especially good technique is to cast the edges of oyster bars and mangrove islands. Although nine days in ten the best bait is a ¼-ounce bucktail jig, there are certain times when the redfish will strike savagely at a small surface plug or at a popping bug cast on a fly rod.

Generally speaking, saltwater fish require a faster retrieve of any artificial lure than does the average freshwater fish, but the redfish is an exception. For this species a lure, whether it be a spoon, jig, plug, or fly, needs to be worked very slowly. Assuming that the fisherman is using jigs, he should retrieve the lures by turning the reel handle very slowly while twitching the rod tip ever so slightly to make the jig bounce naturally on the bottom. Surface fishing must be especially slow and deliberate. Occasionally a fisherman will notice a roll behind a surface bait, a good indication of the presence of channel bass.

Even when the fish does roll, it's important not to speed up the retrieve because the channel bass just need more time to take a top-water plug than the tarpon and the snook that share the same waters.

Except in the surf, no special tackle is needed for Florida redfish provided that all line guides, reels, and hardware are resistant to saltwater corrosion. A light spinning or baitcasting outfit is ideal, with 6- to 12-pound-test line. Use a 12- to 18-inch piece of 30- to 40-pound mono as a shock leader, because small tarpon and snook frequent these same habitats.

BLACK DRUM

Even though a fairly close relative of the red drum, the black drum (*Pogonias cromis*) has a much wider range. It extends from southern New England southward to Argentina, and is common from New York southward. The current IGFA all-tackle record is 113 pounds 1 ounce (Delaware, 1975), but commercial records indicate a maximum of at least 146 pounds. The largest fish have consistently come from the Virginia-Delaware area; at least every one on the record books over 100 pounds came from there. But big black drum, that is, over 30 pounds, are found throughout its range. They've been taken over 75 pounds in such diverse areas as Ocean City, New Jersey, Broad River, South Carolina, and Fernandina Beach, Florida.

The black drum should never be confused with the red drum, yet in spite of some significant anatomical differences, it often is. The younger fish have wide, vertical black stripes and look more like a sheepshead than anything else. As they grow larger, these stripes fade, often disappearing completely by the time they exceed 20 to 30 pounds. The otherwise silvery body, which does have somewhat of a brassy sheen, might be confused a little with the sometimes lighter coloration of the red drum, except for two other differences. The red drum is far more streamlined; the black drum's stocky body is typically less than three times as long as its depth as measured from the belly to the top of its highly arched shoulder. And it has a fleshy "beard" (called barbels) on the underside of its lower jaw—a red drum has no barbels. And the red drum rarely is without a black spot (sometimes several) at the base of its tail. The black has no such spot.

Unlike the red drum, which will aggressively take an artificial lure if properly presented under the

right conditions, black drum will rarely strike anything that doesn't smell like food. The strike is slow, deliberate, often with repeated mouthing of the bait before finally eating it. It is a bottom fish that feeds mostly on crustaceans and mollusks; therefore the best baits are clams, crabs, mussels, and shrimp.

Once hooked, it puts up a stubborn but uninspired fight, rarely making any runs of even medium length. For this reason heavy tackle really isn't needed. Black drum have been taken over 30 pounds on 2-pound test, and over 80 on 8. Landing a big black drum on light tackle is primarily a matter of patience.

The black drum has a strong preference for shoreline habitats, such as bays, sloughs along the beaches, inlets, and lagoons. There is a significant spring run from the Carolinas northward, apparently the result of these fish moving inshore from deeper water wintering grounds. In Florida and along the Gulf Coast it can be found throughout most of the year except during exceptional cold spells.

Like smaller redfish along the Gulf of Mexico shoreline, young black drum up to 10 or 12 pounds frequently move up onto the flats to feed, where like redfish they can often be spotted with their tails protruding lazily through the surface as they grub food on the bottom. Anglers wishing to take them under these conditions can do well with whole shrimp (dead or alive isn't important) threaded on a hook and cast in front of the feeding fish bonefish-style. Tipping a light, weedless skimmer jig with a big piece of shrimp also works.

WEAKFISH

A close cousin of the spotted seatrout, the weakfish (*Cynoscion regalis*) has a range that overlaps considerably with the former. It is found from Massachusetts southward to northeastern Florida, but very rarely at those extremes. The area of best concentration extends from New York to Cape Hatteras, with some of the most productive spots well known in angling history. These include Chesapeake Bay, Delaware Bay, the New Jersey coastline, and Peconic Bay, Long Island.

It is called the weakfish not for its fighting ability, but because it has a soft mouth from which the hook tears easily. Which makes this definitely a fish for the light-tackle angler. It is a slender, silvery fish with a shape similar to the spotted seatrout. It even has spots, tiny, vague, black to dark green or bronze, hardly prominent enough to confuse this fish with the larger, very visible black spots of the spotted seatrout.

The largest weakfish in the IGFA all-tackle record books weighed 19 pounds 2 ounces (Long Island, 1984). Another 19-pounder was taken in Chesapeake Bay in 1983. Almost all of the other large weaks in the record books have also come from Long Island Sound, Chesapeake Bay, and Delaware Bay. Even though it doesn't reach a significantly larger maximum size than the spotted seatrout, its average size is larger. Fish over 10 pounds aren't uncommon.

Its list of preferred food includes seaworms, shrimp, sand lances, crabs, squid, mollusks, and small fish. Such a wide range of food explains the willingness of this fish to leave the sanctuary of the bottom and feed on or near the surface, as well as at mid-depth. It willingly takes any of the natural baits listed above, as well as just about any artificial lure that resembles those baits.

It actively feeds in the surf, often close to shore where it is within easy casting distance of lighter tackle than is often needed for big red drum. But it is also frequently found in channels, inlets, and over the sandflats of bays. By nature it is a schooling fish

Angler about to release a small northern weakfish.

with a decided preference for relatively shallow sandy areas.

Weakfish usually arrive in northern waters in numbers early in May. The first fish appear in Peconic Bay, Long Island, about the middle of May, by which time most available charter boats have already been booked. The typical method of weakfishing in this area involves the use of such live bait as sandworms and squid or shrimp. Although the weakfish is primarily a bottom feeder, it can be attracted into range of the bait and held there by persistent chumming.

They can be taken equally well both day and night in the small bays off the New Jersey, Long Island, and Connecticut coasts. A typical technique of many charter-boat captains in this vicinity is to watch for schools of shiners, menhaden, and other baitfish during daylight and then return to the same area after dark. Almost always a large school of weakfish will have moved into the vicinity. The mouth of inlet to a bay is always a good spot for weaks at high tide and again during the outgoing tide. Any coves in these bays are also good fishing areas.

Many fine weakfish are taken from mid-August to mid-September by trolling with a small bucktail fly, a spoon, or a feather jig. A sinker of sufficient weight is added to troll the bait at a depth of from 10 to 15 feet, which is the zone where weakfish are most likely to be hooked. It's always a good idea, if several weaks are hooked in one area, to drop the anchor overboard and to start chumming and/or casting thereabout. Be careful to lower the anchor gently and then allow the lure to sink to about 15 feet before retrieving it very slowly.

There are periods, especially in midsummer, when bottom-fishing with a slack line and worms for bait is most productive. In these circumstances, a weakfish will usually hook itself. Always give the fish plenty of time to mouth the bait before striking and then do so firmly rather than abruptly. Some of the better baits for bottom-fishing are shrimp, bloodworms, sandworms, squid, and shedder crabs.

Breakwaters and docks are always good places to prospect for weakfish during the middle of the summer and especially on midsummer nights. During this period, be on the lookout for small fish skittering and racing wildly along the surface with no indication that larger fish are following them. Ordinarily this is a sign that weakfish are about, because unlike striped bass, bluefish, and other large fish in pursuit of minnows, weaks rarely splash water even when feeding on the surface.

Chapter 9

PACIFIC SALMON

Unlike the sometimes depressing forecasts for some gamefish on the East Coast, the future of the West Coast salmon fishery looks much brighter owing to improved management techniques and better cooperation between the U.S. and Canada. Thus the Pacific salmon stocks, which decreased alarmingly between 1960 and 1980, have been slowly increasing for the past decade over much of their historical range.

The only dark shadow on this otherwise encouraging picture is the escalating use of drift gillnets in the central Pacific by a huge fleet of commercial vessels. However, there is international pressure to bring that situation under biologically acceptable control, and to eliminate drift gillnetting from that part of the north-central Pacific where most salmon have their migratory routes.

These salmons are truly unique to the north Pacific Ocean, although they have been transplanted elsewhere. The Pacific salmons, of which there are five species available to U.S. anglers (there's a sixth, found only in Japan and Russia), cover many more miles of North American inshore coastline than any gamefish on the East Coast.

At one time some salmon species were found as far south as Southern California, almost to the Mexican border. Environmental degradation has eliminated the salmon from rivers south of central California, and threatens them north almost to Oregon. Siltation, dams, and toxic chemicals in the rivers are the culprits.

But from the northern border of California throughout the Bering Sea they remain plentiful, and they grow to large size. The Chinook (*Oncorhynchus tshawytscha*), also called king salmon, has been taken in nets to over 125 pounds, but as yet the IGFA all-tackle record is 97 pounds (Kenai River, Alaska, 1987). It is also interesting to note that in prehistoric times there once was a huge sabretoothed salmon (*Smilodonichthys rastrosus*) which possibly grew to at least 400 pounds.

Unique among the characteristics of the Pacific salmons are their spawning habits, because this is what brings them into the realm of the angler, both in salt and fresh water. Unless otherwise affected by man, each individual salmon returns to the exact same part of the same stream where it was spawned several years earlier. Redds are dug, and eggs deposited within yards of where these very fish got their start in life. Then, without exception, every salmon dies. There is no second chance, no return to the sea to spawn again another year as the Atlantic salmon usually does.

As they near the coast, they become the targets of anglers fishing from boats. And as they draw closer to the mouths of their natal rivers, they even come within reach of shorebound fishermen. As long as they are in saltwater, they remain bright, silvery, vibrant, fresh, strong. Once they enter the rivers, they begin to lose some of that zip as nature prepares them for the rigorous spawning ritual ahead.

Of the five salmons, four are of particular interest to the saltwater angler. They are the Chinook, silver (coho), pink (humpbacked), and chum. The fifth is the red salmon, also known as the sockeye, a plankton feeder that rarely strikes bait or lures in saltwater.

CHINOOK SALMON

Truly the king of salmons because of its great size and strength, the Chinook remains closer to the coast than any other of its genus and is thus available to the boating angler throughout most of the year (state fishing regulations permitting).

The Chinook makes two major spawning runs up coastal rivers. Spring Chinook, as they are called, begin to appear in late April and remain concentrated through June. A few are left during July, but in

A chinook salmon caught by jigging in saltwater. (Photo by Terry Rudnick.)

rapidly decreasing numbers. A second but smaller migration of fall Chinook takes place in Washington and Oregon from September through October, but most Chinook fishermen in those states consider the prime time to be from May through September. But the farther north you go, the later the run may start, and definitely the sooner it is over. Alaska doesn't have a fall run of Chinooks, and for the most part theirs is almost over by the end of July.

According to angler/writer Terry Rudnick of Olympia, Washington, who is also the information officer for that state's Department of Wildlife, there's a saying among serious Chinook anglers that sums up the best time of day to fish. "If you can see the bait, it's too late." In other words, don't plan to pull away from the docks at daybreak; you should already be fishing by daybreak. The hottest Chinook bite of the day usually occurs at first light, and in July or early August that means sometime between 4 and 4:30 A.M. If you do sleep in until 5 and miss the day's best fishing, there's still some hope. Usually there will be a period of feeding activity on the tide change, especially a flood tide.

Unlike most other Pacific salmon species, the Chinook tends to be a creature of the bottom, found within a few feet of the sand and rocks and sometimes with its nose right down in the mud. Successful Chinook fishermen keep their baits and lures within a foot or two of the bottom, always aware of the depth, and doing what they need to do to stay down in the strike zone.

Fishing bottom, though, doesn't necessarily mean fishing extremely deep. Many of the Northwest's top Chinook salmon spots are in 125 feet of water or less. The key is to find certain kinds of structure that draw baitfish, which in turn draw hungry Chinooks.

"Breaklines," for example, are places where a flat or gently sloping bottom suddenly breaks off into much deeper water. Chinooks often patrol the edge of a breakline in search of baitfish and sometimes use such lines as migration routes. A trolling path or tidal drift that carries you along such breaklines will often put you right in the thick of things. Plateaus are flat or gently sloping tabletops where the water is shallower than surrounding areas. Baitfish such as herring or candlefish sometimes congregate on these plateaus, and the Chinook come looking for them. Baitfish also collect in the current breaks formed by points of land, creating a natural attraction for hungry Chinooks. The "edges," where fast and slow water meet on the downstream side of these points, are often best.

Sometimes the best Chinook structure of all is the shoreline itself. Mature Chinooks headed for freshwater are like wolves on the prowl, often patrolling coves, small bays, and kelpbeds in search of the oil-rich baitfish that will sustain them through the rigors of spawning. When they find schools of bait, they'll charge right in, trapping the little fish against the shoreline and slashing through like runaway chainsaws, first crippling and disorienting their prey, then bursting back through to pick off the cripples. "Pocket fishing" for these near-shore Chinook provides some of salmon fishing's most spectacular action. Anyone who has gone hand-to-fin with an 8-pound largemouth bass in a tangle of lily pads can only imagine what it's like to do the same with a 40-pound Chinook in a jungle of thick kelp.

"Mooching" is one of three angling techniques that take Chinooks, and is perhaps the most deadly of the three when done right. Mooching is the local term for still-fishing with bait, and the bait is most often a herring that has been "plug cut" (the head is sliced off at an angle). Such a bait, usually fished on a tandem hook rig four to eight feet behind a banana-shaped "mooching sinker," is hooked fore and aft with a slight bend in the body, so that it spins like an injured baitfish when pulled through the water. Most serious Chinook fishermen like their bait to make wide, slow barrel rolls as it goes through the water, but some like a faster, tighter roll more commonly associated with coho fishing.

Fresh herring makes the best bait, and it's often possible to catch a day's supply in the area you're fishing. Strings of small, beaded herring jigs are available at most tackle shops, and when you locate schools of herring it doesn't take long to jig enough for the day's fishing. Besides being fresh and firm,

locally caught bait happens to be what local kings are used to eating, so you're "matching the hatch" and not offering some odd-sized bait that the fish aren't used to seeing. Using the right sized bait for the occasion often makes an important difference.

Many use hooks as small as No. 1 or 1/0 with 3-inch baits, while others insist on going as large as 4/0 or 5/0 with a 7-inch herring. With small baits, some fishermen abandon the tandem hook rigs altogether and thread a single hook twice through the front end of the bait, at the top, then push it into the body cavity, out the side, and finally into the side of the bait just in front of the tail.

Happy anglers with a Chinook salmon taken by trolling in a West Coast bay.

Unlike cohos, which often hit a mooched herring with all the finesse of a demolition driver, Chinooks tend to take a bait slowly and deliberately, and you don't want to get overanxious. Pay out line when you feel those first two or three tap-tap-taps, then, as the fish moves steadily down or away with the bait, drop the rod tip until the line tightens and make sure there's steady pressure before setting the hook.

There was a time when trolling for big Chinooks meant dragging a bait or lure around behind a sinker weighing up to several pounds, fished with a rod that was better suited to towing cars than to fishing. Downriggers have changed all that, and it's now possible to get down to where the kings are while still enjoying the thrill of catching them on light tackle. A troller willing to "work" his downriggers can follow the contours of those breaklines and rocky points within a few inches of the bottom, keeping a bait or lure right down where it belongs. Some fish whole or plug-cut herring (just like those used for mooching) behind their downrigger balls, while others prefer spoons, wobbling plugs, large streamer flies, or plastic squid (often referred to as "hoochies"). Flies and hoochies have little action of their own, so they're usually trolled behind a flasher, a metal or plastic attractor that rotates in a wide arc and gives the trailing lure an erratic, darting action.

Vertical (deep) jigging is the newest Chinook fishing technique, growing steadily more popular the past half-dozen years or so. About a dozen different jig styles, all of them simulating or approximating the size, shape, color, and wiggle of an injured herring, anchovy, or candlefish, will take Chinooks consistently when fished by an experienced angler. The standard technique is to freespool the lure to the bottom, then jig it up and down in two- to six-foot sweeps of the rod, dropping the rod tip quickly on the downward stroke to allow the lure to move briefly in a horizontal plane. In this position the jig seems to be most attractive—wiggling, spinning, wobbling, and darting from side to side as it falls through the water.

Salmon strikes on a jig are subtle, often nothing more than a slight slackening of the line as the fall of the jig is interrupted, so the angler has to stay on his toes and react to anything that doesn't feel quite right. Keeping those hooks needle sharp is more important in jigging than in any other kind of salmon fishing, to give the lure that extra split second of "hang time" in a salmon's jaw between the strike and the speed with which the angler can react to set the hook.

Very much like other Chinook fishing methods, it's important to keep the jig working near the bottom, but it still should not be any heavier than necessary to reach the desired depth. If you're hitting bottom a bit too easily with a 4-ounce jig, try going to a 3-ounce and see if you can still get there. A smaller, lighter jig is more active, and therefore more lifelike. Just how light you can go will depend on the depth you're fishing, current, drift speed, and line diameter.

As for tackle, most Pacific Northwest anglers prefer a 7½- to 9-foot rod with a sensitive tip, lots of backbone at the lower end and a long butt for leverage. Such a rod will wear down even the most stubborn 50-pounder if you give it enough time to do its damage. A good jigging rod is lighter and stiffer than the rod preferred for mooching or trolling. The reel of preference seems to be the revolving spool type, usually with a levelwind and enough capacity for at least 150 to 200 yards of line. Jiggers and moochers generally do with smaller, lighter, faster reels than those used by trollers. Monofilament line is preferred, ranging from 8- to 40-pound test, with 15- to 25-pound favored by the majority of anglers.

COHO SALMON

The coho salmon (*Oncorhynchus kisutch*), also known as the silver salmon in Alaska, is the second largest member of the salmon family, reaching a top weight in excess of 30 pounds. The current IGFA all-tackle record, however, is 30 pounds 12 ounces, a freshwater transplant (Pulaski, New York, 1985). Any coho salmon in excess of 20 pounds is considered exceptional, but the average size is probably closer to 10.

Many experienced anglers familiar with all of the salmons rate the coho as the strongest, pound-for-pound. Certainly those we've hooked in saltwater were explosive, excitingly aerial, and tough. On a light casting outfit or fly rod they can be a real handful.

Since they feed voraciously right up to the time they enter freshwater, they will readily take streamer flies, especially the more colorful, flashy variety. Red, white, and purple is a good combination; so is pink, white, and silver, or orange and yellow. The same applies to lures. Metal spoons are usually deadly for these fish. It pays to go with the lightest and smallest that will get down to their level. Espe-

This male coho salmon was caught by casting from the beach at dusk.

cially if it's calm and clear, where heavy lures are certain to scare them. A selection of several different sizes is good to have on hand at all times.

Whatever reel you choose, fly, spinning, or casting, it should have at least 125 yards of line or backing and a reasonably smooth drag. It doesn't take a lot of drag, except possibly where currents are strong, so even if the reel is capable of a strong drag setting, set it lightly and use fingers or palming to add what extra you need.

Coho salmon cover a lot of coastline, from northern California to Asia, and are frequently found near the mouths of even very small streams. In fact, they're really more of a coastal fish since they seldom wander very far out to sea from their natal streams. Thus they're usually inclined to spend more time in nearby saltwater bays than other salmon, and in many areas this makes them available to anglers weeks before they actually start heading into freshwater to spawn.

The best coho salmon fishing normally occurs early in the morning or late in the afternoon, but if they're present in large numbers the action can stay hot through the middle of the day—especially if it's overcast and a little drizzly. Tides affect some areas

more than others, and while the higher stages might be best in one spot, lower water levels are often better in another. Some streams have bars that are so shallow across their mouths that fish stack up just offshore, waiting for high water to cross.

As a rule, coho salmon are a late summer and fall fish. They start as early as middle or late July at the northern extent of their range, and as late as October/November farther to the south. And while they are usually listed in most books as a freshwater fish, in our opinion they are truly a saltwater species. After all, they only spend a short period of time in streams after they're born and another when they spawn. The rest of their time is at sea, where a good diet and lots of exercise develop them into a solid, strong, chunky gamefish with lots of energy.

CHUM SALMON

Without a doubt this salmon (*Oncorhynchus keta*) is at once both the most misunderstood and least appreciated member of the Pacific salmon family. It is also sometimes referred to by the less flattering name of "dog" salmon, because of the Eskimo's historical practice of feeding this fish to their sled dogs. The fact of the matter, however, is that chum salmon do *not* all arrive at a great many river mouths in spawning condition, especially those in Alaska and British Columbia. There are even some river mouths in Washington and Oregon that produce silvery chums.

Some years ago, while fishing tidal water at the mouth of a river on the Bering Sea with Ron Hyde, we got our first taste of what a real run of bright chum salmon is all about. And we quickly learned, via lots of bruised knuckles, that without question a chrome-plated saltwater chum salmon is one of the finest gamefish in North America.

Although they feed on small baitfish at sea, they still require a little finesse to make them strike once they reach the coast. Small spinner-type lures, especially in chartreuse, black, and purple, in various combinations, will usually do the job. Use the smallest size you can get by with.

Chum salmon like shallow water when they reach the coastline, usually picking sloughs that keep them out of the strongest currents. This means that deep-running lures are rarely needed, and in fact they can often be spotted because they have a strong tendency to roll on the surface (porpoise), just like little tarpon.

The chum is definitely a light-tackle fish; you'll get the most strikes with the lightest lines you're willing to use. We've taken them readily on 4- and 6-pound-test line, ideal because you're sure to get lots of great jumping action. The best lure or fly presentation is right at the level they are holding; they seldom seem to be inclined to go down or up to intercept anything moving past.

Chum salmon average 8 to 12 pounds. The IGFA all-tackle record is 26 pounds 8 ounces (Canada, 1987). Anything over 15 might be considered a trophy. They are a summer and early fall fish throughout their range, appearing in Alaska in mid-July and in Washington or Oregon often as late as October or early November.

PINK SALMON

The pink is the smallest of the salmon tribe, averaging around 4 or 5 pounds. The IGFA all-tackle record is only 12 pounds 9 ounces (Alaska, 1974) and anything over 8 is considered big. The largest are always the males and the bigger these "bucks" get, the deeper the body and the more pronounced the shoulder hump (from whence comes the "humpie" nickname) becomes. They remain bright and silvery right up to their entrance into freshwater, and while at sea willingly eat a wide variety of trolled or cast lures.

Pinks, if they are in the area, are usually easy to find. They travel in large schools and often feed right on the surface, sometimes attracting seagulls in the process. Small wobbling spoons or jigs, light in color, seem to produce best. This is truly an ultralight-tackle fish, a good fighter on light rods and lines testing 8 pounds or less.

Pink salmon arrive near shore in late June or early July and continue their shoreline prowl until late August or early September in many areas.

A pink (humpbacked) salmon caught in tidal water in western Alaska, still bright and silvery.

Chapter 10

BOTTOM FISHES OF THE ATLANTIC AND GULF OF MEXICO

CODFISH, POLLACK, SHEEPSHEAD, BLACK SEA BASS, TAUTOG, SUMMER FLOUNDER (FLUKE), WINTER FLOUNDER, ATLANTIC HALIBUT, WHITING, GROUPER, SNAPPER.

Every seaport has its list of readily available bottom fish. Some species are found only in the open ocean, others mostly in more protected waters, and of course there is always a lot of habitat overlap among them. Many prefer the temperate waters of the more northly part of our eastern seaboard, others like the tropics. Rarely do fish from temperate waters roam southward into the tropics, but surprisingly quite a few tropical species make sporadic forays far to the north of their normal limits. Usually this latter event is caused by warm currents that stray far north of their usual latitudes, bringing more tropical fish with them. That's why such tropical bottom species as grouper and snapper sometimes suddenly become abundant for a while as far north as Cape Hatteras, then disappear for years.

CODFISH

Most anglers along the north Atlantic seaboard have good reason to despise cold weather and winter. High winds, rough seas, and a stinging salt breeze make any kind of fishing extremely unpleasant.

Most sane fishermen sit this season out, but cod fishermen are not particularly sane. On the worst days of January and February a surprising number of "codballs" leave the comfort of warm living rooms to suffer on cold and slippery boat decks just to catch a mess of cod.

The codfish, found on both sides of the Atlantic Ocean, is one of the most important fish in the world. Early American colonists depended on cod for food and income. The species was so highly considered that it is pictured on the Colonial Seal of Massachusetts. Today the figure of a codfish still hangs in the Bay State legislature.

On the North American side of the Atlantic, cod range from the Arctic Ocean southward to Virginia. Preferring cold, deep water, they inhabit certain offshore banks almost the year round. South of Cape Cod they are sometimes found inshore, especially from November to April. (An exception is Coxes Ledge off Block Island, where cod may be found in July and August.) Generally they are most plentiful in water from 50 to over 250 feet deep.

Cod are extraordinary travelers. One tagged in Iceland was caught off Newfoundland two thousand miles away. All codfish seem to make extensive migrations to forage for food and to spawn. In addition, they make shoreward movements each fall and spring. Tagging has revealed that most cod caught in New Jersey and New York waters come from summering grounds in the Nantucket Shoals area.

The brown-spotted, yellow-bellied, chin-whiskered cod is known by many names, including Atlantic cod, black cod, rock cod, and scrod (this last is actually used to designate immature cod). Its scientific name is *Gadus callarias*, but no expensive or elaborate tackle is necessary to catch the species. The cost of a winter fishing trip on a party boat, for instance, may be as low as 20 to 35 dollars a day, bait included.

Cod are not terrific fighters, but you will still need sturdy (rather than elaborate) tackle because of the strong tides, deep water, heavy sinkers, and rocky bottoms you will be dealing with. Many fishermen prefer a simple, stiff, one- or two-piece boat rod; others use regular surf rods.

The reel should hold 200 yards of monofilament line testing about 30 or 40 pounds. The best hooks are size 7/9 or 8/0 in Sproat or O'Shaughnessy types. These are knotted onto heavier (than the line) test nylon leaders, each about 24 inches long, then to a spreader or to a three-way swivel.

Many anglers use two hooks, with the bottom one tied about a foot above the sinker and the top one tied just about 2 or 3 feet above the first hook. Sinkers from a half to one pound are sometimes necessary to reach bottom depending on the depth of the water, the velocity of the current, and the tide.

Virtually any bait is good enough for codfish, including clams, shrimp, lobsters, mussels, conchs, starfish, sea urchins, sea cucumbers, worms, or pieces of cut bait. The bait most often provided aboard party boats is the surf clam or skimmer, the "innards" of a couple of these being placed on a single hook. Codfish entrails also can be used.

Some of the best codfishing along the Atlantic seaboard occurs almost within sight of New York City. Party boats are based at such nearby ports as Sheepshead Bay, Canarsie, Freeport, and Montauk. Other boats fish out of bases along the New Jersey coast. During mild winters they go out almost daily, even through January and February, but the most fruitful fishing months are November, December, March, and April. Most party boats, at least the larger ones, have heated cabins and small coffee shops on board. Many also rent fishing tackle. Even when the weather is at its worst, codfishing offers a pleasant change of pace.

More important than tackle is good warm clothing. The winter fisherman should wear woolen or insulated underwear, heavy outer clothing, a cap with earmuffs, large-size boots or overshoes which can accommodate extra pairs of woolen stockings, waterproofed gloves and waterproofed parkas or foul-weather gear. The more raw and cold the day, the more important it is to be dressed properly.

Cod prefer rocky, pebbly bottoms or mussel beds. Near New York, the Cholera Bank, Angler Banks, and 17 Fathoms are the best-known areas. Cod are also always found around sunken, off-shore wrecks.

POLLACK

Winter codfishermen sometimes encounter a bonus in the pollack, a relative of the cod which frequents the same waters. Sometimes called Boston bluefish, the pollack (*Pollachius virens*) ranges from about Cape May, New Jersey, to Nova Scotia and perhaps beyond.

Pollack are taken on the same tackle and by the same methods as are cod along most of the Atlantic seaboard, but they have the fortunate habit of rising to the surface just before dark and just before daybreak at certain times of the year. When this occurs, pollack become excellent light-tackle fish and the fisherman who finds them on the surface, either while surfcasting or while fishing from a boat, is lucky indeed.

The best pollack fishing occurs in October and lasts well into November, a foggy time along the Atlantic coast when visibility can be poor. The presence of pollack is always easy to detect, however, because of the wild commotion they make chasing small fish on the surface. They are usually accompanied by gulls, which feed and circle above them.

Surface-feeding pollack, which average 5 pounds but which can reach 20 or 30 pounds, will strike different artificial lures. Large saltwater darting plugs are effective, as are feather jigs and bucktails when retrieved with short sharp jerks. Occasionally during calm weather, pollack feed actively and extensively on the surface at night.

SHEEPSHEAD

The sheepshead (*Archosargus probatocephalus*) of the Atlantic and Gulf coasts is found anywhere from Texas to the Bay of Fundy but it is abundant only on the southern Atlantic coast. The greatest concentrations are found along the East Coast from Florida to Virginia.

A member of the porgy family, the sheepshead is closely related to the familiar scup or porgy, an important commercial fish northward from Virginia. It should not be confused with the freshwater sheepshead that is a member of the drum or croaker family.

The sheepshead is most often captured around wharves, breakwaters, and sunken wrecks. It has a weakness for crabs, oysters, and other shellfish which it crushes easily with its strong bridgework. In inlets it moves in and out with the tide and, at least in the southern part of this range, does not seem to migrate extensively. During the spawning season, which occurs in the spring, sheepshead assemble into schools and move into shallow water to deposit their eggs. Many are caught at this time.

The largest sheepshead of record weighed about 21 pounds, but the average is only about 2 pounds. Larger fish should be filleted and smaller ones cooked whole. The meat is white, tender, and pleasantly flavored.

A fisherman should look for sheepshead along rocky, irregular bottoms, over reefs not too far from shore, and inside channels. The most notable physical characteristics of the fish are the sheeplike lips and the protruding teeth. The inside of the mouth is equipped with grinding teeth which permit easy feeding on such bivalves as mussels and barnacles.

Sometimes the sheepshead is so fast in taking live bait that it is difficult to hook. Over reefs it will quickly seize baits the minute they are dropped to the bottom. One exciting way to catch sheepshead is to thoroughly chum an area with shrimp or bits of shellfish and, after the sheepshead have begun to feed actively, to cast with small ¼-ounce jigs. On light tackle it is a sporty fish.

BLACK SEA BASS

June through August the black sea bass (*Centropristes striatus*) is plentiful along our eastern seaboard. It is usually found in shallow water over rocky formations with weeds, ledges, sandbars, and reefs. During dog days the black sea bass may be the only really abundant fish. Striper, bluefish, or trout fishermen can always find bass even when these other species are uncooperative.

Averaging only a pound or two, but occasionally reaching 8 or 9 pounds, black sea bass are strong and a pleasure to catch. On light tackle they never seem to stop fighting and, once caught, they can inflict cuts on a fisherman's hands with their very sharp fins. The best way to handle this fish and remove the hook is either to hold it firmly by the lower lip or to put fingers into the eyes to grip it solidly.

Black sea bass prefer sea clams or squid but will take almost any bait offered. Larger bass are taken by bottom-fishing from boats, while the smaller ones are usually taken from shore. In either case, it isn't necessary to use heavy tackle. Most fishermen use two or three baited hooks at one time.

The flesh of the sea bass is white, sweet, and firm

and can be prepared like any other panfish. Large ones should be filleted and smaller ones cooked whole. Excellent in chowders, sea bass are especially good served with hush puppies.

TAUTOG

The tautog (*Tautoga onitis*) is equipped with extremely strong jaws and powerful, conical teeth far back in its mouth. With this double-barreled apparatus, the tautog feeds on the hardest of crustaceans and shellfish along the Atlantic coast. About the middle of May the tautog begins to move from deep water to feed and spawn in big bays and inlets along our middle Atlantic coast. This is a good time to fish for the species.

Fairly heavy tackle should be used for the tautog for two good reasons. In the first place, it is necessary to use considerable force to set the hook, and, secondly, once hooked, the fish will certainly take refuge among any rocks or underwater obstacles it can find. The tautog reel should hold at least 150 yards of 30-pound-test line. This may seem heavy for a fish that averages only 3 or 4 pounds and seldom exceeds 20, but once in sanctuary among the rocks, there is no way to horse it out.

The first fishing of the season is done from small boats or party boats and the best water to explore is over rocky ledges, among rocks and shoals, and over mussel bars. Never look for tautog far from this type of habitat.

Early in the season a tautog is a reliable target for surfcasters where the flood tide covers up an isolated area of rock. It doesn't have to be a large area because half an acre of rocky "island" will hide many fish.

The most productive fishing months are April and May, and again from September until the end of October. When very warm or very cold weather arrives, the tautog goes into deeper water and does not return until spring or fall. Winter and summer it's found on the bottom in from 50 to 150 feet. Occasionally it will rise to chum.

Shore-fishing can be effective. Tautogs in search of food swim along rocky and weedy shores, where they tend to congregate in certain holes. Find such a place and it will afford fast fishing throughout the season, maybe for many seasons to come. A wide variety of baits are acceptable, but the best is a piece of cut crab. Sea worms, squid, and cut fish are also good.

The tautog is often called blackfish, confusing because blackfish is also another name for the pilot whale.

PORGY

The northern porgy (*Stenotomus chrysops*) called scup or northern scup, ranges from Maine along the Atlantic coast to South Carolina. The southern porgy (*Stenotomus aculeatus*) also called scup or southern scup, ranges from North Carolina to the Florida Keys and to Texas. Most abundant in southeast waters, it is prized as a food fish everywhere.

The best fishing season for porgies runs from May through October. Throughout summer and fall, special porgy boats drift back and forth over long-established fishing grounds and on good days fill up with porgies. The fish caught at sea weigh 1 to 3 pounds; those taken in shallower bay waters usually weigh less. They bite best when the tide is slack or early during an incoming tide.

Strictly bottom feeders, porgies are found over shellfish beds, sandy bottoms, around wrecks, reefs, and the entrance to bays. Scups take any bait, but prefer shrimp, skimmers (the favorite), crabs, small pieces of squid, and soft-shell clams.

No matter what bait is used, taking porgies requires a specialized fishing technique. The first trick is to find the bottom. Then lower your line and give quick, short jerks of the rod tip up and down, being careful that the bait does not rise higher than a foot above the bottom. Care must be taken not to move the bait too swiftly. Since porgies have extremely small mouths, the bait should be small. Once hooked, a porgy is a stubborn fighter with a tendency to turn broadside and bore to the bottom.

Porgies rarely exceed 4 or 5 pounds. But while fishing the Bermuda reefs our party once caught several weighing more than 10 pounds apiece. Very large porgies tend to have an iodine flavor and make poor table fare.

SUMMER FLOUNDER (FLUKE)

The summer flounder or fluke (*Paralichthys dentatus*), actually a halibut, dwells in shallow shoreline waters from Cape Cod to Georgia, but it is most numerous from New York to North Carolina. It frequents sandy and muddy bottoms of the Atlantic seaboard and is taken in muddy estuaries where the water is only moderately brackish.

Like all the other flatfish of both oceans, the summer flounder has its eyes and dark color on one side. In the case of the summer flounder this happens to be the left side as opposed to the winter flounder (a true flounder), which has them on the right side. The fluke can camouflage itself against any background. Placed on a red background it becomes red, on blue it becomes blue, and so on through all the colors anyone could use on the bottom of an aquarium.

Although the flesh of this flounder is dry, it has good flavor, especially when fried or baked. This is one of the fish that passes for fillet of sole in most fish markets.

The fluke is curious and will investigate any silvery or flashing movement in the water. Though it may not strike, a fluke will at least investigate a foreign object, and most of the time will suck it into its mouth. If it happens to be a lure, the fluke may be hooked, but a fisherman must strike back immediately. In no way does the summer flounder resemble any classic game fish, but still it is a strong, vigorous fighter. It feeds on both the bottom and the top and is caught in a variety of circumstances.

Summer flounder occasionally reach 25 pounds but the average specimen would weigh 2 or 3 pounds. The best way to find out if and where flounder are striking is to watch the outdoor columns in local newspapers. Another tip is to go fishing following a bad storm. Some fishes strike well during heavy weather, but fluke are among the species notorious for feeding after a storm. Also fish for fluke just before dusk and just after dark when they are most likely to surface; much sport is possible at these times by casting ⅛- or ¼-ounce feather or bucktail jigs. Cast and retrieve these lures as slowly as possible, using a wire leader. One variation to the technique is to cast the jig behind a large wooden float, setting the jig about 3 or 3½ feet deep, and retrieving the combination in very slow, sharp jerks.

WINTER FLOUNDER

The winter or blackback flounder (*Pseudopleuronectes americanus*) inhabits shallow water from northern Labrador to Cape Lookout during the coldest winters. Though absent during the summer, it is fairly abundant in winter in Chesapeake Bay.

Like other flatfish, it swims and rests on one side, in this case on its left side. It is caught in a similar manner to the summer flounder and on similar light tackle. New England fishing begins in March and lasts until the end of May when the best spots are "bottom holes" in the middle or near the mouth of a bay. The best period is on the outgoing tide. Fishing is productive until the tide changes.

Usually in June the blackbacks stop striking until fall, but they return in September or October and are plentiful along North Atlantic beaches and bays until it's too late and too unpleasant to fish them any longer.

There is no reason to use heavy tackle. A reel with 100 yards of 15- or 20-pound-test line is good enough. Hooks in sizes 8, 9, or 10 with a 10-inch leader are sufficient. Best baits are blood- and sand-worms, night crawlers, soft- or hard-shell clams, mussels or tapeworms. A ribbon worm will often catch fish when other baits fail (reddish in color, this worm is found by digging into mud flats at low tide). The one drawback here is that you must use these worms when procured, as it is difficult to keep them alive more than a few hours.

ATLANTIC HALIBUT

Only a very few fishes, the swordfish, marlin, some sharks, and the tuna among them, exceed the Atlantic halibut in size. The largest member of the flatfish family, the Atlantic halibut (*Hippoglossus hippoglossus*) inhabits all northern seas, southward along our Atlantic coast to New Jersey. Like the winter flounder, its eyes and color are on the right side of the body.

Although large halibut brought into New England ports range in length from only about 4 to 6 feet and in weight from 50 to 200 pounds, a few weighing 300 and 400 pounds are taken every year. A 9-foot 2-inch jumbo weighing 625 pounds dressed was caught 50 miles from Thatcher Island, Massachusetts, in 1917.

The Atlantic halibut is voracious. Feeding mostly on crabs, lobster, clams, and mussels, it is able even to capture seabirds occasionally and is well known as a scavenger of refuse thrown from vessels at sea.

Although most Atlantic halibut are taken by commercial fishermen on set lines, it is possible to take them on sportfishing tackle. They will strike a variety of baits, particularly in spring and summer, which

seems to be spawning time along the New England coast. Once a halibut is hooked, it's a long hard drawn-out struggle rather than an exciting fight.

WHITING

The whiting (*Menticirrhus saxatilis*) belongs to the drum family of fishes, which includes the weakfish, channel bass, croakers, and others. It is found along the Atlantic coast from Maine to Florida, but it is common in the northern half of this range only in the summer.

From May through August, surf-fishing for the whiting is popular and rather good along New Jersey and Long Island shorelines. Best time to fish is during high tide, as it follows the surge inward toward shore. It is also caught during flood tides in bays and inlets.

Southward from North Carolina the whiting disappears from shallow inshore waters during cold spells, but it reappears when the weather warms up. In the Carolinas this species and a barely distinguishable relative are taken in abundance along the shore in winter or early spring.

The whiting is a light-tackle fish. An angler is most likely to be successful using shrimp, crabs, small mollusks, worms, or small fish for bait. It is possible to take them on yellow feather jigs, but the bait fisherman will have better luck. Whitings usually run from 12 to 18 inches, and 6 pounds is about tops for the species. The largest ones feed most actively at night. Whitings are rated highly as food fish.

GROUPER

These popular fish belong to part of the sea bass family called Serranidae, which incidentally also includes the black sea bass as well as the numerous groupers. There are at least a dozen species of grouper actively sought by sportfishermen, the larger of which include the black, red, yellowfin, gag, nassau, and jewfish. All of those are found in relatively shallow water from depths of just a few feet to sometimes over 200 feet. They range in maximum size from 30 to more than 100 pounds; then there is the jewfish that may even approach the half-ton mark.

A yellowfin grouper taken by deep-jigging with baitcasting gear.

The IGFA all-tackle record is 680 pounds (Florida, 1961), although divers have reported seeing jewfish that were much larger.

Then there are some smaller groupers that share that same habitat, such as the rockhind, graysby, coney, and yellowmouth. Most of those stay well under 20 pounds, with an average closer to 3 or 4. As a rule they are excellent table fare, but keep in mind that some of the smaller groupers may not meet Florida's maximum size requirement. It's a good idea to read up on the current saltwater fish laws of the coastal states before keeping any fish.

Jewfish, for example, as of 1990 can no longer be killed in Florida, regardless of their size. The species has been dangerously overharvested, especially by scuba divers with spearguns.

There are also some deepwater groupers that are of angling interest. The largest is the warsaw, which reaches a weight of 500 pounds. Other big deepwater groupers include the snowy and misty. These fish are taken with electric reels and wire line, usually in well over 200 feet of water. That's not a particularly sporting way to catch any fish, but in this case the reward is in the eating.

All groupers are essentially a tropical fish. They range from the equator northward throughout the Gulf of Mexico and the southeast coast of the U.S. to sometimes as far north as Cape Hatteras whenever warm water happens to reach that far for a long enough period of time.

They are a bottom fish, highly structure oriented. Rarely found over sandy or even smooth rocky bottom, they prefer ledges, rockpiles, wrecks, and anything else with a substantial vertical profile. Depth isn't nearly as important as structure. We've seen (and hooked) jewfish up to 500 pounds in water less than 8 feet deep. Unfortunately big, stay-at-home fish like that are easy targets for all types of anglers and divers, especially in shallow water. So today a big grouper of any species is rare in shallow water except in very remote areas.

Nowadays the most productive big grouper water is 60 to 200 feet deep, and usually the deeper you put your baits, the larger the fish you're likely to catch.

Big groupers also like big baits. Live baits, such as snappers, mullet, blue runners, small bonito, etc., produce best of all, but all types of whole and cut dead bait work well, too. Usually it's a matter of locating the structure with a depthsounder and dropping the bait on tackle of suitable size to keep the fish from getting into the rocks after hookup. Big hooks (4/0 and up), strong leaders made of wire or heavy mono, and a stiff rod are called for. Plus enough sinkers to get the bait down and keep it there.

Another way of taking these fish is called deep jigging, and this is a technique where much lighter tackle can be used. See Chapter 17 for details on this technique, which has proved so effective that grouper of over 70 pounds have been taken on lines as light as 10-pound test. One of the reasons why the lighter gear has been so effective is that some species, particularly the black grouper, which exceeds 100 pounds, are aggressive enough to leave the sanctuary of the rocks and rise well above the bottom to attack a tempting baitfish. A school of baitfish will often cause this to happen, and if it does the grouper might even be visible on the depthfinder.

We've hooked black grouper over 60 pounds in almost 200 feet of water with 12-pound-test tackle this way, but those we landed were usually hooked a long way from the bottom. By the time the fish realized it really was in trouble, home was too far away.

THE SNAPPERS

Like the groupers, all true members of the snapper family (Lutjanidae) are tropical fish. In some parts of the world other species of fish are also called snappers, even though they belong to entirely different families of fish. An example is the so-called red snapper of the Pacific northwest, a member of the scorpionfish (Scorpaenidae) family, which is actually the vermillion or yelloweye rockfish. Some members of the wrasse family are also called snappers in other parts of the world.

Undoubtedly the most popular member of the snapper family is the gray snapper, much more commonly known as the **mangrove snapper**. It is very abundant throughout the western Atlantic tropics, including the Gulf of Mexico and southern Florida, although its range extends sporadically into the Carolinas. One of the smaller members of the species, it rarely exceeds 10 pounds, although the IGFA all-tackle record is 16 pounds 8 ounces (Florida, 1988). The largest species of snapper in the Atlantic is probably the cubera, which exceeds 100 pounds. The IGFA all-tackle record for this sabertoothed beast is 121 pounds 8 ounces (Louisiana, 1982). The "true" red snapper is a deepwater species of the Atlantic and Gulf of Mexico, more likely to be caught in depths exceeding 100 feet. It reaches weights of almost 50 pounds. There is also a West African red snapper that we encountered around the river mouths of Angola while fishing there in the early

This big mangrove snapper fought very hard, in spite of missing most of its tailfin, which was probably bitten off by a shark or barracuda.

Mutton snappers are among the largest members of the snapper family.

1970s. It definitely approaches 50 pounds, and maybe more. Another common large snapper in the Caribbean and western Atlantic is the mutton, which on rare occasions tops 20 pounds.

Most experienced anglers consider the mangrove to be the most wary of its tribe, giving it the nickname of "sea lawyer." It certainly seems to learn quickly, especially where it has frequent contact with man. Legends abound of oversized mangroves that live around docks and voraciously wolf down anything that appears remotely edible, yet never give the most tempting morsel attached to a hook even a cursory glance.

Those who especially like to fish for mangroves rely heavily on chum, light leaders, live bait, a cautious approach to the fishing spot if it's in shallow water, and often even the cover of darkness. Chumming with crippled live sardines is one of the best way to get a wary school going; the more excited it

gets, the darker the diagonal black stripe that passes through its eye.

Mangroves that live on offshore structure and see little of man are a lot more easy to fool—at first. But they too learn soon enough. We've fished some wrecks that were hotbeds of big snapper activity, yet until resorting to chum and live bait, getting a strike was almost impossible, especially from the larger fish. We also remember fishing around some oil rigs many miles off the Louisiana coast, where big mangroves were also very abundant. Hooking one during the daytime was rare, but at night we took them to 10 pounds with relative ease. Under those conditions jigs tipped with fresh bait even worked quite well.

Daytime anglers will do better with the lightest lines and leaders possible, and small hooks. Even though all true snappers have ferocious-looking teeth, unlike the razor-edged barracuda's they are conical in shape, with a sharp point, and rarely cut even light mono. The big problem is that snappers hang tightly around structure, and that can be the death of a light line or leader. Still, as a rule, you're better off take your chances with light gear; you'll get a lot more strikes because of the more natural appearance of the bait.

Mutton snappers, easily recognized by the dark spot high on the back almost halfway between the head and tail, are found in both shallow and deep water. In some areas they move up onto the flats like permit, often following feeding stingrays. Although as a rule not nearly as wary as the mangrove, once on the flats they become suspicious of anything unedible that moves. Taking a big one on the flats by flycasting is today perhaps a bigger challenge that even permit, but a well-placed small live crab is seldom refused.

Unlike mangrove snappers, the larger of which will rarely strike an artificial, big muttons will crash a noisy surface lure like a runaway fire truck under the right conditions. The edges of deep green channels that bisect the flats of the Florida Keys and the Bahamas are ideal for such activity. This is not the place to use very light lines and leaders, because a big mutton will take you through the underwater jungle of coral heads and sea fans at rocket speed, given the chance. We once hooked one near Deepwater Cay in the Bahamas that our guide estimated at close to 30 pounds. It took a topwater plug in a big explosion of whitewater and cut the 12-pound-test line on nearby sea fans two seconds later. No other mutton we've ever caught (up to 20 pounds) looked anywhere near that big!

Mutton snappers will respond to live and cut bait fished in the same manner you would for grouper. Deep jigging also works extremely well. See Chapter 17 for more details on that technique.

Red snappers are best fished in water that's 100 feet deep or more. They are far more common in the Gulf of Mexico than off the Florida Keys or southeast Atlantic coast. At one time just about any ledge or even small bottom structure in the northern Gulf of Mexico held seemingly endless quantities of big reds, but during the last two decades heavy pressure by sport and commercial fishing has taken its toll. Now the federal government and most states have imposed strict regulations on minimum size and bag limits, so know before you go.

Live bait is by far the most productive for red snappers. Chumming helps a lot, too. And the best fishing is usually very early or very late in the day, or at night.

Yellowtail snapper rarely make it to 10 pounds, but they are top table fare and usually very abundant.

The lesser snappers that are also caught from time to time include the lane, a mutton lookalike, **schoolmaster**, and **silk** (mostly deepwater). But the **yellowtail snapper** is another matter.

In appearance, the yellowtail does not have the stout body shape of the typical snapper. It is more slender, and the forked tail is much larger in relation to its body size, which suggests both power and speed. Anyone who has ever hooked a big cubera or mutton on light tackle will attest to the strength and speed of those fish, but pound-for-pound the yellowtail is definitely faster and possibly even more powerful. It is a fine gamefish in every sense.

Yellowtails are most common in U.S. waters in the Florida Keys, rarely straying much north of Palm Beach. They are also extensive through the Caribbean and Bahamas. Bermuda has a few yellowtails, too, most of them much larger than average. In 1978 we took an unusually large 'tail on the Challenger Bank near Bermuda that weighed 10 pounds even, and it fought very hard even on the stiff 15-pound-test gear we were using for medium-size yellowfin tuna.

Yellowtail fishing is a specialty among some anglers throughout the Florida Keys. The most dedicated go at night, but good results are possible during daylight hours too. The most productive procedure involves chumming along the outer edge of the reef in 60 to 120 feet of water. Some current is necessary, but not too much. Ground chum and/or small glass minnows are sometimes mixed with sand for a faster sink rate. Once the feeding yellowtails gather in the chum line, very small hooks tied directly to light lines (8- to 15-pound test) and baited with a piece of cut bait or a glass minnow are used with as little weight as possible for the most natural sink rate. Live shrimp and small live baitfish are also extremely effective. Small lures, especially jigs that have been tipped with bait, or even small flies that resemble bits of chum or small minnows, can often be used successfully.

Cubera snappers are the tough guys of the family. Not particularly abundant throughout most of their range, they average close to 30 pounds, in U.S. waters (the Keys and Gulf of Mexico) tend to stay deep, usually 80 feet or more. Most anglers fish for them at night with live bait in areas where they are known to frequent, usually during the summer months. Further south, along the Yucatan Peninsula and down through Belize and Honduras, they often come into shallow inlets with the flooding tide. We've caught them up to 52 pounds on casting tackle in less than 15 feet of water, using both artificial lures and live bait. They're strong, and when hooked on light tackle, the fight is sure to be a long one. A closely related species on the Pacific side of Central America is the **Pacific dog snapper**, virtually identical in size and appearance. The Atlantic has a dog snapper too, also similar, but rarely exceeding 10 or 15 pounds.

This big cubera snapper was taken by Lefty Kreh at night from an inlet along the Yucatan coast.

Chapter 11

BOTTOM FISHES OF THE PACIFIC COAST

CORBINA, HALIBUT, KELP BASS, LINGCOD, THE ROCKFISHES, SEA BASSES, SHEEPSHEAD, SURFPERCH

We tend to think of the tropics as the richest in fish life, but actually that isn't so. There are more fishes in the temperate and subartic waters of the north Pacific than probably anywhere else on earth. Thus of all seas adjacent to North America, the Gulf of Alaska and the north Pacific Ocean are the most prolific of all, especially in terms of numbers of gamefish. Besides the five species of salmon, there are many, many varieties of very large bottom fish.

The Pacific halibut is one of the world's largest bottom fishes, ranking in size just below several of the giant sea basses. Then there are some of the rockfishes, and also the lingcod, many of which will top 30 pounds. All of these fishes are normally very abundant except in those areas close to major seaports where fishing pressure is extremely heavy.

CORBINA

This is a general name applied to a wide variety of Pacific Ocean representatives of the drum family (Sciaenidae) which on the Atlantic coast includes the red and black drum, croaker, weakfish, spotted seatrout, etc. In California, when an angler mentions corbina he's usually referring to the California corbina (*Menticirrhus undulatus*) a close relative of the Atlantic northern kingfishes (or whiting). Other pacific "corbina" (or "corvina," if you prefer) include the orangemouth corvina (*Cynoscion xanthulus*), found mostly from southern California to Mazatlan, the spotfin croaker, the white seabass (*Atractoscion nobilis*), the totuava (Gulf of California), the yellowfin croaker, and California kingfish. The last two are found further north than the others, often as far as San Francisco. Of these the white seabass attains the largest size, reported to be as much as 80 pounds. And the orangemouth corbina may reach weights of well over 30 pounds. It has, by the way, also successfully been transplanted to the Salton Sea, where it thrives.

Although the California corbina is particularly popular among surfcasters along the southern shore of that state, it is among the most difficult of the surf fishes to hook. There are times when an entire school will actively feed on soft-shell crabs all around a fisherman's bait, ignoring the sand crab with a hook in it. Some say that hooks that are too large keep the fish away. Others maintain that the corbina is spooked by a too heavy and too stout leader. Possibly it's a combination of both and perhaps the corbina is just extremely selective.

A single fleshy chin whisker on the lower jaw distinguishes the California corbina from all the other croakers, except the yellowfin. The corbina has only one or occasionally two weak spines and its body is rounded. A bottom fish, the corbina lives along sandy beaches and in shallow bays. Occasionally it is found in muddy estuaries where freshwater enters saltwater, a condition that occurs most frequently in Central America. Corbinas travel in small schools in the surf in from only a few inches of water to depths of 50 feet. The average depth in which a fisherman can expect to find them is about 6 feet. They move offshore into deeper water during winter and when spawning. But they tend to move closer inshore during high tides at night.

In August 1945 a 7¼-pound corbina, which measured 28 inches, was taken at San Onofre and this remains the largest verified record in California. However, corbinas twice this size have been captured in the Gulf of California.

Male corbinas mature at about two years of age and females at about three years of age. The spawning season extends from June through September but is heaviest during late July and early August. This activity apparently takes place offshore, as ripe females are seldom found in the surf zone by fishermen.

About 90 percent of the corbina's diet consists of sand crabs, with the remainder composed of clams and other crustaceans. Nearly all feeding is done in the surf, sometimes in water so shallow that the corbina's back is exposed. After scooping up mouthfuls of sand and then separating the food from it by sending the sand through the gills, the corbina spits out bits of clamshell and other foreign matter, swallowing only the meaty parts. This mouthing of food explains why fishermen are seldom rewarded with a really hard strike. The angler must have a good sense of touch or highly developed intuition to detect the slow bite of a corbina.

An experienced surf-fisherman's tackle includes a 6-ounce or smaller pyramid or triangle sinker, whichever size is heavy enough to hold against the undertow or current of the tide. This is tied to a 48-inch 2-pound leader with two loops on the leader a foot apart. Two shorter leaders, each about 8 inches, are attached to the loops and to these are knotted No. 1 or No. 2 short shank hooks. Most fishermen bait with sand crabs, but there are times when pileworms or rock worms are effective.

Most surfers prefer to fish on an advancing or flood tide, or at least an early-morning low tide. This gives them a chance to collect the mussels, sandworms, or sand crabs they need.

An early low tide also gives an angler a chance to select his spots. These are the deep holes or depressions along any beach which will be under some depth of water at later high tide. It is always extremely valuable—and this point cannot be stressed enough—to locate these hollows or depressions before actually fishing. If they are not discovered before the tide comes in it is necessary to do much extra casting and probing with a heavy sinker to discover such spots. Good surf-fishing depends very much on finding the right holes.

Once a good corbina or croaker hole is located, whether in the surf or fishing in a bay, a unique method of baiting or chumming can be used. Open a dozen or so mussels and, without removing the meat, toss them into likely holes or depressions. This will attract numerous small fishes and the commotion will in turn attract corbinas. A hook baited with a mussel is then dropped within a short distance down the tide from the bait.

The goal here is to arouse the competitive feeding instinct among fishes. If one fish in a school can be tempted to strike, others will become wildly excited and probably begin striking with abandon. Corbinas are especially susceptible.

During the warm period of midsummer a wise corbina fisherman tries his luck at night. Most surf fish are very active night feeders and the corbina is no exception. Furthermore, there is evidence that they are attracted by a light, especially on a very dark night. A lantern is like a magnet and is likely to bring corbinas close to the caster if any are feeding nearby.

Corbinas and all croakers feed closer into the beach at night. An angler cannot see the fishes feeding as in daylight and must work by the touch system. But sometimes at night it's possible to hear fish feeding close to shore, which has accounted for many extremely fine catches.

HALIBUT

There are at least two species of halibut that are popular among anglers along the West Coast. The smaller of the two is the California halibut, a member of the lefteye flounder family *Bothidae*, although about half of those caught are actually righteyed. It grows to less than 100 pounds; the IGFA all-tackle world record is just 53 pounds 4 ounces (Santa Rosa Island, 1988). Its coloration is greenish to grayish brown, occasionally mottled. It ranges from central California southward just below the Mexican border, and also along the northern third of the Gulf of California. It is mostly a nearshore flounder, found in less than 60 feet of water. It prefers sandy bottoms, but they may be taken in channels and even occasionally in the surf.

Like the others of its kind, the California halibut is an aggressive feeder, rushing up from its hiding place on the bottom to grab unwary baitfish between powerful jaws ringed with large, sharp teeth. Fishing techniques are essentially the same as for other flounders or halibut, essentially a matter of getting a large enough hunk of fish close enough to the bottom to get its attention. This can be done via lead weights or by threading the bait directly on the hook of a large lead jig.

The Pacific halibut is the largest member of the righteye flounder family, *Pleuronectidae*. Its range extends from the Bering Sea all the way across the Gulf of Alaska and southward to central California. It is apparently comfortable within a wide range of depths wherever it is found, from less than 10 feet of water to over 3,000, mostly over sandy or flat rocky bottom, which can be very close to reefs or other structure, too.

By far the best fishing for this species is the Gulf of Alaska, as we learned in July of 1989 while fishing with Al Sullivan, owner of Tanaku Lodge, in the waters around the north end of Chicagof Island. Al's lodge is located in Elfin Cove, about 80 miles west of Juneau, just minutes from Cross Sound and the Icy Straits. Our boat took many big halibut (up to 250 pounds) and lingcod (up to 60 pounds) every day. Some of the giant flatties came out of water less than 20 feet deep.

The Pacific halibut has a dark-brown back and a paper-white belly. Because the head is relatively small for its body size, it may come as a surprise that the heavily toothed jaws on a 100-pounder can easily open far enough to swallow most of a 5-pound salmon in one gulp. They're aggressive and quick for a very short distance, but lack the power for a long sustained run. Except in very shallow water, the fight is essentially an up-and-down affair, with short, strong rushes back toward the bottom as the angler struggles to lift it toward the surface. Eventually its efforts get weaker and weaker, until finally becoming mostly dead weight as it nears the surface.

It is standard procedure to shoot any halibut much over 100 pounds between the eyes with a handgun or shotgun as it floats on the surface next to the boat, because although it has quit fighting, it is by no means dead. Even after being shot it can still thrash around dangerously for a minute or two, so because of its great size it should always be handled very carefully.

Smaller halibut are aggressive enough to take an unbaited artificial lure. We repeatedly caught them up to 60 pounds using 2- to 4-ounce Florida-style leadhead jigs. White and green were the best colors. Bigger fish seem to want big pieces of meat and are much less inclined to attack a "bare" artificial.

Deep water and strong currents may dictate heavy weights to reach bottom. More than a pound in extreme situations. A particularly popular rig is a 4- to 20-ounce leadhead jig, unpainted, with no skirts, and a 5/0 to 12/0 hook. Often a second hook is added with Dacron or heavy mono so that it is positioned 6 to 12 inches behind the first. Heavy leader is not needed, except when using very light lines. For example, we found using 3 feet of 50-pound-test mono as leader for 15-pound-test line was quite adequate.

An unbaited jig is simply fished deep-jigging style (see Chapter 17). If bait is added, drop it down to the bottom and raise it up a few feet, then yo-yo it up

A Pacific halibut caught near Elfin Cove, Alaska.

and down very slowly with the rod. The strike of a big halibut is anything but subtle.

KELP BASS

Although kelp bass (*Paralabrax clathratus*) also known as rock bass, sand bass, calico bass, bull bass, and cabrilla, do not compare in size to black sea bass, they are an extremely fine game species. Unfortunately, this almost sedentary fish becomes scarcer every year, even though commercial fishing has been prohibited since 1953.

Kelp bass are mostly caught around kelp beds on live anchovies or sardines fished near or just under the surface. Recently more fishermen have been catching them on trolled plugs, spoons, and streamer flies because these fish will take a variety of artificials. Best catches are made with yellow or brown plugs or streamer flies. But more important than type of bait is knowledge that kelp bass are almost never caught far away from a kelp bed. Many kelp beds where bass are most plentiful are not visible from the surface of the water.

Kelp bass are distributed from San Francisco south to Abreojos Point, Baja California. They are not abundant north of Point Conception, California, but at kelp beds elsewhere within their range, usually the most abundant game species in residence.

Calico bass, a common name for a smaller kelp bass, can be caught practically the year round. But the period from May to October is best for the larger variety, frequently called bull bass.

The kelp bass and black sea bass have cousins along the Pacific coast worthy of mention here. First is the broomtail grouper (*Mycteroperca xenarchus*) a colorful, spotted fish also called the garrupa (in Mexico), gray broomtail, pinto broomtail, or spotted broomtail. Especially plentiful in scattered spots off Baja California, it can be taken on strip baits, live baits, or trolled spoon lures. The broomtail grouper has been caught up to 75 pounds, but probably grows larger.

Another bass cousin, this one reaching a weight of 125 pounds, is the gulf grouper or garrupa de baya (*Mycteroperca jordani*). Less colorful than the broomtail, it is more abundant south of San Quintín Bay and in the Gulf of California. Only a few have been taken north of San Diego. Largely a bottom feeder on live bait, it will take an artificial lure trolled slowly.

The sand bass (*Paralabrax nebulifer*) can be taken the year round south of Monterey on various kinds of strip baits, live anchovies, queenfish, small sardines, shrimp, and mussels. It feeds on the bottom and reaches almost 2 feet in length. The spotted bass, (*Paralabrax maculatofasciatus*), also called spotted cabrilla or pinto cabrilla, reaches about 1½ feet in length. It ranges from Point Conception, California, southward in nearly all bays, sloughs, and stream entrances to Mazatlán, Mexico. It is taken on a wide variety of live and cut baits.

LINGCOD

Whatever the ling lacks in good looks it surely more than makes up for on the table. It is one of only four species belonging to the greenling family (*Hexagrammidae*) in North American waters, and the largest. It probably reaches weight in excess of 75 pounds, because fish up to 60 are not uncommon, and the IGFA all-tackle record is 64 pounds (Elfin Cove, Alaska, 1988). Its range extends throughout the Gulf of Alaska and southward to at least Central California. Like the halibut, it is also found in both shallow and deep water, at least down to 400 or 500 feet.

Lingcod are extremely aggressive. Since they tend to run in large schools where there's an abundance of bait, competition for food can get formidable. It's not uncommon to hook a big ling and fight it all the way to the surface, only to find that another of equal size is fiercely clamped onto the one that's hooked. They have a large mouth and big teeth for their body size, and a face that only another ling or an angler could love. Unlike rockfish, lingcod seem to be totally unaffected by changes in pressure; fish brought quickly to the surface from 200 feet down have no ballooned swim bladder problems and can return immediately to the bottom with ease.

Locating lingcod is a matter of locating structure. The greater the structure's vertical extent, the better they like it, because that's where the bigger bait concentrations usually are.

Fishing for lingcod is exactly like fishing for halibut. They readily take artificial lures, as well as bait-tipped jigs and whole baits. Live baits are especially good for big fish. They are an excellent light-tackle fish, and while they fight fairly hard they can still be easily taken on lines testing 20 pounds or lighter.

Like many species of fish, the really large lings

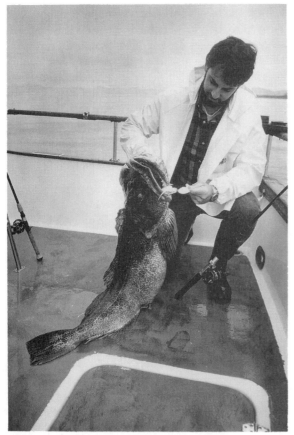

A lingcod caught near Elfin Cove, Alaska.

(over 25 pounds or so) are females and should be released whenever possible to serve as brood stock. Also like halibut and other coldwater fish, they tend to grow slowly, and a 50-pound female could be 25 to 30 years old, or more.

THE ROCKFISHES

The *Scorpaenidae* (scorpionfish) family consists of at least 250 different species, most of which are too small and some of which are too dangerous to be of interest to anglers. A few species found throughout the Gulf of Alaska and southward along the California coast to Mexico are of interest to anglers because of their flavor, size, and availability. None are particularly strong fighters, and they do not tolerate being hauled rapidly to the surface from more than 50 or 60 feet down without suffering the "bends," visible as a badly distended swim bladder protruding

through the mouth. Puncturing the swim bladder with an ice pick or sharp hook point sometimes deflates it enough for them to eventually go down, but as a rule any fish brought up from more than 100 feet isn't likely to make it.

The **black-and-yellow rockfish** is found primarily along the California coast, and rarely exceeds 15 inches in length, but it is excellent table fare. The **black rockfish**, which looks almost exactly like a largemouth bass, grows to over 10 pounds and schools heavily. It is so aggressive that it will, in water where the depth is 30 feet or less, readily chase an artificial lure all the way to the surface. And sometimes even leap clear of the surface to strike, as we found out in southeast Alaska.

Bocaccio are typical of the larger rockfish found in the Pacific northwest, and the fishing techniques discussed below would also apply to the rest of that family as well. It reaches a length of 36 inches and a weight of 21 pounds, but an extremely good fish would be half that size.

Almost any rocky or rubble bottom from 250 to 750 feet deep is likely to yield a good catch of bocaccios. The secret lies entirely in finding the right type of bottom.

The usual fishing rig consists of from four to six hooks above a sinker heavy enough to take all to the bottom on a fairly straight course. The rig can be fished from a large specially built reel attached to the rail of the boat, or from a large-capacity reel as used for large billfish and tuna. Because of the depths (adult bocaccios sometimes go as deep as 1,000 feet), it takes considerable time just to lower the line and haul it up again. So the bait should be sufficiently tough to remain on the hook while being chewed by bocaccios and other deep fishes. Squid makes an ideal bait.

Once the angler finds the bottom, he should leave the rig there long enough to catch a fish on every hook. This is difficult because the impulse is to strike immediately when a nibble is felt. Bottom fishermen have caught bocaccios from Queen Charlotte Sound, British Columbia, to Ensenada, Baja California.

Another rockfish caught in great numbers is the **olive rockfish**, often confused with kelp bass. It reaches a weight of 7 or 8 pounds, and some kelp beds around Santa Barbara and San Nicolas islands are almost paved with them. Olive rockfish have been taken as deep as 480 feet.

Another important rockfish is the **blue**, which ranges from the Bering Sea to Santo Tomas, Baja California. It never reaches more than a few pounds in size, but can be caught in quantity near rocky shores, around breakwaters, sunken ships, piles of rubble and similar localities along the entire California, Oregon, and Washington coasts. Best baits are mussels, clams, crabs, shrimp, or squid. For their size, blue rockfish put up an excellent battle on light tackle.

Vermilion rockfish have been caught from Vancouver Island south to Baja California. They reach 30 inches, about 15 pounds, and occur in water 180 to 500 feet deep over irregular, rocky or rubble bottoms. Vermilion rockfish usually make up a majority of the bag of southern California anglers. The same rig, bait, and technique can be used as for bocaccios.

Because a good rockfish hole may yield a dozen or more kinds of rockfish any day, rockfishing is colorful, interesting, productive, mysterious, and good exercise. And it yields very unusual fish. The strangest member of the rockfish family is the **sculpin**, which

A colorful canary rockfish, locally called red snapper, caught in southeastern Alaska.

reaches a maximum weight of about 4 pounds and is an excellent fish for chowders and soups.

Fishermen should handle sculpin carefully because the sharp fin spines—dorsal, anal, and pelvic—are mildly poisonous and can cause an extremely painful wound if the skin is punctured. Immersion in hot water in which Epsom salts have been dissolved will help alleviate the discomforts from a sculpin wound. If undue swelling, nausea, dizziness, or fainting follow, a doctor should be called immediately.

The **canary rockfish** is one of the most colorful and one of the larger members, reaching a length of at least 30 inches and a weight of 12 or more pounds. It has an orange body, three bright orange stripes across the head, and bright orange fins. Probably the largest is the vermilion rockfish, similar in appearance to the canary rockfish, but reaching a length of more than 3 feet and a weight of over 20 pounds.

It is possible that the majority of rockfish are caught by anglers fishing for other species. The same tackle and techniques used for lingcod are equally effective for rockfish. Probably most overlooked of the species as a gamefish is the black rockfish, very reachable with light tackle. They look almost exactly like a freshwater largemouth bass. We've caught many that ran 8 to 10 pounds on light spinning tackle, and they fought very hard on that gear.

SEA BASSES

The temperate sea basses of the Pacific coast include two species that grow to large size and are distributed over a wide range. The largest is the giant sea bass (*Stereolepis gigas*), also known as the black sea bass or California bass, which may exceed 600 pounds. Then there is the white sea bass (*Atractoscion nobilis*), a sea bass in name only because it really belongs to the drum and croaker family. It may reach weights of almost 100 pounds.

The giant sea bass belongs to a relatively small branch of the saltwater basses called the temperate bass family (Percichthyidae). Its closest relative is, somewhat surprisingly, the striped bass. And the third member of this small group is the wreckfish, which looks like the tripletail so common to the Gulf of Mexico, but reaches weights of over 100 pounds and is most common along the eastern Atlantic coast from Norway to the Canary Islands. The giant sea bass ranges from Monterey, California, southward to the Gulf of California. The IGFA all-tackle record is 563 pounds 8 ounces (California, 1968).

Most abundant at Anacapa, San Nicolas, and Los Coronados islands and between Oceanside and San Clemente on the mainland, giant sea bass prefer a rocky bottom just outside of a kelp bed where the water varies between 19 and 25 fathoms deep. But they can frequently be found in inshore areas from 5 to 10 fathoms deep where the bottom is sandy. These inshore blacks average smaller in size.

Giant bass do not mature until they are eleven to thirteen years old, between 50 and 60 pounds. A 320-pound female ready to spawn was found carrying an estimated 60 million eggs that weighed 47 pounds. The main spawning season occurs from July to September.

Because of their size and extremely bulky shape, they may appear slow and clumsy. Actually, they are capable of catching some of the fast fishes of the Pacific in a short chase, as is evident from the wide variety of items found in their stomachs. Included in a bass's diet would be mackerel, jack mackerel, sheepshead, ocean whitefish, sand bass, cancer crabs or red crabs. There's no way to estimate the longevity of this fish, but California biologists recently examined a 435-pounder and determined that it was between seventy-two and seventy-five years old.

There is no shortcut to landing a black sea bass once hooked. Most sea bass specialists use a big game rod with a 14/0 hook; about 500 yards of 80-pound-test line on a 10/0 (600-yard capacity) reel, and wire, mono, or cable leader testing about 100 to 150 pounds and about 6 feet long.

The bait can be almost anything, but one favorite is a small barracuda or mackerel, split and tied to the line with a section of nylon. This is done to hide the hook with the point left embedded near the tail. Besides mackerel and barracuda, giant sea bass readily take sand dabs, smaller bass, large sardines, queenfish, or a fillet of any of the other fishes that live in the same water. The bait need not be fresh and anglers prefer it a bit ripe from sitting in the sun.

Sometimes the strike is barely noticeable, but a wise fisherman plays out a small amount of line anyway, just in case. As soon as this much slack is taken up and the line taut, he sets the hook sharply.

The secret to landing this species is to maintain all the pressure the tackle will stand. If the fish is given any slack at all, the bass will shake its head violently from side to side. Either the hook will be pulled free or the line will snap.

Sport fishermen can afford to copy a trick used by market fishermen to catch big bass. The tail is chopped off a large live sardine, jack mackerel, or ocean whitefish. The idea is to inhibit the swimming ability of the baitfish and at the same time permit the release of blood into the water where a hungry bass may be hiding. They have an excellent sense of smell.

The IGFA all-tackle record for **white sea bass** is 83 pounds 12 ounces (Mexico, 1953). The location of that record is perhaps a little misleading because it could thus be assumed the species is primarily tropical or subtropical in nature, but actually it ranges north as far as Alaska and as far south as Chile, although it is uncommon north of San Francisco.

It is taken near kelp beds, over shallow submerged banks, and on the edges of banks with such live bait as sardines, anchovies, small mackerel, and strip bait. Sea bass will take lures trolled at a fairly slow speed.

The recommended hook size is from number 1 to 2/0. Although white sea bass are not ordinarily as wary and shy as some other Pacific offshore fishes, they can become quite selective. Occasionally sea bass will strike only fairly large, live Pacific mackerel. Other times a live squid is the only successful bait.

Once white sea bass were far more plentiful than today. Large numbers were taken years ago in the San Francisco Bay area, but their presence there is now a thing of the past. Spawning is presumed to take place in late spring and on into the summer months. The shore areas in Santa Monica Bay, Belmont Shore, Dana Point, Oceanside, Coronado, and similar localities appear to be important nursery grounds for white sea bass. But in many of these same areas the white sea bass population is seriously threatened by pollution.

Larger fish frequently gather into large, loosely grouped schools, and are most common over sandy bottoms and around the offshore margins of kelp beds on the mainland coast. They are most numerous offshore around San Clemente and Santa Catalina.

An adult white sea bass is a strong fighter. The species is also long-lived. The record fish must have been very old, because 40-pounders taken in Mexican waters will average about twenty years.

Many saltwater species of fish are vastly more active at night than in daylight and the white sea bass is one of these. Fishing for big whites at night is among the most unforgettable experiences available to an angler along the Pacific coast; still, this technique is not yet fully exploited.

Some anglers find night fishing for game species exciting. Summer nights on the Pacific are often calm except for the activity of fishes and marine animals that suddenly surge to the surface. Sometimes the activity is so great that the sea appears to be boiling. At such times white sea bass lose much of their caution. They not only venture closer to a boat in darkness, but also feed nearer the surface and strike any lure or live bait with more abandon.

CALIFORNIA SHEEPSHEAD

The California sheepshead (*Pimelometopon pulcher*) is in no way related to its Atlantic namesake. It is instead a member of the wrasse family Labridae, which includes many of the small colorful fishes so popular among those who maintain saltwater aquariums. The California sheepshead grows to large size; although the IGFA lists no record for the species, it probably reaches weights of close to 40 pounds. While fishing in Australia in the late 1970s we caught many large fish locally called snappers, which were in fact wrasses with the characteristic forehead bump. Although not nearly as colorful as the California sheepshead, they nevertheless were delicious eating.

This Pacific sheepshead is among the plug-uglies of the fish world. As though its caninelike teeth and its lantern jaw are not enough, the male sheepshead develops a forehead hump during the breeding season. His scientific name means "beautiful fat forehead."

Even the body colors of the sheepshead are weird. At all stages, ages, and sexes, sheepshead can be distinguished from the other wrasses by their unique coloration. The young of both sexes are a solid orange-red except for roundish black blotches. Adult females are a dull red or rose, and adult males have a bluish black head and tail with a red midsection. Both males and females have light or whitish chins when full grown.

Most abundant near the bottom, particularly around dense kelp forests, sheepshead are taken from 29- to 100-foot depths, though they are occasionally caught in shallower water. They also tend to congregate along rocky shores, especially near mussel beds. Never abundant north of Los Angeles, they have been taken from Monterey Bay to the tip of Baja California and throughout the Gulf of California.

Male or dog sheepshead are said to reach more than 30 pounds, but most sheepshead caught by fishermen are less than 15. They are taken on 3/0 to 5/0 hooks baited with mussels, rock crabs, lobster, shrimp with the shell on, clams, abalone, and fish strips.

Although they seldom strike a trolled or cast lure that is retrieved in a normal manner, sheepshead can often be tempted to strike even a shiny bare hook or a small metal jig that is jiggled up and down in an enticing manner within a few inches of the bottom. They are expert bait thieves and their large jaw-teeth can cause the hook to slip out after an angler strikes.

Any fisherman who hooks a sheepshead is in for a strong, tugging battle. It can end in disaster when the fish runs through or around kelp or ducks beneath a rocky ledge. It's possible in some rocky areas to hook sheepshead all day long but never land one. The best fishing areas are around kelp beds south of Point Conception, California, and around the offshore Pacific islands south of Santa Cruz Island.

SURFPERCH

There are no less than twenty different kinds of surfperch along the Pacific coast, all belonging to the family Embiotocidae. While most live in the surf, tidepools, bays, or just about anywhere else close to shore, there is one species that is found only in the freshwater streams of northern California, and another that resides solely in very deep water.

From an angling standpoint, the most important is the barred surfperch. Two others that are also popular are the calico and redtail, which are similar in habit and often confused with one another. The barred surfperch are usually found in the surf along sandy beaches, where they congregate in certain holes or depressions along the bottom. They constitute about 50 percent of the surf angler's bag in southern California, but their range extends from Vancouver Island southward to the tip of Baja, California. The largest taken in California was a nine-year-old weighing only 4¼ pounds. Any fish over 3 pounds is an extremely good one, since the average catch will weigh a pound or less.

Barred and all other surfperches are viviparous, which means they give birth to living young. As many as 113 embryos and as few as 4 have been found in female surfperch, but the average is about 33 per individual. The fertilization of the eggs is entirely internal; these eggs hatch and the young develop in saclike portions of the oviduct. The young surfperch are usually born between April and July, and are about 2 to 3 inches long at birth. Some mature when they are only 6½ inches long, between one and two years of age.

An analysis of stomach contents of barred surfperch caught by fishermen revealed that their diet, like the corbina's, is 90 percent sand crab, with the remainder consisting of other crustaceans, particularly bean clams.

Thousands of barred surfperch have been tagged by California Fish and Game biologists and results revealed that, like corbinas, they travel very little. Their average movements are less than two miles and only one had traveled thirty miles from the place it was tagged.

The tasty, white-meated, barred surfperch can be taken any time of the year, any time of the day or night. The largest are usually taken in midwinter (January is the best month). Best baits are soft-shelled sand crabs, bloodworms, mussels, and pieces of mackerel. In some areas, entrails of freshly caught sardines are used. The barred surfperch in particular will readily strike certain artificial lures. Small jigs are effective, so are small streamer and nymph flies, such as the Pink Shrimp. Flycasting on relatively calm days is a sporting and lively proposition.

The most consistent area for barred surfperch are sandy beaches between Point Mugu and Pismo Beach, but there are other hotspots. Calico surfperch fishing is best along beaches of Monterey Bay while redtails are most abundant northward from San Francisco. Some especially good areas are along the coastlines of Humboldt and Del Norte counties.

Other members of the surfperch family taken in numbers along the Pacific are: the walleye, which is especially abundant around open rocky coasts and fishing piers; the black perch, which ranges from Bodega Bay to Abreojos Point, Baja, California; and the shiner perch, which reaches a maximum of 8 inches and is taken from shore, docks, piers, rocks.

Another fish, the opaleye, which superficially resembles the surfperch, is a year-round resident of rocky shorelines and kelp beds between Monterey Bay and southern Baja. Opaleyes live in caves and among seaweed-covered rocks in shallow water, but are also found at mid-depths and in offshore kelp beds. Spincasters and flycasters have found they are extremely game, dogged, light-tackle fish. They occasionally reach 6 pounds. Opaleyes will bite on mussels, sand crabs, and pieces of other fish.

Another Pacific coast fish that resembles the surfperch is the half-moon. Half-moons have been caught as far north as Eureka, California, but are most abundant on the southern California coast and in the Gulf of California. The greatest number of half-moons occur around the Channel Islands where they are year-round residents of kelp beds, shallow waters, and rocky shorelines.

Chapter 12

UNUSUAL GAMEFISH

BLUEFISH, COBIA, DOLPHIN(FISH), TRIPLETAIL

The gamefish discussed in this chapter are unusual in that they all are one-of-a-kind. They're all also somewhat unique in their habits, and they have no close relatives. Much like the snook covered in Chapter 3, they are in a class all by themselves, and they deserve special treatment.

BLUEFISH

Bluefish are truly one of the world's great mystery fish, sometimes disappearing entirely for years at a time and then returning suddenly in rapidly increasing numbers.

Although we tend to think of the bluefish in terms of the East Coast of North America, actually they are found in all major temperate seas worldwide except possibly the north Pacific. In the western Atlantic as far south as Argentina, and in the eastern Atlantic from Spain to South Africa. The largest specimen to date, according to *McClane's Field Guide to Salt-water Fishes of North America*, is a 45-pounder from the Mediterranean off the coast of North Africa. The current IGFA all-tackle record is 31 pounds 12 ounces (North Carolina, 1972). Bluefish are also commonly found in the Indian Ocean, the Black Sea, the shores of the Malay Peninsula, plus southern Australia and New Zealand.

In spite of this widespread distribution, *Potatomus saltatrix* is the only member of its family, strangely devoid of even any close relatives. It is a matter of historical record at least as far back as 1764 that this fish is subject to population extremes in cycles of roughly forty years or so. The most recent disappearance occurred during the 1920s. The cur-

Big bluefish are exciting sport on any light tackle.

rent high began during the late 60s and early 70s, and thus far oddly shows no signs of diminishing.

Thus, earlier dire predictions to the contrary, the East Coast of the U.S. all the way from Maine to Florida has for over fifteen years been enjoying a bluefish bonanza unlike any before in the history of modern angling. Even the Gulf of Mexico coastline has perhaps more blues than normal, although they aren't nearly as plentiful (or usually as large) there.

Many bluefish experts, citing the forty-year cycle theory, maintain that the current boom is long overdue for a bust. Thus far no one has apparently informed the bluefish of this, so they continue happily to do their thing, producing even more and bigger members of their finny tribe.

South Florida, for example, until about fifteen years ago wasn't known for big bluefish. A 5-pounder was considered big, and one that hit 10 was a news event. Then suddenly offshore charterboat skippers began to find huge schools of big blues migrating up and down the coast, from one to at times twelve miles offshore. They sometimes appear on the surface heading rapidly south rather sporadically in March, staying up for very short intervals. These fish are exceptionally large, running sometimes 20 pounds or more. They are also fat and full of roe.

A month later, with considerably more regularity, big schools again show on the surface, this time staying up for often hours at a time, heading rapidly northward at the same distance offshore as when southbound. Now, however, these fish are the same length but slender, weighing only an average of 12 to 16 pounds. And to make the situation even more bizarre, now and then a marlin or two can be seen crashing and feeding in one of the schools that has wandered far out into blue water.

Whenever one of these rapidly moving schools is encountered, the angling action exceeds your wildest imagination. These fish are extremely ravenous (even more so than usual!) from their intense spawning activity and will eat almost anything that moves, regardless of size.

Fishing a school of big bluefish the size of a football field is about as exciting as light-tackle angling can get. Especially when casting artificial lures or flies into the brilliant green mass of fish and watching your offering disappear in a washtub-size explosion of white foam. The trick here is to place the lure or fly right at the edge of the school, otherwise lure, leader, and a substantial part of the line may get eaten too.

A big bluefish on light tackle is a real handful, capable of making long runs and typically ripping off 50 to 100 yards of line (or backing from a fly reel) before it stops.

By early May the rapidly moving bluefish schools are as far north as the Carolinas and Chesapeake Bay. Late in that same month they're usually rampaging Long Island Sound. It only takes them another week or two to reach the Cape Cod area, and by late June they may be as far north as Maine.

Except for the rapid offshore passage typical of Florida's short "big bluefish" season, once they show up along the northeast Atlantic coast they are there to stay throughout the summer and fall.

Large numbers of big blues in Maine were somewhat of a novelty until they started showing up there with regularity in the middle 1970s (for the first time in fifty years or so). Now they are abundant from July through September, often staying until early or mid-October. Few small fish are taken there; the average is 8 to 15 pounds.

In spite of their typically ravenous appetite, they can also be evasive and spooky. Small lures and long casts will catch more fish in such situations. Vertical jigging with light lines over ledges in 30 to 100 feet of water also produces well. More and more fishermen are coming to the conclusion that in many situations light tackle will produce more fish.

Certainly the East Coast from Cape Cod southward to the outer banks of North Carolina is well into the light-tackle bluefish revolution. Some charter boats and many private vessels are now going for blues in a big way with lighter and lighter gear. Fly fishing for them has also become the "in" thing to do, which makes sense because these fish are perfect for that gear.

Even in the surf, where a big blue can be a tough opponent on the long rod, most fly fishermen use 7 to 9-weight rods and poppers or brightly colored streamer flies. Complicated patterns aren't necessary, but those with lots of mylar produce especially well.

Bluefish are plentiful in the Cape Cod area until late October or early November. In addition, as a bonus it's not uncommon for a light-tackle angler to hook a big stripper while fishing for blues. Quite a few large striped bass have been taken this way. Another exciting way to fish for blues in this area is to sight-cast to big fish visible in tide rips with fly or light spinning (or baitcasting) gear.

The rigging needed to fish big blues with light tackle isn't complicated, but it does require some sort of shock leader to protect the line from those extremely sharp teeth. Quite a few anglers have in recent years switched from wire to heavy monofilament leader material, typically 60- to 80-pound test, maintaining that in many situations it produces a lot more strikes. Our experience verifies this, but we've also learned that if short lures are used with mono, you can lose a fish now and then. Especially if you don't cut back past frayed sections of leader and retie the lure. Longer lures, like some pencil poppers, as a rule keep the blue's dental equipment reasonably well separated from the mono leader.

Bluefish respond readily to the same casting, trolling, chumming, and live bait techniques as mackerel. Almost any lure will hook them readily, but if you use plugs it's a good idea to remove the treble hooks and substitute a larger single for each treble. Or, in a pinch, mash all of the barbs flat on the trebles. You'll lose extremely few (if any) fish this way, but trying to remove fully barbed trebles from a large, thrashing, angry bluefish's mouth is just begging to get lots of blood on your hands—most of it yours.

COBIA

Also known as the ling, or crabeater, *Rachycentron canadum* is the sole member of the family Rachycentridae. It is found in tropical waters almost world wide, except perhaps the eastern Pacific (e.g. the west coast of Central America). In the western Atlantic its range extends from Argentina northward through the Caribbean, the Gulf of Mexico, and up the U.S. East Coast as far as Massachusetts and Bermuda. It is most commonly found from Chesapeake Bay southward.

The cobia grows to large size. The IGFA all-tackle record is 135 pounds 9 ounces (Australia, 1985). Cobia of over 100 pounds have been taken in Florida, Alabama, Kenya (Africa), and Virginia. The average is more like 30 pounds, but over 50 pounds is likely throughout its range.

In Australia it is most commonly called the black kingfish, and when fishing there in the late 1970s we encountered them from Brisbane northward along the Great Barrier Reef, typically hanging around marker buoys and other structure just as they do in U.S. waters.

Anglers who know the species well realize that it is not among the smartest or most wary of fishes. It will often swim right up to an anchored or drifting boat and simply take up residence in the shade. It frequently follows large sharks, and seems especially to enjoy the company of giant manta rays. Why they like the big rays is a mystery; perhaps they regard the mantas as "moving structure" rather than a likely provider of food. Cobia look a little like a small shark to the casual observer, but they don't have any teeth, they do have scales, and they don't have the shark's fin structure.

Miami angler Dick Moore happily shows off his 60-pound cobia. It was a fly-rod world record at the time.

Cobia follow the sun in U.S. waters, ranging northward during the summer months and southward when the first of the fall cold fronts come through. A popular wintering spot is the southern tip of Florida and the Keys, especially the ship wrecks so abundant in the waters around Key West. In March they start their annual northward migration up both coasts of Florida and along the western shoreline of the Gulf of Mexico. They usually reach the northern Gulf by April, where they are often fished close to shore from small boats by anglers who cruise the shoreline looking for the more easily spotted massive dark shapes of the big manta rays. Casting a live bait or lure in front of the ray draws no interest from that ponderous creature, but if there are any cobia hitchhiking along for the ride, they will usually respond quickly.

When it comes to food, the cobia is rarely difficult to please. Just about any baitfish, crab, or shrimp it can get into its mouth is acceptable. Anglers do well with live bait, such as small mullet, pinfish, large sardines, live shrimp, small crabs, etc. A float can be used if the cobia is close to the surface, as they often are when following rays or hanging around buoys or channel markers, but for the most part that isn't necessary. Most anglers simply attach a 4/0 to 7/0 hook to a short piece of monofilament leader (50- to 80-pound test), and the leader directly to the line without a sinker or float. This technique is often called "free-lining," "live-lining," or "fly line fishing" (not to be confused with flycasting, where a fly rod and artificial fly are used).

Cobia can be easily lured away from wrecks or other structures, where they may otherwise become deliberately entangled after hookup, by chumming from a short distance upcurrent. Or sometimes by casting a noisy surface lure near their position, and then working it just fast enough that they cannot easily catch it until it is far enough from the structure to improve your chances after hookup.

The cobia is a favorite among saltwater fly fishermen. It takes poppers and streamers readily. Just about any pattern will do, but those that resemble baitfish have a slight edge. Size is more important than color; streamers 4 to 6 inches long are better for the bigger fish. Working in pairs, one angler will use a hookless live bait or hookless noisy surface plug to get the cobia excited and within easy casting range for the other.

Once hooked, the Cobia puts up a strong, stubborn fight and thrashes around a lot after being boated, so keep a billy club handy as an immediate pacifier.

DOLPHIN (FISH)

These are true fish, not to be confused with the marine mammals also known as dolphins (or porpoises). It is perhaps unfortunate that the dolphin name persists for these fish in the light of the confusion it sometimes generates, but the more colorful and appropriate Spanish name of dorado (it means golden) has somehow never caught on.

There are at least two members of the family Coryphaenidae, maybe more. The largest and by far the most predominant is simply called "dolphin" (*Coryphaena hippurus*). Smaller and possibly less frequently encountered is the pompano dolphin (*C. equisetis*), which resembles the common dolphin so closely it may not be recognized when

Dolphin (fish) are great fun on light tackle.

caught. Rarely exceeding 5 pounds, it is usually a somewhat more slender fish.

The common dolphin is prevalent in blue water in all tropical and subtropical seas worldwide. It will also follow warm-water gyres spun off a major tropical current like the Gulf Stream far to the north of its normal range, and for this reason has been caught as far north as the southern edge of the Maritime Provinces of Canada. It grows to large size, the current IGFA all-tackle record being 87 pounds (Costa Rica, 1976). It exceeds 50 pounds frequently, and fish in excess of 75 pounds have been caught in such widely diverse locations as Florida, North Carolina, the Bahamas, Africa, and Mexico.

Everywhere it is found, it is considered by fishermen to be both an aggravation and a blessing. Those who seek it for the wonderful light-tackle gamefish that it is in its own right loudly sing its praises, while any billfisherman who has had carefully prepared baits destroyed by these "green hornets" will seldom have anything good to say about the species.

For example, during a recent trip to Golfito Sailfish Rancho in southwestern Costa Rica, we were fly fishing for sailfish. We had just successfully teased a big sail to within flycasting range and put the big streamer just a few feet in front of its elongated nose, when suddenly out of nowhere a 30-pound dolphin appeared and in a flash of green pounced on the fly before the sailfish could even get close. A dolphin that size on a fly rod is always a worthy adversary, except when you really wanted the billfish in the first place.

Dolphin often vigorously attack just about anything that moves, appearing without warning right behind a bait, which it mangles in seconds with its small but needlelike teeth. For that reason more and more anglers are using high-speed offshore trolling lures for these fish, instead of going to the trouble of rigging natural baits. The lures seem to work just as well.

Dolphin are very structure oriented. They tend to follow weedlines, and hang around floating debris, because that's where small baitfish otherwise helpless in the open ocean seek shelter. Sometimes all those weeds offer little protection for the baitfish, because a hungry dolphin will push its way through a lot of vegetation to get to its prey.

There are several ways to fish for dolphin. One way, when trolling baits for billfish, is always to have a medium-weight casting or spinning rod handy, rigged with a ½- to 1-ounce bucktail jig (yellow or white). If a dolphin appears near a bait and you're quick enough, you can cast the jig nearby and it will often pounce on that. This not only saves a laboriously rigged natural bait now and then, it also adds an extra dimension of action to the day. It is also interesting to note that it is not uncommon for a marlin or sailfish to appear suddenly while someone is busy fighting a dolphin.

Trolling is always a good way to cover ground, but on days when there are likely to be sargassum weedlines offshore, you often do better if you keep going at cruising speed until you get to that area. Then start trolling along the edges of those weeds. Jigs, feathers, and lures all work. So do streamer flies and poppers. We have had especially good results with noisy surface plugs like chuggers and floater/divers. Also pencil poppers and other "walking"-type lures.

Drifting with live bait (shrimp, small fish, etc.) also produces well. Dolphin are attracted to the boat's shade. Some anglers create shade by spreading newspapers on the surface near the boat (pick

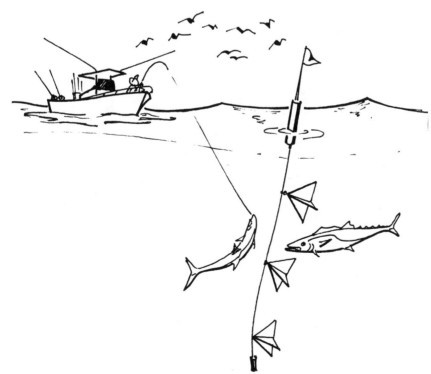

Fish-aggregating device (FAD), a floating structure that attracts fish. The one illustrated here is a commercially made FAD by McIntosh Marine of Ft. Lauderdale, Florida, and called a Sea Kite. It attracts both baitfish and gamefish.

them up before you leave), or perhaps a plastic tarp of some kind with enough floats around the edges to keep it from sinking. Dolphin are especially attracted to just about any type of floating FAD (Fish Aggregating Device), and there are even some commercial models available just for that purpose.

Big dolphin (over 30 pounds) are found alone or in pairs. If they're under 20 pounds, they're more likely to be in schools. As a rule, the smaller the fish, the bigger the school. There may be over a hundred in a school of 3-pounders. Once a bonanza like that is encountered, the angler will do well to remember that the bounty of the sea is not endless. Kill only a few for the table, and let the rest go to maintain the species. This especially applies to large fish, because when they top 15 pounds or so the flavor diminishes rapidly.

Almost every female dolphin we've ever seen over 10 pounds was full of eggs. The cow of the species is easy to distinguish from the bull; the former has a sloping forehead, while the latter has a high, rectangular, very blunt forehead.

TRIPLETAIL

Another loner as far as its family tree goes, *Lobotes surinamensis* is also known as the buoy fish, buoy bass, blackfish, and chobie. It is classed in the family Lobotidae, which also includes a close relative, *L. pacificus*, found from Mexico to Panama but apparently not plentiful anywhere. In the western Atlantic Ocean, the tripletail's range extends from Argentina northward to Massachusetts and Bermuda. But it is most common throughout the Gulf of Mexico and on Florida's east coast near Cape Canaveral.

In appearance this fish looks very much like a freshwater crappie of gigantic proportions. The IGFA all-tackle record is 32 pounds (Florida, 1988), although there are reports of fish that exceeded 40. In spite of its unusual appearance, the tripletail has firm white flesh and is excellent eating.

This is not a school fish, but it often does show up in an area as a loose, widespread group. Anglers in Florida and elsewhere in the Gulf of Mexico look for

The unusual tripletail looks very much like a giant version of a freshwater black crappie.

these fish near any floating object. Buoys are a popular haven, as well as channel markers. Also floating debris, almost no matter how small. And sharp-eyed anglers often spot them floating in open water, looking for all the world like a dead fish as they drift along motionless, on their sides, heads slightly down. But cast a bait or lure so that it drifts or swims past the "dead" fish's nose, and it is usually accepted readily.

This fish tends to be rather wary at times, and must be approached with caution or it will become alarmed and head for the bottom. It is best to idle the boat carefully to just outside of casting range, upwind or upcurrent as the situation requires, then make the rest of your approach by drifting with the engine off. Place the bait or lure a few feet beyond the fish so that the retrieve will bring it close by the fish's nose. The strike is quick, sometimes preceded by a shallow dive to a position just below the bait.

A skimmer jig, which has a wide, flat head in a horizontal position so that it sinks slowly and with a fluttering action, is an excellent lure. White, brown, light green, and yellow are popular colors in just about any combination. It should not be too heavy, ¼ to ½ ounce is best. Use a light spinning or baitcasting rod, and 12-pound-test line or lighter so that you can make an accurate cast. Most anglers find they hook more tripletail by tipping the jig with a small piece of shrimp or fish to give it a more attractive smell.

If it's not too rough, tripletail may announce their presence by skyrocketing baitfish from below. They sometimes even jump when hooked. If you see one skyrocket, look the area over carefully; there could be many more.

Live baits that work well include small baitfish such as finger mullet and sardines. And of course live shrimp. They will also take just about any streamer fly that resembles a baitfish.

Chapter 13

SHARKS, LARGE AND SMALL

Unlike all of the other gamefish discussed in this book, sharks belong to a class of fishes called Chondrichthyes. That's because they have no hard, bony skeleton. Theirs is made entirely of cartilage, and in fact the only hard parts in their supple bodies are the teeth. The skin is usually rough (exception: an open-ocean species known as the silky shark because of its smooth skin), actually made up of very tiny, specialized placoid scales. Fertilization occurs internally, although some sharks lay their eggs in the sea and others bear their young alive (called "pupping").

As a family, sharks are truly the world's greatest survivors among the larger animals. They have been around for more than 300 million years, having appeared long before the first dinosaur. They may even outlast man, unless we succeed in senselessly eradicating them before we too become extinct. Most sharks have changed little since the age of the giant reptiles. The great white shark (*Carcharodon carcharias*), suspected to reach a length in excess of 30 feet, is considered by at least some scientists to be the direct descendant of the prehistoric *Carcharodon megalodon*, a 60-foot monster that once roamed the tropical seas.

Of the more than 200 shark species world-wide, only a handful grow to very large size, but that seems to be enough to challenge the interests of many big-game anglers. The two largest species are of no importance to anglers, except for curiosity's sake. The tropical/subtropical whale shark grows to more than 40 feet and a weight in excess of 12 tons. The basking shark, found mostly near the arctic circle, is almost as big and heavy. Both are plankton feeders and fortunately harmless to man.

But of those sharks that can truly be considered gamefish, many of huge proportions are available in waters where the other giants of the gamefish family, the marlins, swordfish, and tunas, are not found. There are four other species, besides the great white, on the IGFA record books that exceed the half-ton mark. They include the Greenland shark (1,708 pounds 9 ounces, Norway, 1987), the mako (see below), the sixgilled shark (1,027 pounds, Azores, 1987), and the tiger (see below).

Just below the 1,000-pound mark, there's the hammerhead, the IGFA record for which is 991 pounds (Florida, 1982). That relatively low weight is somewhat surprising, since hammerheads have been repeatedly sighted in lengths which would seem to indicate 1,500 pounds or more. Some years ago while fishing in Boca Grande Pass, Florida, a tarpon hotspot, we watched a 18-foot hammerhead leisurely swim right alongside our 16-foot skiff. Fortunately it was looking for tarpon, not fishermen.

The IGFA record thresher is 802 pounds (New Zealand, 1981), but it definitely exceeds 1,000. The dusky also grows very large; the current IGFA all-tackle record is 764 pounds (Florida, 1982). Bull sharks reach 500 pounds, and the blue goes well over 400. The porbeagle undoubtedly tops 500. Even the lemon may reach 400 pounds.

Fortunately for the shark family, the attitude of a gradually more enlightened public and a definitely more knowledgeable angling community has changed considerably over the past decade. It is rapidly becoming less fashionable to drag the dead, foul-smelling carcass of a big shark back to the dock to serve as an object of fascination for a gaping crowd. More and more conservation-minded anglers simply cut the leader and let them go. After all, they play an important role in the balance of the sea.

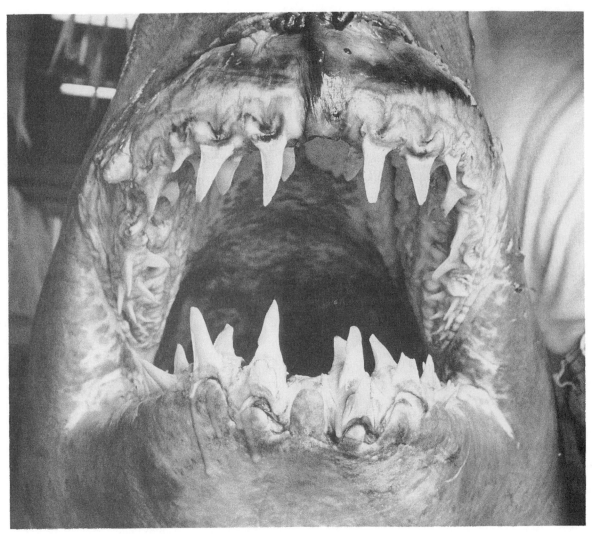

Dental equipment of a 1,000-pound mako shark.

OFFSHORE SHARKS

A 2,664-pound **great white shark** caught in 1959 by Australian Alf Dean is the officially recognized world record, though it is not the largest fish ever taken on rod and reel. In 1977 an even bigger shark was caught by Clive Green of Brisbane, but it was not officially recognized by the International Game Fish Association. Using 130-pound-test tackle off Albany, Western Australia, Green caught a great white shark that measured 16 feet in length, 10 feet 2 inches in girth, and weighed 3,388 pounds.

Boating the fish took five long and difficult hours. Under the strain of the fight, the gamefishing chair collapsed, tumbling Green onto the deck. Before the first gaff could be planted the shark was brought close more than twenty times, only to tear the wire leader out of the crewman's hands each time. Three gaffs in the shark's jaw and a wire noose around its tail finally subdued the fish. During that fishing expedition, Green also "lassoed" two other great white sharks alongside the 45-foot fishing cruiser. According to Green, "The action was quite unbelievable. One fish about 2,500 pounds was close to coming into the boat, and it reared eight feet into the air, attacking our boat with terrifying savagery. After these fish quieted down, we released both unharmed."

The **common thresher** is one of five members of the thresher family, so named because of a tail almost one half its total length. The common thresher runs from bluish gray to brownish gray on the back, shading to white on the belly. It has a small mouth and relatively small, weak teeth for a shark, but there are about forty teeth in a row in each jaw.

The common thresher isn't limited to California offshore waters. A pelagic species living in clear blue water, it's found in nearly all temperate and tropic waters around the globe, sometimes far offshore. It is often observed on or near the surface and as deep as several hundred feet.

All sharks are very interesting, somewhat mysterious creatures and the common thresher is no exception. Though little is actually known about it, the thresher is believed to reach a length of over 20 feet and a weight exceeding 1,000 pounds. There is evidence that it doesn't mature sexually until it is at least 14 feet long. The young are born alive and usually about two to four at a time. An 18-footer caught off Newport Beach in 1954 contained four young sharks weighing from 11 to 13½ pounds apiece and measuring from 4 feet to 4 feet 6 inches long.

Though the average thresher taken in California waters will measure from 5 to 8 feet long and average less than 100 pounds, commercial fishermen in 1948 reported two threshers which weighed in at 1,094 pounds and 968 pounds. The best places to find threshers include the San Francisco Bay area, the inshore coastal waters between Point Conception and Hueneme, Santa Monica Bay, and in Los Angeles Harbor. They seem most abundant during summer when they are observed swimming slowly on the surface or even jumping clear of the water.

When hooked on light or medium tackle, some thresher sharks will put on a display of aerial jumping not unlike a marlin of the same size. Others do not jump and depend on a sub-surface, brute-strength fight which can tow a fishing skiff for many miles.

Best baits for threshers include live sardines, anchovies, and mackerel, but there are examples of the fish taking artificial lures or salmon plugs. Also large whole squid. No matter what bait is used, it is important to use a stout wire leader of 10 to 20 feet. Such leaders are a necessity in every type of shark fishing—to cope with the teeth of the shark and because an ordinary nylon line will wear through after long rubbing against the abrasive hide of a shark.

There is no known record of an unprovoked attack by a common thresher shark upon a human being. Because of its habit of sometimes swimming on the surface and waving its large tail above the water, it

has been mistaken for some strange kind of sea serpent.

Another shark familiar to sportsmen is the **blue**, which belongs to the requiem shark family and which is a close relative of soupfin and tiger sharks. It is readily identified by its brilliant blue topside, which fades to white below. Found in all temperate and tropic seas of the world, the blue shark is occasionally common off southern California but rarely appears north of Point Conception unless currents of abnormally warm water bathe that area. Often it is observed swimming on the surface some distance from shore.

The blue shark is not considered a dangerous man-eater, but no doubt is responsible for some attacks on swimmers and skin divers. It should be approached with caution because of its great abundance and because it is so quickly attracted to blood.

An 11½-footer is the largest blue shark of authentic record, but no doubt the species grows to much larger size. Most of the blues taken in California waters are shorter than 6 feet and weigh less than 50 pounds. Interesting to note is that during a recent southern California shark derby, all of the hundred blue sharks taken were male. This may indicate a geographical distribution or segregation of the species by sex, at least during part of the year.

March through October, blue sharks are easy to capture off the southern California coast. They are not as exciting or difficult to land as threshers, and it is possible to handle even the largest on light tackle. But once a blue is brought to the surface, it twists and rolls in such an ugly manner that wire leaders become tangled almost beyond further use.

In natural surroundings, blues feed on crustaceans, fish, squid, and octopuses. They will also take flying fish and pelagic crabs. Blues also have the reputation for being readily attracted to garbage from ships and they will gorge on anything small enough to swallow.

Along our Atlantic coast, the **mako** is considered the most desirable shark. Found in such widely separated parts of the earth as off New Zealand, Ceylon, Cuba, Puerto Rico, and northward along the Atlantic coast to about New York, it is the most popular shark among east coast charter boats.

A large mako is certainly a formidable adversary. It reaches 800 pounds or more, and is difficult to land because it mixes a deep, dogged fight with sudden and spectacular jumps. There have been cases where it made a last-ditch attempt to turn upon the man trying to gaff it alongside a boat.

You should use heavy tackle for makos. The best recommended outfit is a 7-foot overall big-game rod with a reel with a capacity for from 800 to 1,200 yards of 80- to 130-pound-test line. Use such whole live baits as menhaden, mackerel, whiting, or herring on 10/0 to 14/0 hooks. A stainless steel cable or piano-wire leader should be at least 15 or 20 feet long.

The largest mako shark of which there is a record was a 1,080-pounder measuring 12 feet which was caught near Montauk, New York. A far more remarkable catch, however, was the 261-pounder taken in 1953 by Chuck Meyer off Montauk, New York. Meyer's line tested only 12 pounds!

Another shark familiar to Atlantic fishermen is the strange and awesome **hammerhead**, named for the elongated nostrils that give its head the shape of a hammer. This unique feature enables the fish to use its head as a rudder and to make sharper turns in pursuit of prey than any of the other sharks.

The hammerhead is often seen swimming with dorsal and caudal fins above the surface and can be found almost anywhere in warm waters on the high seas. We have also found and hooked hammerheads, and big ones too, far inshore around the Isle of Pines, Cuba, while fishing for tarpon and bonefish. And also in the Florida Keys.

Few fishes have as remarkable a sense of small as the hammerhead. Since it is able to scent blood at a great distance, it is generally the first shark to arrive when a hooked fish is badly hurt and begins to bleed. Chances are that most of the game fish lost to sharks are lost to hammerheads.

Though the average hammerhead caught offshore will average from 8 to 10 or 12 feet in length, they are known to reach almost 18 feet. No completely accurate weights for the largest fish are available, but it's assumed that they will reach 1,500 pounds. Ordinarily the food of a hammerhead consists of live fish, but you can hook a hammerhead simply by tossing or trolling a large chunk of fish or meat close by its head. Hammerhead females produce extremely large, live families. Thirty-nine young were found in one hammerhead caught off the Texas coast.

The great **white shark** that furnished Alf Dean with the current record for largest rod and reel fish also occurs in warm temperature waters along the Atlantic coast. Occasionally found as far north as eastern Nova Scotia, it prefers a diet of sea turtles and large fish and has been known to attack man, whales, and sea lions on many occasions.

The stomach contents of the great whites have included the following: a Newfoundland dog (in Australia); two 6- to 7-foot sharks inside a 15½-foot female (Florida); and a 100-pound-plus sea lion (California).

Tiger sharks are plentiful in just about all tropical and subtropical waters. The IGFA all-tackle record is 1,780 pounds (South Carolina, 1964). Tigers average about 12 feet in length, but there are a few reports of individuals that reach over 20 feet. They feed mainly on sea turtles, on large fishes and other sharks. They're greatly feared as man-eaters around the world, especially in the West Indies.

The **salmon shark** is a Pacific member of the mackerel shark family, which makes it a close relative to the great white, mako, and probably closest of all to the porbeagle. A cold-water species, it is reported to reach a length of more than 12 feet, and it occurs from San Diego northward to Alaska and westward to Japan. It is a strong, fast swimmer and puts up a hard fight when hooked. Since it feeds voraciously on salmon, anglers use whole or large pieces of salmon as bait.

There are specific methods that work best for each shark species. Makos respond well to live or whole rigged baits that consist of or at least resemble the species of prey they prefer. Interestingly, swordfish is very high on this list, and while obviously it is both physically and economically impractical to troll a rigged swordfish as mako bait, many very large makos have been caught by anglers who happened upon one feeding on a recent swordfish kill and simply used a hunk of the unfortunate prey as bait. A big mako can disable an even larger swordfish's propulsion system by biting off its tail, after which it dines on the helpless fish at leisure.

Anchoring or drifting and chumming in deep water is very effective for both makos and great whites, and the process is liable to attract many other species of sharks, and even other gamefish as well. Baits can be fished either on or near the surface, or on the bottom.

It should also be pointed out that the IGFA does not accept entries for records of any species of fish if the chum contains any type of mammal blood or parts (other than pork rind or animal hair). And also the federal Marine Mammals Protection Act makes it illegal to use any part of any marine mammal for chum or bait (to protect porpoises, seals, manatees, etc.).

In years past blood and refuse from slaughter houses was popular among serious shark fishermen. And in fact it was the on-shore processing stations of the whaling industry that attracted so many giant white sharks to the east coast of Australia. Most of the giants caught in that area during the 1950s were hooked close to these stations, using refuse from them as chum and bait. But the processing stations were abandoned years ago as whaling activity declined sharply, and the great white population of that area has consequently shifted elsewhere.

Anchoring in known productive locations and simply fishing a large bait on the bottom is very effective for big hammerheads, bull sharks, and sand tigers. Often no chumming is necessary. Both charter and private boats have been fishing for sharks successfully all up and down the East Coast, and throughout the Gulf of Mexico, for many years.

INSHORE SHARKS

Many big sharks, often some of those species considered primarily as offshore game, come into surprisingly shallow water close to shore. Giants in the tiger and hammerhead families are often caught from piers, jetties, and around inlets by anglers deliberately fishing for them from small boats. Even some surfcasters dedicated to fishing for them have scored with some that exceeded 500 pounds. In all cases these big fish still require the same heavy tackle used offshore.

The **sand tiger**, formerly known as sand shark, grows to over 300 pounds and is within easy reach of the shore-bound angler. It is found in the western Atlantic from Maine to Brazil, where it feeds close to shore and often ventures into estuaries. Occasionally it will even ascend coastal streams to the beginning of fresh water. It is primarily a bottom feeder, which means that fishing dead bait on or close to the bottom is the most effective way to get a hookup.

Compared to other sharks, the sand tiger is rather sluggish in its habits, but because it averages around 6 feet in length, it can put up a dogged fight by sheer size alone. Its principal diet consists of small fishes, including mackerels, bluefish, flounders, trout, porgies, and others of similar size. It will also eat crabs, shrimp, and squid. As it has a formidable set of teeth, use a strong wire leader and extreme care when handling it at close quarters.

Until relatively recently the sand tiger was not considered dangerous to man, except through the potential risks of dealing with a large specimen after it has been hooked. But during the past two decades

some evidence has implicated it in several nonfatal attacks on humans. And a close relative in Africa may have even caused several fatalities.

There is also a lot of fun to be had with the far more abundant smaller inshore sharks on light tackle, especially by sight-fishing for them where the water is clear enough. This is not to be confused with "sight-fishing" by chumming them to the surface in deeper water, because that really amounts simply to seeing them before hooking them, as compared to both searching for and locating them by sight in shallow water without the concentrating effect of scent. This type of shark fishing has become quite popular in the inshore waters of Florida, especially the Keys and Florida Bay, as well as some scattered spots along much of the Gulf of Mexico shoreline. And even here and there along the East Coast as far north as the Carolinas.

The most common shallow-water species are the **blacktip**, **lemon**, **bull**, and **nurse** sharks. The nurse is a relatively mild, inoffensive beast that when hooked fights like a discarded automobile tire and

This big bull shark, caught off Miami Beach, weighed just under 400 pounds.

has only very fine teeth. It rarely takes artificials, but is easily caught on bait. As a rule, most anglers pass it up in search of more active and exciting game.

The average inshore shark is perhaps 4 feet in length, but during the fall when the southbound mullet runs create an abundance of forage, it's not uncommon to see a lemon or greater blacktip that pushes 150 to 200 pounds. And in the spring, when schools of tarpon migrate northward, hammerhead sharks that may reach as much as 15 feet are occasionally seen in water less than 6 feet deep.

Being primarily tropical species, the sharks mentioned above are more likely to be encountered if water temperatures are in the middle 60s or higher. Anglers fishing south Florida and the Keys can expect to find sharks on the flats almost all year, except when strong cold fronts push water temperatures down temporarily. The very best skinny-water sight-fishing for the jaws tribe is in spring, summer, and fall.

One of the reasons so many anglers enjoy this phase of the sport is because when hooked in shallow water, the beast has no recourse but to try to run away. It cannot dive deep and "dog it." Another reason is that because the water is clear, it is possible to watch the strike in all its fascinating detail.

The most energetic shark is the blacktip. Easily distinguished because of the prominent marks on dorsal and pectoral fins that give it the name, this species is an excellent runner. The somewhat smaller member of the blacktip family, known most commonly as the spinner shark (lesser blacktip—seldom tops 75 pounds), is a spectacularly acrobatic leaper when hooked. Even occasionally seen free-jumping, it rotates as it leaves the water, much like a bullet fired from a rifle. The spinner is also the most colorful member of this toothy group when alive and active, displaying at times an almost shimmering bronzy appearance—especially when chasing a bait or lure.

Shallow-water sharks are excellent game for the light-tackle angler. Both lemons and blacktips will take a variety of artificial lures, including large, highly visible streamer flies. The plugs that work the best are the floating/diving variety, finished in bright silvery colors or yellow/red combinations. While hollow plugs with mirrored interiors will perhaps draw the most strikes of all, sharks have enormous crushing power in their jaws (even the smaller ones) and will usually drive their teeth right through the plastic shell. Punctured plugs quickly fill with water and don't work very well after that.

Serious shallow-water shark pluggers opt for the wooden variety over hollow plastic for the above reasons. Some lures that we've seen and even used have been badly chewed and repainted many times. Not pretty to look at, but functional—and durable, unless the beast runs off with it. A few anglers even make their own out of 6-inch pieces of discarded wooden broom handles.

As aggressive as sharks are portrayed to be in popular literature and on the silver screen, in only two to six feet of water they can be *very* wary and even downright shy. The right noises will definitely attract them, but many sudden sounds will send even a 7-footer bolting for deep water. Banging the boat, or splashing the lure or bait noisily down in the critter's face, will almost always scare it, at least momentarily. Working a surface plug too loudly when a shark is very close to it is another way to discourage strikes.

However, if used properly, noisy lures will definitely attract sharks at surprising distances. Since they seem to have poor eyesight, their hunting tactics utilize highly developed senses of sight and hearing. Chugging a surface lure noisily when the shark is 15 to 100 feet away is a good way to get its attention, but once it begins to close the gap down to 10 feet or less, the noise output of the plug should be softened to a gentle gurgle.

Noisily splashing an oar or pushpole will sometimes attract a shark passing in the distance. As the toothy beast passes within casting range, place the lure just beyond its path of travel and about 5 feet or so ahead of it. Retrieve the plug or fly with a gentle, darting action. Sometimes the strike is so quick it's over in the blink of an eye, but more likely it will be a little more deliberate. It's important *not* to try to set the hook until you're sure the shark has the lure in its mouth.

The best flies for shallow-water sharking are those that are highly visible. Tied with lots of bucktail or artificial deer hair (i.e. Fishair), they should be full-bodied. Four inches, on a 2/0 or 3/0 hook, is none too long for the average flats shark, and 6–7 inches (4/0 to 5/0 hook) is more likely to attract anything over 5 feet long. Adding some strands of flashy silver or gold mylar helps, too.

The best colors for lures, whether flies or plugs, seem to be white, yellow, silver, or orange. These colors can be used by themselves or combined with other colors, such as green, red, blue, or black. A good combination that resembles many baitfish found in the shark's environment is white or silver with a green, blue, or black back.

Like most other gamefish that prowl the flats, sharks tend to move into shallow water with the rising tide and work their way back to deep water with the ebb. A sure place to find them is in and around mullet muds, milky white patches often an acre or more in size, where mullet are actively feeding on bottom algae. Admittedly, a shark on the prowl inside a mullet mud is about as easy to spot as a black cat in a closet, providing evidence of its location only by the occasional explosion where an unfortunate mullet has been ambushed. The best way to get your shots at sharks under these conditions is by poling the boat around the edges of the muds.

There are two methods for locating sharks in the shallows that work particularly well. One is to search the area in a boat powered by an electric motor, or use a pushpole. The soft noise of the motor's propeller actually seems to attract them. Staking or anchoring in a good location and chumming also works, and offers a viable alternative if the first method isn't producing.

Locating shallow areas that have fishable shark populations is a matter of trial and error, or hiring a guide. Unless you have plenty of time on your hands hiring a guide for at least one day is a practical way to become familiar with the area. Also, a guide will have all the necessary tackle, lures, bait, chum, etc.

On a size-for-size basis, the tackle needed to subdue a shark in the shallows is essentially the same you would use for any other gamefish of similar size. In order to maximize your sport, it is essential *not* to overgun the shark with tackle inappropriately heavy for its size. A small shark (10 to 20 pounds) calls for light gear: baitcasting or spinning rods with 8- to 10-pound-test line and reels with at least 200 yards capacity and a smooth drag. Tarpon-size sharks—40 pounds and up—are best handled with tarpon gear: 12- to 20-pound-test line, suitably stiff baitcasting or spinning rods, and reels with 200 or more yards of line. The same criteria apply to fly tackle.

Wire leaders are an absolute must. If you're interested in following IGFA regs, the wire trace on a fly

Small sharks are gamefish too, if taken on light tackle. Many species willingly strike artificial lures.

leader cannot be more than 12 inches long. For other tackle, it's only a matter of the maximum length you can comfortably cast, usually 15 to 24 inches. Since many sharks tend to roll up in the line, a secondary leader of heavy mono (i.e. 40- to 50-pound test) is needed. For spinning or baitcasting, the secondary leader should be about the length of the rod from the tip down to the reel; this prevents knots from hanging up when casting.

In the best interests of safety, treat all sharks as *very* dangerous, regardless of size. Even a 3-footer can inflict a serious, often disfiguring wound that can require extensive reconstructive surgery and still leave nasty scars.

PART II

SALTWATER TACKLE

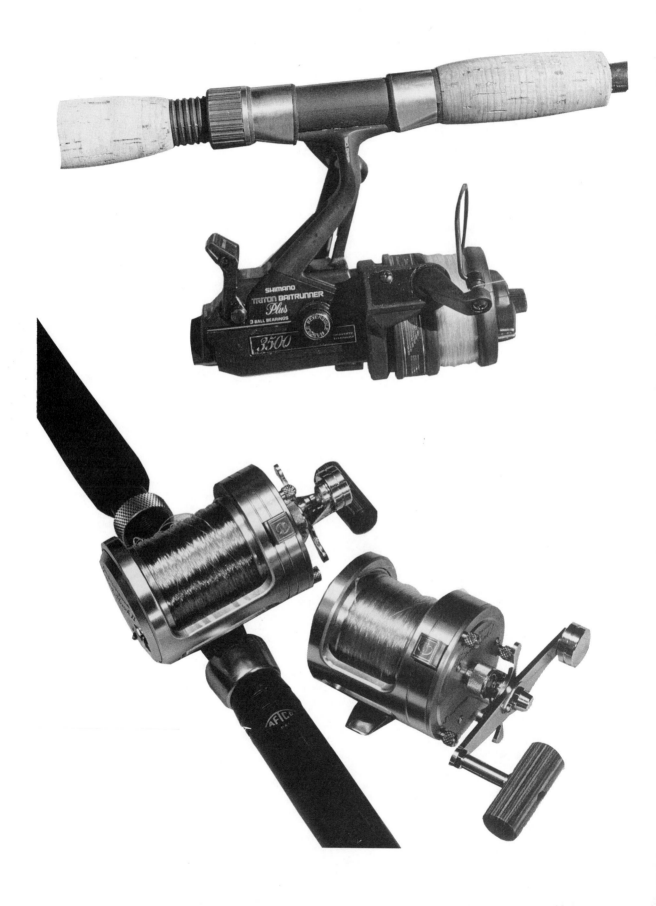

Chapter 14

SPINNING AND BAITCASTING TACKLE

Without a doubt the most popular form of tackle in saltwater today is spinning. It has been thus for over three decades, and still the tackle undergoes constant refinement. But during the 1980s several other forms of tackle gained in popularity. One is standup gear for big-game fish (see Chapter 16). But on the light-tackle scene, both baitcasting and fly tackle (see Chapter 15) have made tremendous strides.

SPINNING TACKLE

Don't confuse this with *spincasting* tackle, which employs a closed-face reel mounted on top of a baitcasting rod. A spinning reel is open-faced and is mounted on the *underside* of a spinning rod. Spincasting tackle is designed primarily for freshwater fishing, and although usable for many smaller saltwater fish, it really isn't the best choice. Unless the reel is exceptionally well made with salt-resistant materials, it will soon fail.

Spinning tackle has replaced the so-called "boat rod" for much saltwater fishing, mostly because it is lighter, in some instances also less expensive, and especially because it is to easy to use. But it does have one major drawback: line twist.

Twist occurs because the line is pulled off a revolving spool by a fish running against the drag, but replaced on a stationary spool by the angler when the handle is cranked and line is regained. And if the angler turns the handle while the line is going out or not being placed back on the spool, twisting becomes rapidly worse. What's so bad about line twist is that it weakens the line significantly if there is a strong pull on it at the time the twisting occurs. Monofilament line typically stretches from 30 to 40 percent under heavy load, and if at the same time it

is being twisted badly, as much as 30 percent of its strength is eventually lost. That's why an angler fighting an exceptionally big fish for a long period of time is facing steadily increasing odds that the outcome will favor the fish. This problem does not occur with revolving-spool reels (also called baitcasting reels), and is one reason why they are making such a strong comeback on the saltwater scene.

There is only one way to get rid of line twist. If aboard a boat or fishing from a stationary location where there is a strong current, simply cut off all terminal tackle and pull all of the twisted line off the spool so that water drag can untwist it. Only a few minutes are required to accomplish this. But if the line is badly twisted and consequently damaged, replace it. Monofilament, especially in bulk spools, is certainly one of the least expensive items in your tacklebox.

The big reason for spinning's sudden surge to universal acceptance shortly after WW II is its ability to cast very light lures or baits with no risk of backlash. And there are many situations where this offers a tremendous advantage to the angler.

The spinning gear in use today ranges from ultralight to medium, using monofilament lines from 2- to 30-pound test. By far the most popular lines are 6- to 20-pound test. The heavier stuff is sometimes used for bottom fishing, but anything over 20-pound test casts poorly. Actually, the smaller the line diameter, the easier it will cast.

The three factors of most importance in choosing spinning tackle are rod length and stiffness, reel capacity, and drag.

Short rods restrict casting distance. A rod that's too long quickly becomes heavy and unwieldy, and there's a definite point of diminishing returns when it comes to rod length versus casting distance. As a rule the rods most popular for ultralight use—that is, with lines under 6-pound test—are the shortest. If the rod is to be used in close quarters, it might be as short as 5 feet. In open water, where maximum casting distance is needed, it might be 6 to 7 feet.

The term "light" covers 6- to 12-pound test, and the rods typically vary from 6 to 8 feet in length. "Medium" means 12- to 20-pound test, and covers a very wide range of applications. For boat use where shorts casts are the rule, the rod might be only 7 feet long, while a surfcaster would need a stick that's 9 to 12 (or more) feet in length.

Even billfish can be landed on spinning gear, as Walt Stearns shows with this 128-pound Pacific sailfish.

The best spinning rod materials today are graphite or in some instances graphite/fiberglass composites. Fiberglass rods are still used, but their action is softer and they are much heavier. The saltwater angler should pay particular attention to the hardware on the rod: guides that cannot rust, and reel seats that won't soon become locked up by corrosion. Even with the best of materials, it's wise to rinse all of your tackle with freshwater at the end of the day.

Action is critical to both casting and fighting a fish. Contrary to popular opinion, very soft rods do *not* cast farther than medium-stiff rods because the tip flops up and down after the casting stroke is completed, adding more friction to the outgoing line. Ideal stiffness for casting is a tip that returns immediately to the straight position as soon as the lure is launched. That means rod stiffness should be selected with two things in mind: line strength and lure weight. A rod that's too soft doesn't fight a big fish very effectively, either.

Considering the ever present possibility of hooking a big fish just about anywhere in saltwater, the reel should have plenty of capacity—at least 200 yards, and maybe up to twice that in situations where you might hook a long-runner. An example of a well-balanced outfit that has a very wide range of applications is a 7 to 7½ foot medium-action rod, and a reel loaded with 200 yards of 8- or 10-pound-test line. Just about any gamefish under 20 pounds can be landed with that gear, ranging from bonefish and permit on the tropical flats to stripers from a small boat or pier. Many much bigger fish have also been landed on that gear, including tarpon over 100 pounds.

On the other hand, suppose you plan to be deep-jigging over a blue-water wreck or reef in 100 to 200 feet of water. You'd want a stiff rod 7½ to 8 feet long, and a reel loaded with 300 to 400 yards of 10- to 15-pound-test line. Thousands of very big groupers, snappers, amberjack, king mackerel, blackfin and yellowfin tunas, and even sailfish and small marlin have been beaten with that tackle. It's a matter of proper rigging, good knots, and always using line that's in tiptop condition—plus a drag that's smooth and easily adjustable to the desired level of resistance.

BAITCASTING TACKLE

Of all forms of light tackle—and we're not including standup gear in this consideration because it has a

Light baitcasting tackle makes catching a middleweight tarpon even more exciting.

special place of its own—baitcasting is by far the most efficient for fighting a big fish. Fly tackle is next, and spinning third. Of course, this ranking assumes high-quality gear in the hands of a proficient angler.

In terms of capacity, a baitcasting reel holding 250 yards of 16-pound-test mono is far more compact and about half the weight of a spinning reel of equivalent capacity. And a skillful caster with properly balanced baitcasting gear can cast the same lure significantly farther with the same rod length and line test as an equally competent spinning angler.

With baitcasting tackle, also called plugging tackle in some areas, there is no problem with reel-induced line twist. That's because the line is both cast and retrieved by a revolving spool, and even pulled by the fish from a revolving spool. Thus when fighting a big, stubborn fish over a long period of time, an angler is not also racing against the "line-twist clock."

But what makes baitcasting gear so effective as a fish-fighting tool is the way an angler can apply drag. It is possible to use the left thumb as additional drag pressure while always keeping the right hand on the cranking handle. No hand shifting is necessary, as is the case with spinning, to get instant extra drag pressure on the reel while pumping to gain back line from a stubborn fish. Also, as a relief from the muscle-cramping effect of a long fight, an angler can reach many inches above the reel seat to grab the rod blank for a different leverage position, and yet still maintain extra thumb pressure on the reel spool with the other hand. That's difficult to do with spinning gear.

Backlashing is no longer the problem with these reels that it once was. When we first started using them in the 1940s, an educated thumb was your only protection against the overspin gremlins. Then came the inertial braking system in the early 1950s, eventually followed by the magnetic casting brakes of the late 1970s and 1980s. The magnetic system has been developed to the extent that it is virtually foolproof—as long as an angler adjusts it to his or her casting capabilities.

Modern baitcasting reels have two different level-wind systems for spooling line evenly. The traditional method involves a wire lineguard that's moved from side to side by a worm gear. It moves back and forth when the line goes out and also when line is recovered by cranking the handle. A newer system has a smaller circular or oval ceramic lineguard that

Angler with big tarpon on light baitcasting gear.

moves only when the handle is cranked and line goes back on the reel. It is stationary during the cast, and also when the fish takes line. A more recent variation (first introduced by Daiwa) of the latter system involves a lineguard that automatically splits apart during the cast or when the fish takes line, and closes to normal size when the handle is cranked.

A reel with a wire lineguard works just fine as long as it is kept properly lubricated with light oil (never grease!). It also seems to cast just as well as any of the newer versions. Thus it is the design of preference among baitcasting anglers who seek exceptionally big fish. We have used this gear many times to land tarpon and other large fish with 15-pound-test line.

However, reels with the newer magnetic brake system and semi-stationary lineguard design work best with very light lines. For many years we've used these reels with 200 yards of 6- or 8-pound-test mono to catch bonefish, permit, barracuda, small tarpon, big bluefish, red drum, and many other species in shallow water. They cast light lures very well, and the ultrathin line doesn't get between the spool edge and frame.

Some of the new small baitcasting reels will handle line as light as 2-pound test if they aren't overfilled. Certainly 4 and 6 are no problem. For really tough fish in tight places, lines as heavy as 30-pound test may be used with some of the larger reels.

Rod stiffness and materials follow the same basic patterns as with spinning tackle. But guide placement is more critical when it comes to baitcasting. A 7-foot spinning rod can function effectively with just five running guides, plus the tiptop guide, and their placement isn't terribly critical. But a 7-foot baitcasting rod should have seven to eight running guides, and they should be properly placed for optimum casting efficiency and to keep the line from rubbing against the rod blank when the rod is sharply bent by a big fish.

Baitcasting rods are a little shorter than most spinning rods. A 7- or 7½-foot baitcasting rod would typically be used with the same line test as a 7½- to 8½-foot spinning rod. Stiffness still depends upon line test and lure or bait weight, and also the size of the fish.

Chapter 15

SALTWATER FLY FISHING

Although a few anglers had been dabbling in the salt with fly tackle as far back as the 1890s, that early gear was intended for freshwater use and barely up to the task of taking a 25-pound salmon if the angler was both skilled and lucky enough that everything held. Certainly it was never designed for a really big fish, like a grown-up tarpon. Yet around the turn of the century one angler, A. W. Dimock, managed to subdue a silver king of around 80 pounds, most likely the first large tarpon taken on fly tackle in the history of the sport.

After WW II Joe Brooks, Lee Wulff, and other legends of the long rod began to write about the excitement of fishing for bonefish, tarpon, snook, seatrout, and many other species with fly tackle. Be-

fore too long the concept began to spread, and even billfish have now become frequent targets of the avid flyrodder.

Fly tackle has improved tremendously over the years. Fragile, heavy, easily damaged bamboo rods were gradually replaced by fiberglass, which was soon displaced by ultralight-weight graphite. Reels evolved from storage devices designed merely to hold the fly line to high-quality sophisticated instruments with very smooth drags and the capacity to hold as many yards of Dacron backing as needed to catch fish well over 100 pounds. Today's fly tackle, from the lightest 2-weight outfit to a billfish-taming 13-weight, is no longer designed for freshwater *or* saltwater. Owing to the high quality of the materials,

Big Pacific sailfish and the large popping fly that took it. Today, anglers fish for most saltwater species with fly tackle.

any rod can be fished anywhere; it's just a matter of matching the weight of the rod and line to the size of the fish and the fishing conditions.

CHOOSING THE BASIC SYSTEM

More than a decade ago a company called Scientific Anglers came up with the "system" concept because it made choosing perfectly matched rods, reels, and lines a simple process. The premise of the system concept is based upon the weight of the fly line; everything else that goes with it is simply matched to that line size in order to provide optimum performance. Thus, when we mention a System 10 outfit, we are simply saying that the line is a 10-weight, that the rod used with it is designed specifically to cast a 10-weight line, and that the reel will hold all of the 10-weight fly line plus a suitable amount of backing.

Fly lines are graded according to the weight of the first 30 feet. Breaking strength is not measured. Fly lines are graded in weight from 1 to 13; the larger the number, the heavier the weight. There are a number of reasons why an angler chooses a specific line weight, often to the exclusion of all others, but for saltwater use we'll consider only two.

In spinning or baitcasting, if wind becomes a problem, frequently we only need to add weight—a heavier lure or sinker—to combat it. Since fly-line weight rather than lure weight is used to propel a fly, a heavy line is needed to beat the wind.

Line weight is also critical in that it is difficult to cast a large fly with a light line; there just isn't enough weight in the line to overcome the air resistance caused by the fly. For the most part, flies used in saltwater fishing are larger and often more bulky than those used in fresh, so a heavier line is needed.

On the other hand, if the line is too heavy it is more difficult to control and the matching rod is tiring to cast. So, while a System 12 or 13 might not seem overly heavy when dealing with a 100-pound tarpon, it feels like an unwieldy club if you're trying to cast to a tailing bonefish or redfish.

CHOOSING THE ROD

Rod selection starts with line *weight* selection. The process has to start somewhere, and most anglers with lots of coastal fishing experience feel that the best all-round line weight for just about any fish under 40 or 50 pounds is either a 9 or a 10. And if you have to choose just one as a "do-all," particularly as a first outfit, it should be a 9-weight. A better-

Happy angler with a big bone-fish taken on fly tackle.

than-average caster might get by with an 8, and there are certainly times when it's unusually windy and the additional weight of a 10 offers some advantage, but in the long run it is still hard to beat the 9-weight as a close to perfect compromise.

A 9-weight outfit is relatively light, yet still quite capable of making surprisingly delicate presentations, even to a nervous bonefish in ultra-thin water on a bright, calm day. A long leader and topnotch casting skill are certainly called for in this extreme situation. On the other hand, even a caster of modest skill can deliver the fly to a fish 40 to 50 feet away under typically windy situations (i.e. 15 mph or so). And getting that close to a fish as flighty as a bonefish isn't difficult under such choppy conditions.

Assuming you don't have an unlimited budget to spend on your first fly outfit, consider the rod as the item deserving the most careful deliberation. Go with the very best you can afford, because even the best fly line will yield only a poor to mediocre casting performance if the rod isn't of quality design and construction. Today's graphite rods are by far the best choice, unquestionably capable of superior casting performance, and also lightest in weight.

Assuming you have no real flycasting experience, consult with someone who has before choosing. Not only do fly rods come in various line weights, they also come in different lengths. Some are as short as 6 feet, and others as long as 12. Those two extremes, by the way, represent specialized applications. For most of us the happy medium for all-round use ranges from 8½ to 9½ feet, with around 9 feet as the most popular choice for general saltwater fishing.

CHOOSING THE LINE

Since we've (at least theoretically) chosen a 9-weight line as a starting point, and also based our rod selection upon that size, we must now decide what *type* of 9-weight line we need to go with it. Fly lines

either float or sink, depending upon their design. Those that float will stay on the surface indefinitely, while those that sink do so at varying rates depending upon their respective densities. In most cases, the beginning saltwater fly fisherman will do better to start with a floating line because it is easier to learn how to cast with.

Fly lines also come in different shapes, which actually are nothing more than simple variations in diameter along the length of the line. If the diameter is precisely the same from one end to the other, the line is said to be *level*. If the line is thinner at the front end (where the leader is attached), then progressively thicker for the next few feet, then constantly the same larger thickness for the next 12 to 20 feet, and finally gradually thinning to a uniform diameter for the remainder of its length, the line is said to be *tapered*. The line just described is actually known as a *forward taper*, since the heaviest part is contained in the first 30 feet or less.

A line that is tapered in the forward end, whether floating or sinking, is called a *weight-forward line*. The designation for this is the abbreviation "WF". If the line is a floater, the designation for that is the letter "F", while a sinking line would be "S". The number between the taper and the floating or sinking designation is the weight of the line. Here are some typical examples:

WF 9 F   means weight-forward, 9-weight, floating.

WF 9 S   means weight-forward, 9-weight, sinking.

L 9 F   means level (no taper), 9-weight, floating.

And so on.

At times the line has an additional designator to indicate some special function:

WF 9 F SWT means weight-forward, 9-weight, floating, while "SWT" means saltwater taper.

SWT indicates that the forward taper is a little

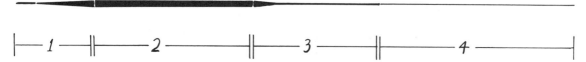

A weight-forward (WF) tapered fly line. Section 1 is the forward taper, the end of which is attached to the butt section of the leader. Section 2 is the belly, the part that carries most of the casting weight of the line. Section 3 is the rear taper. Section 4 is the smaller diameter level running line.

shorter and a little thicker, so that the same weight is compressed into a slightly shorter length for easier casting of bulky flies in windy situations. Most new-comers to saltwater fly fishing will find SWT tapers a little easier to learn to cast, so they make a good beginning fly line.

Incidently, the weight of the fly line has nothing to do with its breaking strength. In all cases the inner core of the fly line is far stronger than the weakest part of the leader (called the *class tippet*), and it's the latter that fails should you put too much pressure on the fish.

CHOOSING THE REEL

While a top-of-the-line, handmade, machined, an-odized aluminum fly reel can easily cost $300 or more, there are reels in the $100–$150 price range that are quite capable of catching just about any saltwater gamefish you're likely to hook on fly tackle. For example, tarpon over 100 pounds have been rou-tinely taken on the Scientific Anglers System 2 fly reel, model 1011. And anything that can be taken on a 9-weight system can be easily handled with many reels of slightly smaller size and capacity.

There are even less expensive reels capable of suitable performance in saltwater, but in order to go the distance, and last through many years of service, they should be specifically designed for saltwater use. Many popular freshwater models are not, al-though the trend nowadays is to make more and

more reels suitable for use in both fresh and salt water. And by the way, a good saltwater fly reel is equally at home in freshwater.

There are several features to look for in a saltwater reel. Most important are capacity, drag, and finish, in that order.

The reel *must* have enough capacity for line and sufficient backing. Otherwise, sooner or later you're going to hook that big fish of a lifetime and watch it run away with everything on the reel. Most experi-enced saltwater anglers believe the minimum capac-ity, for any size reel, should be no less than 200 yards of Dacron backing plus the full fly line. For lines in the 11–13 weight range, the backing should be 30-pound test. If you're using lines from 7–10 weight, 20-pound is sufficient. And for 6 or less, 12 will do the job.

Dacron, which has no stretch, is the backing of choice. Mono will stretch too much, building consid-erable pressure on the reel spool as it is cranked back under tension. And sooner or later the spool will be damaged, often with disastrous results.

A strong drag, like the type you'd expect in an offshore big-game reel, is hardly necessary for fly reels, even in saltwater. The most important charac-teristic is smoothness. Hard-starting or rough-running drags all too often cause the fish to break off. As for tension, if it can produce up to 3 or 4 pounds of smooth drag, that's all you'll need. The thickness of the fly line, plus the length of backing being dragged through the water, all add up to a lot of additional drag.

Except for situations where we are dealing with

Typical medium-sized fly reels suitable for saltwater fishing. From left: a Bill Pate bonefish reel, an Orvis D-XR, and a Sci-entific Anglers System Two.

fish around nearby obstructions, the heaviest drag setting we ever use is 1 to 2 pounds, even for tarpon over 100 pounds. That's the best way to avoid breaking the fish off during the first wild, tailwalking dash. When more drag pressure is needed, it can be easily applied as needed by palming the spool rim if it's a "rim-control" design, or by a little finger pressure on the line inside the spool.

And finally, it just doesn't pay to buy a reel that's not constructed of saltwater-resistant components. If the finish isn't anodized (usually reserved for the more expensive reels), then it should at least be a high-quality baked enamel or epoxy. The screws, foot, and internal components should be stainless steel. The pillars, if there are any, should either be stainless steel or anodized aluminum. In some models there are no separate pillars; they're machined or molded as an integral part of the frame, thereby producing a much stronger and more rigid reel.

FLY LEADERS

The leader is a critical part of saltwater fly tackle. Since the fly is essentially weightless, and is carried through the air by the weight of the fly line, the leader must be in balance with the line and fly or casting becomes difficult. Perhaps even impossible during windy conditions.

Essentially, the leader must continue the forward taper of the fly line. A good rule of thumb is that the diameter of the leader at its thickest point, called the butt, where it joins the tip of the fly line, must be at least two-thirds the diameter of the tip of the line. If the fly line tip is .045-inches, for example, the leader but must be at least .030.

It is possible to buy tapered fly leaders. You can make your own, starting with the heaviest mono needed and connecting increasingly smaller diameter sections. The length of the leader depends upon the fishing situation. As a rule, long, finely tapered leaders are needed for calm conditions, while

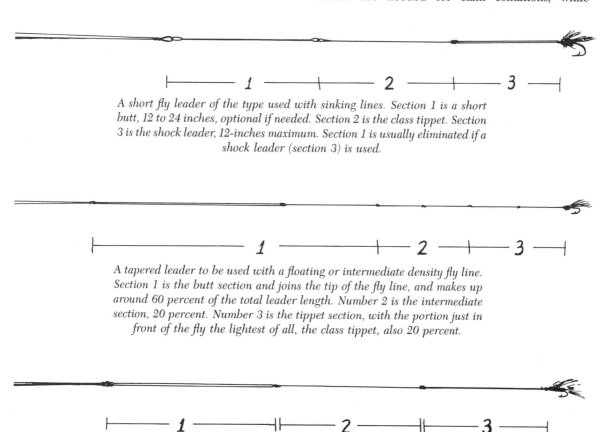

A short fly leader of the type used with sinking lines. Section 1 is a short butt, 12 to 24 inches, optional if needed. Section 2 is the class tippet. Section 3 is the shock leader, 12-inches maximum. Section 1 is usually eliminated if a shock leader (section 3) is used.

A tapered leader to be used with a floating or intermediate density fly line. Section 1 is the butt section and joins the tip of the fly line, and makes up around 60 percent of the total leader length. Number 2 is the intermediate section, 20 percent. Number 3 is the tippet section, with the portion just in front of the fly the lightest of all, the class tippet, also 20 percent.

A big-fish leader, for tarpon, sailfish, or sharks. Section 1 is the butt, used only with floating or intermediate lines. Number 2 is the class tippet section, attached directly to the tip of the fly line if it is a sinking line. Number 3 is the shock leader, heavy mono or wire, usually 12 inches long.

shorter, fast-tapered leaders are needed for windy days.

A bonefish angler might need a 12- to 16-foot leader with a floating line for a calm day but require a 7- to 9-footer for wind. On the other hand, a medium- to fast-sinking line never requires a long leader, and it could be as short as 3 if the water isn't too clear.

There's a simple formula for making most fly leaders. It's called the "60-20-20-rule." The first 60 percent is the heavy part, usually the two heaviest sections. The next 20 percent is the middle, usually two or three sections of medium-weight mono. And the last 20 percent is the tippet section, containing the lightest part of the leader (called the class tippet), plus a shock leader up to 12-inches long if needed.

For example, a 10-foot leader for bonefish or red drum on the flats, to be used with a 9-weight line, would start with 3 feet of approximately .032, about 40-pound test for most monos (except the ultra-thins). Next would come around 18 inches of .026 (around 30-pound test), and about 18 inches of .022. Then a foot each of .018 and .015 as the middle, and finally a foot each of .013 and .011. The last would be around 8-pound test. But if that same rod and line were being used for snook, which requires a larger fly, the leader components might be shortened to 7 or 8 feet and the last section before the fly might be a foot of 40- or 50-pound mono to serve as a shock leader.

CHOOSING FLIES

The most basic of all fly patterns in both fresh and salt water is the streamer, and the most commonly used color in saltwater is white. This simple fly can be used, in one form or another, to catch just about every species—bonefish, tarpon, striped bass, salmon, bluefish, sailfish, seatrout, and so on.

Single-color streamers are also the easiest of all flies to tie, if you're interested in trying that phase of the sport as well. Even when you've later added many more sophisticated patterns to your flybox, there should *always* be room for a few basic whites.

White works so well, of course, because it is the most common color of saltwater baitfish. Rare is the species that doesn't have at least some white or white/silver as part of its color pattern. It is also a color of high visibility under a wide range of water conditions, thus making it easy for predator fish to see and "home in" on.

Of course there are a few other fly types that will prove effective at one time or another. Considering that while the streamer is primarily a subsurface configuration, there are also at least three surface patterns that work effectively: poppers, sliders, and "hair" flies.

And then there are the specialty patterns, each usually designed for one or two species under particular conditions. Examples are crab patterns for permit on the flats (flies that resemble crabs), shrimp patterns for bonefish under the same conditions, and heavily weighted streamers that sink very rapidly.

Hook size has a lot to do with fly behavior in the water. The overall weight of the hook will also be a factor in determining how fast it sinks, if it is a streamer. As for materials, stainless steel is the best choice, with quality plated a distant second. Bronzed or varnished hooks are designed for freshwater and seldom last longer than one or two days after their initial exposure to saltwater, even if rinsed and dried thoroughly after each use.

A good rule of thumb is to use the smallest and lightest hook that is effective for the tippet test and the size of the fish. The thinner the wire that was used to make the hook, the easier it is to drive the point in far enough for a good hookup. But, if the wire is too thin, the fish may be able to straighten the hook too easily and get free.

The best flies for saltwater are usually short and sparsely dressed. The larger and more bushy the fly, the harder it will be to cast under all conditions, especially when there's wind. Unless the pattern design calls for exceptional length, such as some of the eel-like streamers tied for stripers and barracuda, the extra length of body hair and/or feathers can actually contribute to missed strikes.

Species with small mouths are best fished with small flies. The mouth of a 5-pound redfish (red drum) or even a seatrout is huge when compared to the mouth of a 5-pound bonefish. That's why the experienced bonefish angler would choose a fly 2 inches or less in length, tied on a No. 1 to No. 6 hook, while a streamer 2½ to 4 inches long, tied on a 1/0 to 3/0 hook, would be just fine for the red or trout.

Rod and line weight obviously limit fly size. Casting a 3- to 4-inch streamer tied on a 2/0 hook, for even short distances, would be tough with a rod designed for a line size of 6 or less. A 7-weight would be borderline, and 8 would be okay, but a 9 or 10

*Flies for saltwater. Top row: small flies for bonefish. 2nd row: tarpon fly and
permit fly. 3rd row: a penny for size comparison, and a needlefish imitation
for barracuda. Large streamer at bottom is for sailfish.*

would be best of all. Especially when the typical
coastal wind conditions are factored in. It's a good
rule to keep the flies as small as practicable.

Some fish respond best to very large flies. While a
100-pound tarpon will usually react eagerly to a
4-inch streamer, a sailfish of just half that weight will
usually ignore something that small and typically go
for the biggest "mop" you can cast. And that usually
calls for a 12- or 13-weight rod and line, and a very
bulky popper or bushy streamer that's at least 6 to 8
inches long.

A simple white bucktail or artificial deerhair
streamer is more effective if a touch of color is
added. Most minnows and sardines have a darker
back—green, blue, gray, or black, with dark green
the most common. A white streamer with one-third
of its upper body a dark color and the lower two-
thirds white makes a lot of sense. As a further refine-

ment, a few strands of silver mylar or other flashy
material can be added to the sides, and perhaps even
black eyes on the head. Many anglers feel eyes add a
lot to any fly's strike potential.

While most freshwater patterns remain somewhat
on the dull side, many saltwater fish like bright colors. Red, yellow, chartruese, bright (neon, even)
blue, orange, hot pink. A good rule of thumb: If the
gamefish you're seeking feeds primarily on crabs and
other crustaceans, flies in darker colors (browns,
dark blues, dark greens, black) are often better,
sometimes with a tiny bit of bright orange (to look
like attached eggs) or other high-visibility color
added. But if the gamefish feeds frequently on baitfish, then bright flies are often the most productive.
A great pattern for big snook in dark-stained brackish water is a streamer tied with long yellow feathers
and bright red, bushy hackle, even though there is

Angler fly fishing a tidal creek.

no baitfish in that environment with those colors. It's a combination of visibility, motion, and seductive action that attracts the fish.

Basic, very simple patterns (e.g. the all-white streamer) will take most saltwater species at least now and then, but fish in areas that feel a lot of angling pressure tend to gradually become more and more selective. In the long run, patterns that more specifically resemble the food they prefer—even if just superficially—will be the most productive.

HOW TO USE FLIES EFFECTIVELY

Freshwater trout fishermen steeped in the tradition of the drag-free dry fly drift will find saltwater fly fishing quite a bit different. To be sure, there are instances where the fly is fished on a dead drift, such as in certain chumming situations. And there are times the fly can be fished through a downstream current swing with little or no added motion on the part of the angler.

But most saltwater fly fishing is done in situations where currents are weak or absent, and all of the fly's motion comes from the hands of the angler. This is essentially a matter of allowing the fly to sink to the desired depth, then retrieving the line in small strips, ranging from just and inch or two at a time for bonefish to as much as a foot or so for many other species.

The two retrieval factors that seem to be the most important are length of the strip and speed. Some species seem to prefer a long, very slow, deliberate rate of retrieve, others react more rapidly to a quick, darting motion of the fly. Just remember, a live baitfish, which your fly is trying to emulate, will always try to escape from a predator. It pays to experiment with retrieval rate, especially if you can see how the fish is reacting to your presentation.

Chapter 16

BIG-GAME TACKLE

The preferred tackle for big-game fishing has changed a lot in recent years, even though to a casual observer it still might look the same. The most obvious changes have been in fishing lines and rods. Although reels have improved quite a bit, they still look much the same today as they did twenty years ago.

In the early days of all saltwater angling, lines were made of linen and rated according to the number of individual threads in their makeup. Each of those threads wet-tested at around 3 pounds breaking strength, so for example a 39-thread line would break at about 117 to 120 pounds. Or a 9-thread at 27, the early equivalent of today's 30-pound class. Linen is stronger when wet, while all synthetics in use today are slightly weaker wet than dry (by 5 to 15 percent). But linen also rots easily, and after each use had to be removed from the spool, rinsed with freshwater, and dried on a special rack.

The synthetics do not rot at all and so they have replaced linen. They do deteriorate, however, from abrasion and exposure to sunlight. So while the currently popular synthetics, nylon and Dacron, still don't last forever, they will long outlast linen, and they don't require laborious attention after each day's fishing.

Dacron is preferred for some kinds of fishing because it has no significant stretch. But monofilament (single strand) nylon is by far the most popular because it is inexpensive and almost transparent (except when deliberately dyed bright colors for specific purposes). Until mono could be made supple enough to cast reasonably well with baitcasting reels, braided nylon was the most popular for that tackle. It is still used here and there.

Most line companies today rate their product by IGFA line class divisions, which range from 2- to 130-pound test in defined increments. Some lines also carry a "tournament" label, which means the manufacturer guarantees they will not exceed the IGFA line class label that appears on the spool. This means a spool of line rated as 16-pound test "tournament" will wet test at 16 pounds or less. Spools not carrying a "tournament" or "class" label will almost always overtest, some by a big margin.

Not all tackle used for big game necessarily employs line that looks like rope or rods that are as thick as a broom handle. Some huge gamefish have been taken on some surprisingly light gear. For example, the current IGFA black marlin men's record for 20-pound-test line is a whopping 1,051 pounds! And if you think that is some sort of freak accident, consider the women's record for the same species at 998 pounds. A number of blue marlin over 500 pounds have also been landed on 20.

Nowadays big-game tackle can start with lines as light as 20-pound test (or less) in the hands of a highly experienced angler, while just two decades earlier anything under 50 was considered too light for the real big stuff. Better lines, rods, and reels, plus highly refined fishing techniques, have changed all that.

CONVENTIONAL BIG-GAME TACKLE

The typical conventional big-game rod today, whether for 20-pound class line or 130, is around 6½ to 7 feet in length. Of this the butt, that is the lower section as measured from the top of the reel seat down to the bottom of the "handle," will account for 18 to 20 inches. The tip is everything that extends upward from the top of the reel seat.

In the old days, rod tips were made of laminated strips of wood or bamboo, and rated by their various weights in ounces. Today they are made of fiberglass, graphite, or a composite of the two, and a rating by tip weight would be meaningless. Instead, they are classed by the lines they are designed to be used with.

Unlike other rods, big-game rods are not designed

Standup and conventional tackle compared. The rod at left is a conventional 7-footer for use with the fighting chair in the photo; the rod at right is a 5-foot 6-inch standup rod with a much shorter butt and more flexible tip. Shown in the chair is a soft-back harness, a gimbal plate for standup, and a kidney harness for standup.

for casting, but rather for trolling or still-fishing with live bait. The rod tip is as stiff as is practicable for its line size rating, primarily so an angler can put as much pressure as possible on the hooked fish. The guides, from the tip down, are usually of a roller design so that friction and therefore line wear is minimal. Today there are some rods with fixed ring-type guides made of low-friction materials, such as special oxides or ceramics, but a rod with all roller guides is strongly preferred by experienced big-game anglers. Even though roller guides require more maintenance, especially regular lubrication, they won't wear the line dangerously if the fight lasts all day.

Some big-game rods are one piece from tip to butt, but many are two piece with a detachable butt so that when separated the reel seat remains as part of the butt section. The most popular material for big-game rod butts of all line classes is machined and anodized marine-grade aluminum.

Reels are chosen by capacity and quality. The most expensive on today's market, like the Zane Grey series by Hardy of England, can cost as much as some automobiles. Other less expensive reels in the top-of-the-line category, such as Fin-Mor, Penn International, Shimano Beastmaster, or Daiwa Sealine Tournament, are more than adequate for anything that can be caught on rod and reel. In the more expensive but still-capable category are reels such as the Penn Senators, Shimano Tritons, and Daiwa Sealines, all of which have accounted for many extremely large gamefish of all species.

When it comes to conventional big-game tackle, the fighting chair can be every bit as important as the rod and reel. For lighter lines, up to 30- or possibly 50-pound test, the chair can also be light if it is well built. The best fighting chairs are mounted on a single pedestal that has been anchored firmly in a reinforced part of the deck. Light lines do allow the use of four-legged chairs with a rod gimbal mounted on the front edge.

Serious big-game anglers are willing to spend a lot of money on a custom-built fighting chair, built of wood and stainless steel, with a removable back, and removable but ruggedly built footbrace. Stories abound of chairs ripped right out of the deck by giant fish hooked on 130-pound-test tackle, so those who can afford the best usually buy the best, even if the price tag does run into the thousands of dollars.

Successfully beating a really big fish with this gear is the end result of top-quality tackle, the strongest knots and properly rigged leaders, a good fighting chair, and a boat crew that really knows its stuff.

STANDUP TACKLE

Standup tackle differs considerably from the more conventional gear used with a fighting chair. As a rule, the two cannot mix because of their big differ-

ence in rod lengths. Especially the butt. The standup rod has a much shorter tip and butt, and simply won't work effectively (if at all) in a fighting chair. And a conventional trolling rod's tip is too long for effective leverage when standing, while the butt's extra inches are a real backbreaker to an angler afoot.

Standup fishing rods and related equipment evolved aboard Southern California long-range party boats during the late 1970s, where until their inception anglers were routinely taking a beating at the rails from big yellowfin tuna and marlin, losing a dishearteningly high number of these fish on conventional tackle. As both rod tips and butts were gradually made shorter and shorter, the number of successful big-fish landings steadily climbed. These same anglers gradually began using the new gear in other fishing situations, often ignoring the fighting chair on boats equipped for big-game fishing in the customary manner. As others began to see this unique gear in action, acceptance by more and more offshore anglers was inevitable.

Compared to the standard 7-foot big-game fighting-chair rod, the average standup rod is 5½ to 6

Angler fighting a big fish with standup gear.

feet in length. The action is quite different too, with a much softer tip that bends easily under load. The lower half of the rod retains the necessary stiffness so that the angler can still exert sufficient leverage, but the much softer tip serves two vital purposes. It is adequately forgiving to provide shock-absorption against sudden surges by large fish, and when bent it reduces the length of the lever the angler has to pull against.

Keep in mind that the longer the effective length of the rod tip under load, the greater the leverage the fish has against the angler, and the harder that person must work to move that fish through the water. If a standup rod has the right action, when fully bent the angler will be pulling against a lever whose total length is only 4½ to 5 feet (measured from the fulcrum, where the rod butt seats into the gimbal), as compared to 6½ to 7 feet for a chaired big-game rod with a tip so stiff it barely bends.

So why not also make the traditional big-game rod shorter? Remember that an angler in a stationary fighting chair must have enough rod length for the tip to reach sufficiently past the gunwale in order to fight a fish that is straight down. The standup angler has only to stand against the transom to accomplish this.

The right harness and rod belt is to the standup angler what a top-quality fighting chair is to conventional tackle. The harness and rod belt are designed specifically for standup fishing. Over the years they have become somewhat smaller, lighter, and far more effective than the early designs. They are intended to distribute the load of the rod throughout the kidney and pelvic region, and across the top of the legs, giving the angler maximum leverage.

However, as a departure from the standup harness and rod belt, a growing number of dedicated anglers are now using a padded upper-body harness. Extending from the neck down to the waist, this type of harness distributes part of the load of a big fish on a standup rod through the upper back and shoulders. The typical shoulder harness used by the chair-bound angler cannot.

For example, expert standup angler Marsha Bierman of Miami has been using a full body harness with standup gear in the 50-pound class, and this average-size woman has landed and released dozens of big marlin, most in thirty minutes or less. Her largest was estimated to weigh between 800 and 900 pounds. We've used an identical harness on billfish up to almost 400 pounds with similar results. What seems to make a harness of this type so effective,

and incidentally it is also used regularly by fighting chair fishermen, is that it can be adjusted to fit the angler's body. This is an important feature for if it isn't completely comfortable, especially under a heavy load, the angler doesn't stand a chance against a huge, tough fish.

A properly designed body harness will have adjustable padded shoulder straps. Instead of just one adjustable strap on each side, with a snap on the end for the lugs at the top of the reel's two sideplates, the strap system should be in the form of a "Y," with the snap at the single leg of the Y and the other two legs each separately adjustable. This allows the pull angle between the harness and the reel to be adjusted for the angler's optimum comfort level. Fit is extremely critical for standup fishing.

According to Ken Pepping, whose Reeline Company makes the popular Rippoff brand of standup kidney harness and gimbal buttplates, it is extremely important that both harness and gimbal be both properly fitted and mutually compatible, so that they can work together effectively. This is definitely not a situation where one size fits all, although there are several stock sizes that will accommodate most anglers.

The gimbal buttplate comes in two versions, both very well padded for comfort and shaped to rest on the groin area of the upper legs. It is very important that it be correctly fitted, as it will be the fulcrum for a lot of strong leverage. It can also be either attached to the harness by straps with snaps on the ends for quick removal, or it can be a completely separate belt system. Each type has its advantages, but if you're thinking about a full upper-body harness, a separate gimbal belt will be required.

The most popular range of standup tackle seems to be 20- to 80-pound test. Most anglers still feel that 130 is too heavy, although probably there are some exceptionally strong men who could handle 130 with the right harness rig. But even then would it offer any real advantage over 80? Time will undoubtedly answer that question.

Thus far 50-pound-class gear seems to be considered capable of landing just about any fish that can be caught on a standup tackle. And there seems to be little doubt among those anglers familiar with both conventional and standup that the same line test can be used more effectively on the latter. We will get to the reasons shortly.

In addition to a reduced overall length and short butt, there are a few more features essential to standup rods. It is important that the foregrip be

Angler with 363-pound blue marlin taken on standup gear. Tackle for standup is comparatively light.

length, and serves as a big help in keeping your balance when fighting a fish. The tip should have at least five running guides, plus a good tiptop.

The typical total rod length is 5½ to 6 feet. But, if you're under 6 feet tall, we suggest you stick to rods no longer than your height. A number of custom rodbuilders can tailor specialized rods to your specs, but there are a lot of good off-the-shelf sticks that are expressly designed for standup fishing. We've had excellent results with stock rods made by Daiwa, Penn, Shimano, and Magnuflex.

At present there are no special reels built solely for standup rods, nor do any seem needed. Like any conventional reel, the standup reel should have a smooth drag and adequate line capacity. The importance of drag smoothness cannot be emphasized too much. An angler standing on a rolling deck, braced against the pull of a large fish, is very vulnerable to a jerky drag, which could cause a loss of balance.

One comment frequently heard from anglers who have given up the fighting chair and conventional tackle for standup gear is how much they like the relatively light weight of the latter. Even with a machined-aluminum reel packed with 600 to 800 yards of 50-pound mono, the tackle still isn't nearly as heavy and bulky as the full-sized version for the fighting chair.

There is a big difference between fighting a fish from a chair or standing up. In a fighting chair, pumping a fish is done by primarily pulling with back muscles and/or pushing with leg muscles—depending upon the type of harness you're using. With standup tackle, it is entirely done with leg and pelvic muscles. And instead of pushing with your feet braced against a footrest as in a fighting chair, the pumping technique calls for an almost comic burlesque of pelvic thrust and partial deep knee bends, a sort of "bump and pump," the effect of which is to raise and lower the rod tip rapidly with a surprising amount of force. The pumping strokes are short and quick, much faster than possible from a chair. This allows the angler to bring the fish to the transom a lot faster and with minimal or no backing down. We prefer to have the man at the wheel keep the transom pointed toward the fish and let the angler do the rest. The principal advantage of landing a prime billfish so quickly is that it can be released immediately in good physical condition with a better-than-average chance of survival.

very long, at least 16 inches, and extends almost all the way from the reel seat to the first (stripper) guide. This allows the angler to vary the position of both hands up and down as necessity and comfort dictate. The center of the bend of the fully loaded rod should be about 2 feet forward of the long foregrip. This is a result of the soft upper third of the tip

Chapter 17

ARTIFICIAL LURES

INSHORE FISHING

A seemingly endless variety of lures are used in salt-water nowadays, with dozens more being developed every year. In spite of the confusing array, lures still fall into three basic groups: those that float on the surface and make noise; those that float but dive when retrieved, and those that sink. Choosing the right lure for a specific gamefish under certain circumstances is primarily a process of elimination. Size, color, and swimming action are important to the extent that it helps if the lure looks and behaves like a baitfish the gamefish feeds upon. Whether the lure sinks or floats depends upon where the gamefish is found—deep or shallow.

Noisy surface plugs are great for attracting gamefish that home in on noise—bluefish, mackerel, most of the jack family, trout, tarpon (at times), and dolphin(fish). Even sailfish have been caught on light plugcasting gear with surface lures that make a loud chugging noise.

On the other hand, toss a chugger at a bonefish or permit on the flats and most likely all you'll see is a muddy streak accelerating toward deeper water. And while a grouper or snapper might come to the surface for a noisy plug in shallow water, they'll almost always ignore it if they are on the bottom at a depth of over twenty feet.

Floater/diver plugs are great for many fish that feed on the surface, at least occasionally, but don't like lots of noise. Tarpon and snook definitely like them better than chuggers: They also go for the type of plug that "walks" on the surface (sometimes called a jump bait). These can be worked slowly to give them a soft, gentle gurgling action, or more rapidly to get attention at greater distances.

Surface plugs are only effective when conditions are right for them. Sinking lures will catch more fish

This large snapper fell victim to a big diving plug.

Different types of plugs. From top: two floater/divers; a floating chugger-type plug with hooks removed for teasing gamefish within flycasting range; "jumping" floaters that remain almost vertical at rest but jump erratically when retrieved; a fast-sinking Mirrolure.

in the long run, even those that are feeding on or near the surface. But hooking a fish on a surface lure is surely one of the most visually exciting aspects of angling.

Choosing a sinking lure is a matter of matching the size and color with the prevalent baitfish in the area. Knowing how deep the fish are and how fast the lure will sink are also helpful. Some heavily weighted plugs go down pretty fast, but on a weight-for-weight basis jigs will win the race to the bottom every time. That's why if the water is deep, and/or there's a lot of current, a jig is the logical choice.

Sinking plugs are most effectively fished by the count-down method. If you know the fish are likely to be holding or cruising fifteen feet below the surface, and also that the plug you're using sinks one foot per second, then you must let it sink freely for fifteen seconds before starting the retrieve.

Jigs are most often fished in a more vertical fashion. Usually they're allowed to sink unimpeded until the angler feels them hit the bottom; then they're

retrieved at a pace necessary to get strikes (a process of experimentation). They can also be fished horizontally at a fast pace, a method often employed when long casts are needed to reach the fish and especially if there's wind to contend with.

Ask almost any experienced angler which lure he or she would choose if only one were allowed, and 90 percent of the time the answer will be "a jig." If you have a good assortment of jigs you can cover an extremely wide variety of situations.

Head shape has a lot to do with sink rate and action. A round or arrowlike head sinks rapidly. A flat, vertically oriented head sinks even a little faster and has excellent horizontal visibility for its weight. On the other hand, a flat, *horizontally oriented* head sinks relatively slowly and produces a wobbling motion. These so-called skimmer jigs are great for bonefish, permit, snook, red drum, trout, and many other fish in shallow water. But they won't go down quickly enough to fish effectively in water more than a few feet deep, especially if there's any current.

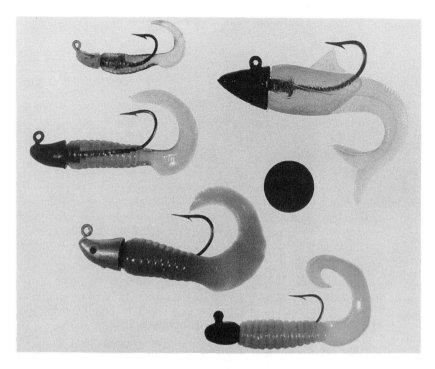

Jig heads with curlytail soft plastic bodies. Curlytails give the lures very lifelike swimming action. The penny is for size comparison.

Unlike plugs, jigs and spoons can be used with other artificials or with dead or alive natural baits. A jig with a long curlytail plastic worm impaled on the hook is a deadly snook combination, so is the lure called a "grub" by freshwater anglers, which is actually a combination of jig head and plastic-worm body. It offers a softer, more realistic feel to the fish. They also tear more easily than the time-tested bucktail or nylon-skirted jig, but the soft plastic bodies are relatively inexpensive and easily replaced. Adding a pinch of shrimp or other natural bait sweetens a jig effectively without changing its action. Adding a strip bait, whole shrimp (live or dead), or even a small whole fish often breaks down the resistance of fish that would otherwise ignore it.

OFFSHORE FISHING

Artificial lures for offshore big-game fishing were first developed by Japanese commercial fishermen. By the middle of the 1950s the technique had been refined by anglers in Hawaii, and it was just a matter of time until the whole world caught on. Lures are now used just about everywhere for offshore fishing. As a result, big-game anglers tend to be divided into two more or less distinct groups: those who prefer natural baits (dead and alive), and those who drag high-speed trolling lures.

Around offshore reefs and wrecks, many offshore anglers are now using jigs with great success. The vessel is anchored or allowed to drift and the lure is worked straight up and down between the surface and the bottom. It's called deep jiggling, and it is truly a great technique for catching big fish on light tackle.

High-Speed Trolling Lures

Every species of offshore gamefish has been caught on high-speed plastic trolling lures. Billfish, tunas, dolphin(fish), wahoo, king mackerel—any fish that will strike a bait on the surface will also strike an artificial. And when a big-game fish decides to eat one of these lures, there is nothing subtle about the strike. It is always quick and hard, because of the lure's high speed.

True to their name, these lures are designed to be dragged much faster than the typical 4 to 6 knots typical for rigged natural baits. High-speed lures work best between 10 and 14 knots, although one angler we know caught a blue marlin in the 300-pound range at almost 18 knots.

There are a number of guidelines for choosing lures from among the plethora of head shapes, sizes, and colors available today.

The faces of the earliest lures were either slanted or dished to provide maximum swimming action at relatively slow trolling speeds. The erratic pushing action of slant-faced lures and the darting action of dished lures attracted attention at such speeds. Lures of this type are still used today, mostly by those who wish to mix natural and artificial baits and troll everything at natural bait speeds.

It became apparent that if speeds were increased the angler would be able to present his lures over a greater expanse of water, increasing the likelihood of a billfish seeing them. The technique proved most effective when the fish were scattered over a large area. Considering that most of the billfish found off the U.S. coastline are scattered rather than concentrated, high-speed artificials made a lot of sense to a great many anglers.

Flat-faced lures became popular for this style of high-speed trolling soon after pioneer Capt. Mike Benitez first hacksawed the slanted front end off a long-head swimming lure called a Yap and proved his design at the famed blue marlin dropoff north of St. Thomas. The broad, flat face tracked straight at high speeds and created fish-attracting turbulence. It made intermittent but frequent trips to the surface to entrain air and create a solid bubble trail, also an occasional roostertail when it pushed water during those forays on top. This is now considered to be the ideal action for most lures.

Capt. Benitez favored the short, flat face of his doctored Yap for yet another reason. Since he knew that most big billfish attack a lure or baitfish at the head and swallow their food head-first, he felt that a relatively short head and the placement of the lead hook as far forward as possible increased his hookup percentage. For that reason he even went so far as to drill out the aft end of the lure's head in order to get the first hook of his two-hook rig farther forward. This up-front placement of the first hook, combined with a short lure head, has influenced lure designs ever since, and one sees fewer and fewer long-head lures each year.

Another early lure designed for fast trolling speeds was the Jet Head. It had a pointed head with holes drilled through it, and it smoked effectively at the surface. Heavier, weighted versions created turbulence beneath the surface. Frank Johnson of Moldcraft combined the benefits of the Jet Head and

An assortment of high-speed offshore trolling lures for marlin and tuna with various head shapes. (Photo by Don Mann.)

flat-faced designs by drilling blind holes in the faces of his soft-plastic, flat-head lures called softheads. The result was the popular Hooker. Its light weight, combined with the holes drilled in the flat head, created an enhanced bubble trail that greatly increased its visibility.

Soon anglers figured that if they could cover a great expanse of water at high trolling speeds, they might as well cover a still greater area by dragging lures while traveling to and from the fishing grounds. Doorknob lures were designed to track at the ultra-high cruising speeds of our modern sportfishing craft, and anglers suddenly became aware of the incredible speeds at which blue marlin could pounce on their prey. These weighted lures, with their exceptionally hydrodynamic shapes, were dragged far behind a high-speed boat, remained in the water, and caught blue marlin at speeds above 14 knots.

Another popular shape is the concave flat face. Fished extensively by Capt. Ron Schatman of Miami, it produces an even greater commotion, especially at trolling speeds from 8 to 10 knots.

In order for a lure to "look right," to be visible to the fish while tracking straight, and to remain in the water at high speeds, numerous adjustments must be made when setting it out. Boat speed must match the lure. Flat-faced chugger-type lures and mildly slant-faced lures can be trolled at a wide range of speeds, while swimming lures must be trolled more slowly. Concave straight runners work well over a broad range of boat speeds, but tend to fly at the upper end or when seas are up. Weighted flat-faced, heavily weighted pointy-heads, and doorknob-styled lures can be trolled at the highest speeds.

Many anglers believe the color of the lure is unimportant when fishing for billfish, especially blue marlin. This reasoning stems from scientific observations which seem to indicate that billfish are capable of distinguishing only light and dark shades. Besides, they believe the question is academic since all lures appear as a silvery blur of bubbles when streaking through the water at high speed.

Certainly not everyone agrees with this, and lure colors are important to some fishermen. Everyone has his or her favorites. As it turns out, many color preferences are regional, and cynics insist that most color preferences are self-perpetuating. They point out that when a particularly noteworthy fish is caught on a particular color at a particular location, almost everyone else in the area begins to troll the same lure and color thereafter. And of course the greatest number of fish are caught on that lure/color.

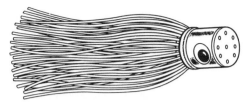

High-speed soft plastic offshore lure called the Hooker (by MoldCraft). It comes in many sizes and is very effective for billfish, tuna, and dolphin(fish).

Perhaps this accounts for the compulsive use of green lures in the Northeast, especially off New Jersey. Or the preference around Baja for green or orange and yellow. Nevertheless, fish are caught on all colors, and who's to say that another color combination might not produce just as well on any given day?

In Florida, the Bahamas, and much of the Caribbean over the past several years, the trend has been toward darker lure skirts. A majority of giant fish, many major tournament winners, have been caught on combinations of black with (in approximate order of preference) purple, orange, dark blue, red, pink, and green. All show a flash of light color beneath the predominant dark outside skirt, or consist of two dark shades. Black over black may become popular in the future, even though such a combination looks dismal on a display rack.

Those few anglers who fish white marlin with lures instead of natural baits seem to prefer blue and white, as do the few Ecuadorian anglers who choose lures over giant ballyhoo for big black marlin.

So, what's best in terms of colors. Unless you have an unlimited budget, it probably would be a good idea to start with a modest selection of darker colors, with perhaps one or two light colors thrown in. We're sort of partial to black over blue or purple, black over orange or pink, blue and white, and green and yellow. Blue/green and yellow are dolphin(fish) colors, and we've done well with that combo too.

Adjustments must also be made for sea conditions. If it is choppy, switch to weighted lures, or slow the boat speed and switch to lures that either swim erratically or create turbulence and smoke at lower speeds. Or try dropping the lures farther behind the boat to keep them from skipping too much.

In all cases the lures should ride the forward face of a wave for best action. Although there are endless "rules" on placement, most pros prefer to set large lures out flat on the second to fourth wake wave behind the boat, and smaller lures on the fifth to seventh wave. Some put out a fifth lure, either very short and center, or far, far back, down the middle.

A word on the hooks themselves. Besides being razor sharp, the size of the hook should be determined by the breaking strength of the line employed, and if possible the distance between barb and shank should be greater than the diameter of the lure head. Just remember that heavy, thick hooks require heavier strike drags, and hence heavier line, if you are going to be able to set them in the bony mouths or bills of large billfish.

Most experienced anglers use two hooks with artificial lures, connecting them with a variety of materials from heavy monofilament (usually snelled) to heavy wire or cable. Even the experts argue between using stiff rigs or loose, swinging "gaffer" rigs, but the beginner would do well to start with ready-made rigs. They're available in most coastal tackle shops that cater to offshore fishermen.

Finally, if you want to be successful at offshore high-speed lure fishing, it is important to stay alert. Especially when fishing with lines up to and including 50-pound test, because the angler *must* set the hook. To do this, he or she must be within a step or two of the rods and must watch the lures at all times. A good skipper will hit the throttles the instant the rod bends and line begins to run off against the drag of the reel in order to keep slack out of the line if the fish should charge the boat. With line of 50-pound test or less, this added momentum of the boat will not always set the hook for the inattentive angler. The angler must take the rod in hand and haul back hard and repeatedly to set the hook. Otherwise the odds of a pulled hook rise considerably. When fishing with 80- to 130-pound-test tackle, the greater drag setting of the reel made possible by the heavier line does increase the chance that the helmsman can set the hook with the throttles.

VERTICAL JIGGING

Also called deep jigging in the southeastern U.S., this is unquestionably one of the most effective light-tackle fishing techniques we know of. There are very few places where it won't work in one form or another, in both fresh and salt water, as long as the water isn't *too* deep. We have used it all over the world, in at least four oceans, to catch everything from bottomfish to sailfish.

The basic techniques work in depths that range

from just a few feet to as deep as you're willing to go. We even know some anglers who claim they enjoy deep jigging (without electric reels) in 300 to 400 feet of water, but that's too much hard work for most of us. As a rule, 200 to 250 feet of water is about the practical lower limit for deep jigging with manual reels. And those depths are practical only under reasonable wind and sea conditions. Most anglers prefer to work in less than 200 feet.

Actually there aren't many fish that cannot be hooked by deep jigging in 150 feet of water or less. Some of the species most commonly caught include bluefish, striped bass, black sea basses, groupers, snappers, amberjack, blackfin tuna, yellowfin tuna, African pompano, bonito, king mackerel, wahoo, dolphin(fish), sailfish, mackerel, and more. It's a super-exciting, grab-bag type of fishing. You seldom know what you're going to hook. Or sometimes don't even know what you *have* hooked until it's at boatside.

While vertical jigging is a relative easy technique to learn, it does require some skill to become really proficient at it. There's more to constant success here than simply tying on a jig and dropping it to the bottom.

The tackle must be strong enough to handle any size fish (within reason) you're likely to hook and also light enough that jigging with it doesn't become a back-breaking chore. Most experienced anglers choose spinning or baitcasting tackle with lines that test from 6 to 20 pounds. Line size is pretty much dictated by the size of the lure, the depth you'll be fishing, and the size of the fish you're likely to catch. With lines heavier than 20-pound test, heavier jigs are required. Heavy lines have so much drag it's difficult to reach bottom in water deeper than 100 feet. And fish often refuse heavy jigs.

One of the first rules you'll learn in the vertical jigging game is to use the smallest, lightest lure that will reliably reach bottom. Smaller lures just seem to hook more fish most of the time. As with any rule, there are exceptions. At times we've found that banging the bottom noisily with jigs seemingly far too heavy for that depth will provoke fish (that have been steadfastly ignoring lighter lures) into striking violently. For instance, we've used 2- to 3-ounce jigs in as little as 10 feet of water to take big grouper and snapper in Florida, the Caribbean, Australia, and even Africa. When bounced across the bottom, the heavier lures kicked up puffs of sand that these fish couldn't resist, especially the huge cubera snapper (often 60 pounds and more) and very large corvina

A member of the seatrout family, this African corvina weighed almost 20 pounds and took a jig bounced on bottom.

that hung around river mouths along the west coast of Africa. Those fish gave us some lumps we'll never forget! Hooking them sure was exciting, though.

Whether spinning or baitcasting, the rod you choose must be both long enough and stiff enough to move the jig when it finally reaches bottom. You shouldn't have to raise the rod tip violently in order to make the lure barely wiggle, as you should be able to set the hook readily despite the long length of stretchy monofilament line between you and the fish. For jigging in deep water, say 80 feet or more, the preferred length for spinning rods seems to be 7 to 8 feet, and for baitcasting rods, 6 to 7 feet. Obviously, shorter rods are just fine for shallower water.

Back in the early days of deep jigging in Florida, twenty or more years ago, we used fiberglass rods almost the diameter and stiffness of a broom handle. Thanks to graphite, boron, and the various lightweight composites, those rods have shrunk considerably in both diameter and weight (but not stiffness). These new materials are also considerably more sensitive to the sometimes soft strike of a fish 150 feet down than their heavier fiberglass predecessors. This adds up to more hookups and less fatigue at the end of a long fishing day.

Reel size is equally as important as rod size. Fishing with a big, heavy reel requires a lot of effort, so keep it as light as possible. The largest fish in the deepest water can be landed if the reel has a filled capacity of approximately 250 yards of 10- to 20-pound-test mono. More capacity just means more reel *and* line weight to content with all day long.

Most of the larger level-wind baitcasting reels will hold 200 to 250 yards of 15- to 20-pound-test mono, which is more than adequate for the deepest water you're likely to fish.

Be sure that your spinning *or* baitcasting reel has a smooth drag. You'll often be hooking fish down near the bottom, so you'll need a lot of drag to keep the beast out of the rocks. That means as much as 4 or 5 pounds of drag with 15- to 20-pound-test lines. If the drag is jerky, or has a very high starting pressure, you can expect to get busted almost every time you manage to hook something with very big shoulders.

Lure size, weight, and shape are usually the important considerations. Color can be important too, especially in shallow water where colors are still visible. Most vertical jigging is done with lead-head bucktail jigs or solid metal lures. Plugs with plastic or wood bodies, regardless of how heavily weighted, just sink too slowly to reach bottom. This is particularly true when the boat is drifting with wind and/or current. Especially wind.

For depths of 100 to 200 feet or more, the best lures are 2¼ to 4 ounces. For shallower water, ½- to 1½-ounce lures should do the trick unless it's really windy. Keep in mind that the faster the boat drifts with the wind, the more weight you will need to reach bottom. It's most important to carry a variety of lures of different weights.

Shape is a matter of what works best for you. Most of the heavier jigs come with heads that are shaped somewhat like an arrow or spear head. There are a few other shapes that depart from these, but these two are the most common. When it comes to jigs below 1 ounce, the most typical head shapes are the "lima bean" and the "bullet."

The color preferred by most anglers for depths below 50 to 75 feet is white for jigs (with sometimes silver mylar strands mixed in with the ducktail) and silver flash for metal lures. Other colors tend to appear dull gray in the depths unless they're fluorescent, while white changes little. In shallower water, bright yellow and bright green have produced well for me.

Many anglers tip their lures with either a plastic worm, pork rind strips, or some form of bait. The same plastic worms that are popular among bass anglers work quite well when added to the jig's hook, especially those with curlytails. Colors that seem to

A 2½-ounce arrowhead jig with a plastic worm added is an excellent lure for deep-jigging.

This large red snapper took a jig fished very deep.

work are white, bright yellow, and bright green. Some anglers even use phosphorescent plastic worms that glow.

If the fishing is slow, it often pays to add a strip of natural bait to the lure's hook. Fresh bonito is hard to beat, but many other fish strips—mullet, mackerel, and even squid—also work very well.

Good vertical jigging action can occur during any part of the day, particularly during the cooler months in more tropical climates. When the heat of summer begins to penetrate even to the deeper reefs of Florida, the best action seems to occur most consistently during the very early morning and late afternoon hours, when the sun is near or just below the horizon.

Most experienced anglers who jig for bottom-dwelling fish, keep a rod handy that's rigged for surface action. Smaller jigs (½ to ¾ ounce) that can be cast long distances are very effective. Noisy surface lures, such as chuggers or 99M series Mirrolures, can be used to attract surface fish from surprisingly great distances. The reason for having the extra rod rigged primarily for surface action is pretty obvious, when you think about it. If a surface blitz erupts while your jig is 100 feet below, it simply takes too long to get it back up in time to fire it off. And even if

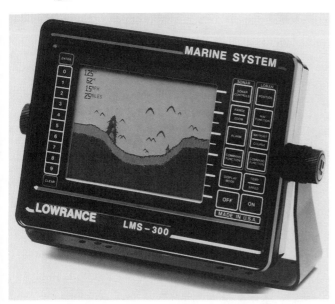

Combination LCD graph/Loran C depthfinder/navigator locates fish, records depth, and shows you the way home. (Photo courtesy Lowrance Electronics.)

you do, the odds are it will be too heavy to work effectively on the surface.

Leader material is critical to success when vertical jigging. There's no doubt that the lighter the leader, the more strikes you'll receive. Unfortunately, there's a point where a leader that's too light becomes counterproductive and results in too many fish lost. Some days you can get by with lighter leaders than others; it's primarily a matter of experimentation.

Except when toothy critters are a particular problem, leaders of monofilament are the best choice. For open-ocean jigging, it might be necessary to use 30- to 60-pound-test mono, which incidentally has proved capable of landing a lot of king mackerel, bluefish, and even, with a little luck, wahoo. Inshore jigging in shallower water might call for no leader at all, or perhaps 20- to 30-pound-test mono. Our rule of thumb is to use the lightest leader material we think we can get by with, and if that doesn't work, go

lighter still. We'd rather lose some of the fish we hook this way than get no strikes at all. In most cases the shorter the leader the better, but there are times when you'll have to suffer with a long leader.

A short wire leader will eliminate the toothy critter problem, but cuts down on the number of strikes. Kingfish, wahoo, even grouper and snapper frequently won't hit a jig—even one tipped with bait—attached to a wire leader.

Many anglers compromise when there are enough toothy critters in the area to make some protection mandatory. You can use 6 to 12 inches of 30- to 50-pound test single-strand wire with a dulled finish. The lighter and shorter the wire, the more strikes you'll get. But if you make the wire too short, you'll begin to lose many fish that inhale the jig past the point where the wire joins the mono.

If you don't know how to tie the mono directly to the wire, then use a small swivel—also *not* shiny. A good deep-water big-fish wire/mono leader combination is 2 to 4 feet of 30-pound mono and 8 to 10 inches of very light wire. Some anglers we know even go to the trouble of painting the lower half of the wire leader the same color as the jig.

A good depthfinder is a big help in locating likely jigging areas. Especially the newer type with a Loran C receiver built into the same housing, a great space saver for small boat consoles. The cost of these combo units is also quite a bit less than if you bought the two separately. The depthfinder doesn't have to be the most expensive graph on the market. Certainly the more sophisticated recorders do offer many advantages, but we've caught many big fish deep-jigging with only a basic flasher. You'll just have to pay closer attention to the dancing blip in order to get the maximum amount of information out of it. And while such structures as wrecks are obviously dynamite spots, often overlooked are small rock piles and ledges that are only two to four feet high.

Although I've heard some anglers complain that deep-jigging is a lot of work, if your equipment is balanced properly, it really isn't all *that* laborious, and the rewards are certainly worth the effort.

Chapter 18

KNOTS, BAITS, AND RIGGING

KNOTS

The old saw about the chain being no stronger than its weakest link is never more accurate than when applied to knots and fishing lines. Knots are the weakest link in all cases except one: when the last few feet of the line has been doubled into a bimini twist, and this double line is attached to the leader. The bimini, when properly tied, retains 100 percent of the strength of the line itself. All other knots are weaker, but a few do come close to 100 percent. Why fill a spool with 10-pound-test line and then use knots that reduce its breaking strength to 7 or 8 pounds? So take the time to learn to tie the bimini because it is the foundation for most of the other knots that are important to the saltwater angler. It isn't difficult, but it does require practice.

Although there are many different knots in use today, the saltwater angler only needs to know how to tie five or six of them to cover just about every situation from flycasting to big-game fishing. It is important to understand these knots in order to tie them correctly. An incorrectly tied knot can lose up to 50 percent of its inherent strength.

How some knots are tightened (drawn down) makes a big difference, because otherwise they slip (especially when wet) and cut themselves internally or simply come apart under steady pressure. That's why all knots should be wetted (saliva is fine if the line will go in the water within a few hours) before they are drawn down tight. Wetting reduces friction damage during the tightening process, and often provides some warning, when the knot fails after tying it, that it wasn't tied correctly.

In this section, we will explain how to tie the most important knots and when to use them. Breaking strengths are given for each. Ultra-thin lines as a rule test toward the low end of the strength range shown

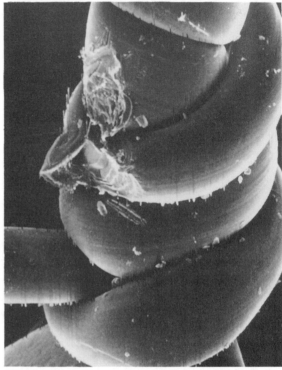

This is what an improved clinch knot looks like magnified more than 50 times. Note damage to the knot when the clipper accidentally nicked it while cutting off the tag end of the mono.

for each knot, while the more typical lines of average diameter test toward the higher end of the range.

Bimini Twist

Sometimes called the 20-times-around knot, this knot, if correctly tied, retains 100 percent of any line's strength (regardless of materials) because it is really more of a wrap than a knot and therefore cannot slip internally. The doubled line thus produced can be tied directly to wire via an Albright knot, to swivels and lures or other terminal hardware with a simple clinch knot, or directly to heavier mono leaders with a connecting type knot. Even though these other knots are less than 100 percent, the bimini's doubled line serves as a cushion and the resulting "chain" of hardware and/or leaders have no "links" weaker than the rest of the fishing line on the reel.

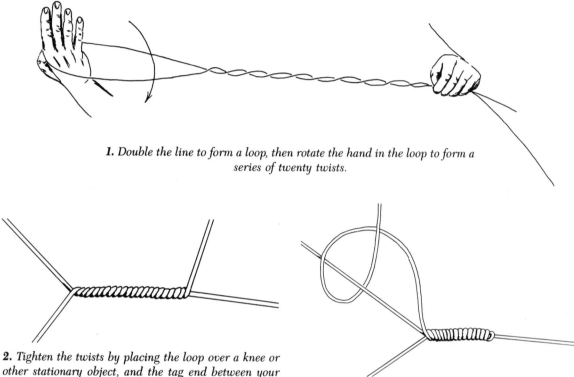

1. Double the line to form a loop, then rotate the hand in the loop to form a series of twenty twists.

2. Tighten the twists by placing the loop over a knee or other stationary object, and the tag end between your teeth. Pull the upper side of the loop upward with one hand placed a few inches away from the twist, while at the same time pushing down slightly with the other hand on the standing portion a foot or so away from the twist.

4. Continue until the twist is completely overwrapped. Then grasp the junction of the wrap tightly between the thumb and forefinger with one hand, so it won't unravel, and make a half hitch, as shown here, and pull it tight.

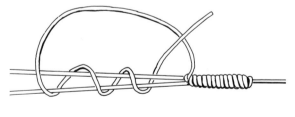

5. Make a two or three wraps overhand . . .

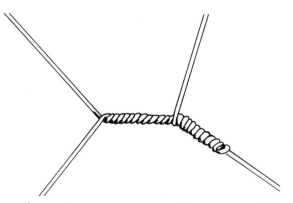

3. The previous maneuver causes line to wrap tightly over the twist, as shown here.

6. . . . and pull the overhand down tight. Cut off the tag end approximately ⅛ inch beyond the finished knot.

Blood Knot

This connecting knot is sometimes called the barrel knot. It is mostly used to join lines of unequal diameter, such as when making up a tapered leader for fly fishing. Usually tied with three or four turns on each side, its wet test is 62 to 74 percent. In order to be reliable, it *must* be wetted and then quickly drawn down as tight as possible. Leave one-eighth of an inch of line sticking out of each side when trimming.

1. Place the two lines to be connected parallel to each other, and begin by wrapping the tag end of one around the standing part of the other.

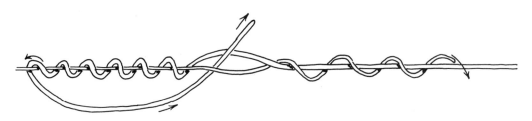

2. Feed the tag end from step 1 through the opening between the two lines, then wrap the tag end of the second line around the first.

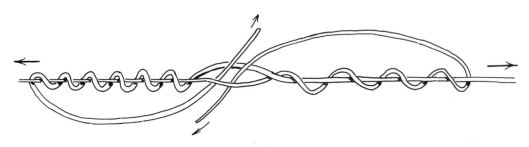

3. Insert the tag end of the second line through the same opening, in the opposite direction from the end of line one.

4. Wet the knot, and pull down smoothly until it is tight. Leave ⅛ to ³⁄₁₆ inch of tag end sticking out of each side of the knot, as shown, to prevent the knot from coming apart under tension.

Surgeon's Knot

When tied with just two overhands, this knot tests 70 to 90 percent. Adding another overhand to the tying process may actually weaken the knot somewhat, so stick to two. It is another excellent knot for connecting lines of unequal diameter, especially if the size difference between the two is great. It is *not* a suitable knot for joining lines of the same diameter; the blood knot is far better for that. But the surgeon's will allow you to tie, for example, 80-pound-test mono directly to 12-pound test. And if the 12 has been doubled with a bimini twist, the resulting "chain" is no weaker than the rest of the 12 on the reel.

Uni-Knot

The uni-knot can be used for the same purposes as the surgeon's, but it is also an excellent knot for tying very heavy mono directly to the eye of a hook or lure. In this case one half of the knot is tied around the standing portion of the leader (with just two turns) after it has been passed through the eye. Saltwater fly fishermen often use it for attaching big flies to very heavy mono leaders. When used for joining lines, it is typically tied with three to five turns on each side, and tests 65 to 79 percent. Use three or less turns for heavier mono, and more than three for light lines.

1. With the heavier and lighter lines parallel to each other, tie a loose overhand knot.

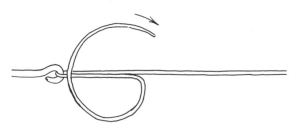

1. Thread the leader through the hook's eye and form a loop.

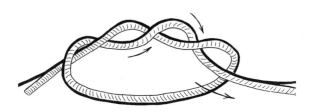

2. Bring both lines back through the loop formed for a second overhand.

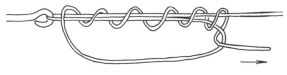

2. Bring the tag end back through the loop to form five or six loose overhand wraps.

3. Wet and pull down snug, but not completely tight.

3. Wet knot and carefully draw tight, making sure all parts draw evenly. Trim, leaving about ⅛ inch of tag end.

4. Slide the knot down as far as you wish, either to form a small loop or completely tight against the hook or lure eye. Then tighten the knot some more, if needed.

Albright Knot

This is the best knot for tying fishing line or light leader directly to wire without a swivel. A loop is first twisted in the end of the wire, and the Albright is tied to that. It only follows that for 100 percent strength the fishing line should be first doubled with a bimini twist. It is also an excellent knot for joining very light mono to extremely large diameter mono. You could tie 6-pound-test directly to 200-pound test if you wished, and it too would be 100 percent if the 6 was first doubled with a bimini.

1. Bend the heavy mono into a loop. Bring the tag end of the lighter line down the loop an inch or so and begin wrapping it around both sides of the loop. (If using wire, twist the tag end around the standing part.)

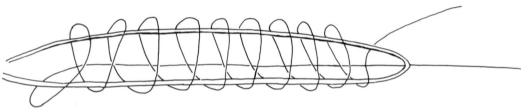

2. Make seven to nine wraps around both loops, then insert the end of the lighter line through the top of the loop, coming out on the same side as the standing part of the lighter line.

3. Wet and pull down tight. Trim off tag end to within ⅛ inch of the knot.

Connector Knot

This is a combination of two knots: one-half blood knot, and one-half uni-knot. It tests 65 to 90 percent. The uni portion is tied with two to three turns, and the blood with four to six turns. We favor it above most other connecting type knots because it slips through the guides of a spinning, baitcasting, or big-game rod better than anything else we've tried. Thus it allows the use of leaders that are longer than otherwise possible under these conditions. Obviously a bimini should be used to double the fishing line to retain 100 percent of its strength. For example, we use this knot to connect a 15-foot intermediate leader for big-game or standup tackle; if 50-pound-test line is used, the intermediate leader is 100- to 130-pound test. The 50 is first doubled with a bimini, and then the doubled 50 is tied to 15 feet of 100- to 130-pound-test mono with a connector knot. The heavy leader above the bait or lure now consists of 5 to 10 feet of wire or 250- to 300-pound-test mono, connected to the intermediate leader via a swivel. This allows the angler to reel the 100 or 130 right through the roller guides and onto the reel, allowing the fish to be brought very close to the boat where it can be handled safely and easily.

Connector Knot

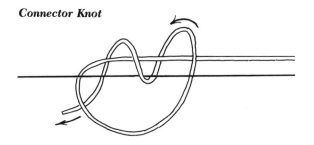

1. This is nothing more than a half-uni and a half-blood knot. Start by tying a two-wrap uni in the heavy mono around the light mono.

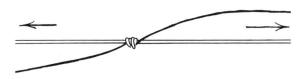

2. Pull the uni down snug, but not to maximum tightness.

3. Tie a half blood knot with the lighter line. It should have at least six wraps.

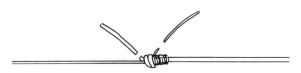

4. Wet and pull the two knots together snugly. Then tighten each separately. Next, cut off the tag ends as close as possible in the heavy mono, leaving ⅛-inch showing.

8-Turn Clinch Knot

This is the best knot for tying light fishing line directly to a hook, lure, or swivel if a doubled line is not desired. Our tests show the 6-turn improved

clinch to be 85 to 90 percent. If the number of turns is increased to 8, the strength factor is 98 to 100 percent. It is an excellent knot for lines up to 20-pound test. Anglers use it often with leader-shy fish like yellowtail snapper, or for tying small flies to light leaders for bonefishing.

8-Turn Clinch Knot

1. Pass the line through the eye of the hook or lure and begin a series of wraps.

2. Continue wrapping until at least five wraps are completed. Eight wraps will make the knot much stronger.

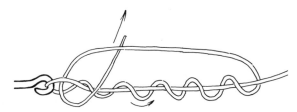

3. For simplicity, a five-wrap improved clinch is shown here. Bring the end of the line back through the opening between the wraps and the eye, then back through the loop formed between the line and the wraps. Adding this last maneuver is what makes the difference between the normal and improved version of this knot. As explained in step 2, eight wraps is the strongest way to tie the clinch knot.

4. Wet and pull the knot down tight. If eight wraps are used instead of five or six, it is usually necessary to "tease" the knot between your thumb and forefinger as it is being tightened, so that it will pull down evenly.

Homer Rhode Loop Knot

If a loop knot is needed in a heavy monofilament leader to allow the lure or bait to swing freely for more natural action, this knot is an excellent choice and easy to tie.

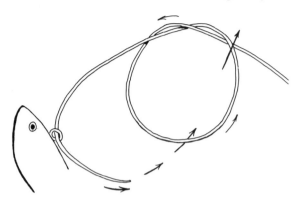 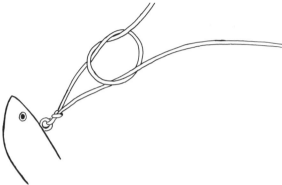

1. Tie a loose overhand knot in the leader and pass the end through the eye of the hook or lure, then back through the loop formed by the knot.

2. Pull the first overhand down to the eye as shown, then tie a second around the standing part of the leader. Pull the second overhand down tight, then pull the standing part of the leader until the first overhand slides up and jams tightly against the second overhand. Trim excess.

RIGGING BAITS

There are probably almost as many ways to rig natural baits as there are places to fish them, so in the limited space we have here we will stick to some of the most popular. This section will show how to rig whole or cut dead baits; rigging live baits is covered in Chapter 19. See also the various chapters dealing with fish species, because in each we have included information about specific baits and lures.

Whole Balao

Every bluewater fish, from dolphin and bonito to tuna and billfish, eats balao. Many inshore fish, such as tarpon, snook, and large red drum, will seldom pass up a drifted balao. It can be trolled on the surface, or just under the surface, or drifted with or without a jig.

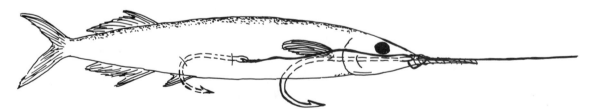

Whole balao rigged for trolling or drifting. *First, insert the hook eye through a small hole in the belly, pushing it forward until the eye reaches the mouth. Next, thread the leader wire through both lips and through the eye of the hook. Make a tight wrap in the leader and lay it flat against the beak. Wrap copper wire around the leader and beak to keep the leader in place. Some anglers break off the beak about halfway before wrapping the wire. Others add a second, usually smaller hook, connected to the eye of the first hook with a short piece of leader. The shank of the second hook can be simply pushed through the skin rather than buried in the body.*

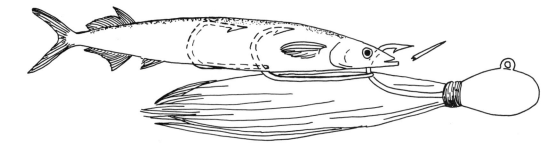

Balao and jig rig, *excellent for drifting and trolling. Two hooks are used by most anglers; some even add a third when fishing for king mackerel.*

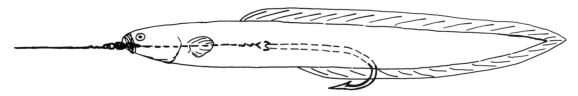

Whole rigged eel. *Soft copper wire is used to keep the swivel in the mouth. A short section of leader wire or heavy mono between the hook eye and the swivel positions the hook as far back as necessary.*

Rigged eelskin for drifting and trolling. *The forward end of the skin is wrapped tightly around a sinker to hold it in place.*

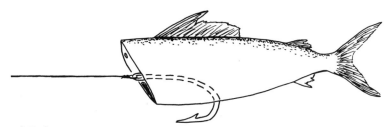

Plug-cut baitfish for trolling and drifting. *Salmon fishermen adjust the angle of the cut so that the bait makes a slow rolling, spinning motion like an injured baitfish as it moves through the water.*

Rigged Eel

A whole rigged eel is the inshore equivalent of balao, unsurpassed as a natural bait for striped bass and just about any other gamefish of similar size. It can be both trolled and drifted.

Sometimes just the skin of the eel is rigged for trolling. Many prefer it because of its especially life-like swimming action.

Plug-Cut Baitfish

Few salmon, especially Chinooks, can pass up the slow roll of a trolled or drifted plug-cut baitfish. The angle of the cut that separates the bait's head from its body is usually around 45 degrees, but it can pay to experiment with that angle.

Shrimp

Whole shrimp, dead or alive, can be used for both casting and drifting. Rare is the inshore gamefish that will pass one up, and many offshore species like dolphin love them too. Small pieces inserted on the hook of a jig are an excellent way to increase that lure's effectiveness.

Whole live shrimp on a single hook, top view. *(Treble hooks are illegal in many states.) Be careful to avoid the black spot (brain) when inserting the hook, or the shrimp will not remain alive.*

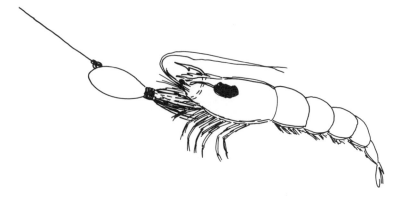

Whole live shrimp on a jig. *In this case the hook is inserted from the bottom, coming out through the top of the head.*

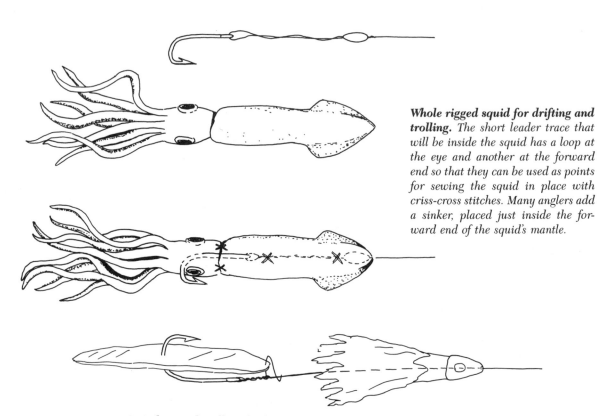

Whole rigged squid for drifting and trolling. *The short leader trace that will be inside the squid has a loop at the eye and another at the forward end so that they can be used as points for sewing the squid in place with criss-cross stitches. Many anglers add a sinker, placed just inside the forward end of the squid's mantle.*

Strip bait and trolling feather. *The strip can be used with or without the feather. Note the "safety-pin" bend in the wire to make changing strips a quick and easy task.*

Squid

Everything eats squid. Rigged whole, this bait is effective for larger gamefish inshore as well as offshore. Strips of squid can also be added to the hooks of jigs and trolling lures as sweeteners.

Bait Strips

Mullet and other baitfish can be cut into strips for trolling. These strips are effective by themselves or when added to a jig or feather. The diagram below shows the strip used with a feather; just omit the feather if it's not needed.

Whole Baitfish

Whole dead baitfish, such as mullet, mackerel, and small members of the tuna family are excellent trolling baits for billfish and large tuna. They can be rigged to skip along the surface, or with an optional chin sinker to swim underwater. If the bait is to be used alive, just make a quick eye loop with a needle and a short piece of Dacron, as shown. See Chapter 19 for more about fishing live baits.

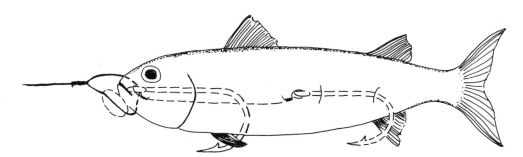

Whole rigged fish for trolling or drifting. Shown here is the classic "swimming mullet." The second hook is optional, as is the egg-type chin sinker held in place by the loop through the lips and the eye of the hook. Some anglers sew the gillplates against the body, or add a few tight wraps of dental floss around the head so that the gillplates are kept tightly shut. Either method prolongs the "life" of the bait considerably if it is to be used for trolling. Most anglers also use an "apple corer," a tubular device that removes the backbone for more lifelike action. Yet another option is to split the bait vertically from the tail forward to the dorsal fin and remove the backbone that way. The body may or may not be resewn together afterward, depending upon the swimming motion desired.

TERMINAL TACKLE

Terminal tackle includes sinkers, leaders, and connectors. As a rule, you'll hook more fish with the least amount of terminal gear you can get by with. Nothing looks more natural to a fish than a live bait on a small hook attached directly to the lightest monofilament line you can possibly use for the species of fish you're after. But for saltwater fish, which usually have rough mouths or sharp teeth, light can be a relative term. A live shrimp on a 1/0 hook tied directly to 6- or 8-pound-test mono is deadly for bonefish, which have rubbery lips. But if a toothy snapper, snook, barracuda, or shark happens upon that bait, the light mono won't last more than a second or two. And so it often becomes necessary to use a leader of some sort.

Leaders

You can use heavy monofilament as leader material for snook, snappers, red drum, striped bass, or anything else that doesn't have sharp *cutting* teeth. For sharks, 'cudas, king mackerel, etc., you'll need wire.

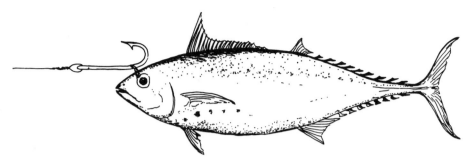

Small tuna or bonito as live bait for slow trolling. *A loop of Dacron line or light wire passed from side to side through the upper edge of the eye sockets does not penetrate the brain, and the bait will live for hours. These baits will not live long if used for drift-fishing; constant forward motion is needed to keep sufficient water flowing across their gills.*

Three-stage casting leader for baitcasting or spinning tackle. *It is designed for taking fish that are relatively large for the line strength you are using. The bimini twist at point 1 ensures 100 percent line strength. The resulting double line is used to connect to the first (lightest) stage of the leader at point 2. This portion of the leader (3) can be any length (subject to IGFA rules for potential world records), as long as the knots will pass through the rod guides. The next stage (4) is heavier, and usually about the length of the rod tip. The final stage is heavy mono or wire as needed, usually 12 to 24 inches long. Section 3 can be eliminated if not needed.*

You can get by with heavy mono (i.e. 50-pound test) when fishing for Spanish mackerel, and you'll get more strikes. If you must use wire, always use the shortest length and the smallest diameter you can get by with. It doesn't take No. 10 wire to catch a 30-pound 'cuda or king mackerel, or a shark under 100 pounds. Usually No. 4 or 5 will get more strikes. And coffee-colored wire usually gets more strikes than bright wire.

Learn to rig a leader properly, but always keep it as light and simple as possible for the species and conditions. The most basic leader is nothing more than a short piece of heavier mono tied directly to the lighter fishing line with one of the knots previously shown. Sometimes more than one stage is needed in the leader system—perhaps a short piece of heavy mono or wire as a shock leader just above the hook or lure and a longer intermediate section to protect the line from chafing against the fish's body. There are even instances, such as when fishing with

ultralight line testing 6 pounds or less, when yet a third stage is needed to put pressure on the fish in close quarters.

Catching a 10-pound bluefish on 4-pound-test line is a lot of fun, but you'll land that fish a lot faster with a three-stage leader that might include 15 feet of 10-pound-test tied to the 4, 4 feet of 30-pound mono to prevent body chafing, and finally a foot or so of wire because of the fish's sharp teeth.

Sinkers

Sinkers come in a wide variety of shapes and weights. It is a good rule never to use more weight than necessary, and in most cases the simpler the rig, the more fish you're likely to catch. Still, the proper use of sinkers is an art and comes with experience. The possible combinations are endless and vary considerably from area to area. While we've covered some of the more basic rigs here, a good way to start learning about some of the more complex arrangements is to visit a tackle shop and ask for the particular rig that's most effective for the species of fish you're seeking.

There are several simple ways to use sinkers to get the bait to the desired depth. Clinch-on or egg sinkers can be added directly to the line rigged on a dropper from a 3-way swivel. Or in the typical "fishfinder" fashion so popular among surfcasters.

In some situations a breakaway sinker might be needed, especially for fishing with bait on a rough bottom or for big fish that jump. A sinker that stays attached to the line now becomes a liability—it could cause the hook to pull free. A simple solution is to attach the sinker with soft copper wire (the type you buy in tackle shops to rig balao), or very light mono, or thread, so that it breaks free at the fish's first jump or if you hang up on the bottom.

Another popular sinker rig is the bottom rig. A 3-way swivel is attached to the line and two droppers attached to the swivel, one for the sinker, the other for the hook. When the sinker hits bottom, the bait floats freely. A second 3-way swivel can be added above for another dropper with baited hook.

Swivels

We prefer black swivels. Shiny swivels often tempt small, toothy predators. To prevent a revolving lure from twisting your line, use *only* ball-bearing swivels. Any swivel you use should always be rated for at least three times more than the line test (i.e. 150-pound swivels with 50-pound-test line). All swivels wear with use, and steadily lose strength. Replace any that look even slightly questionable.

Floats

Floats are often required in bait fishing. Tackle shops carry an assortment of floats that stay permanently attached to your line. We have frequently used a breakaway float, that is nothing more than a small, rectangular piece of scrap styrofoam from a busted ice chest. The float is partially cut in half, and the line wrapped around the slit several times. When the fish takes the bait, the two pieces separate and the fish feels no resistance from the float. It's a very effective way to fish live or dead bait near the surface.

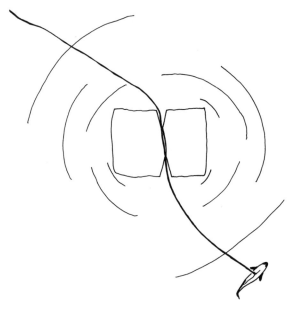

Two methods of attaching a sinker with soft wire so that it can come loose when it's hung up or the fish jumps.

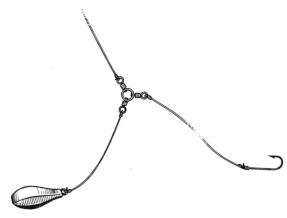

Basic bottom-fishing rig.

Breakaway styrofoam float. *Small pieces of styrofoam are cut into blocks. The blocks are then cut again from the two sides so that about ½ inch of uncut material remains in the middle. The line is wrapped around this middle section. If the live or dead bait thus suspended is struck, the float breaks into two pieces and the fish feels no resistance as it eats the bait.*

Chapter 19

FISHING WITH LIVE BAIT

No one will argue that the most realistic bait for any type of gamefish is live bait. But it's not enough for the bait to be alive. It should be *healthy* too. So while it is true that just about any live bait will eventually draw a strike, the stronger and more frisky it is, the sooner and more likely it is going to get eaten.

Good live baits require a good baitwell, one with sufficient capacity for the number that will be transported, and good raw (outside) water circulation. Live wells that recirculate and aerate the same water over and over again aren't nearly as good, and usually won't keep the bait alive for more than a few hours. That's because aeration doesn't eliminate fish body wastes that contaminate the water, and also because during hot weather the water temperature in the baitwell may rise, and the warmer the water, the less dissolved oxygen it will hold. Accumulated body wastes also seriously deplete dissolved oxygen.

Some live baits require a high flow rate of outside water, enough to create a strong current. Live mackerel and small bonitos fall into this category. This means a high-capacity pump should be part of the system.

Baitwells with rounded corners are better than those with sharp corners; otherwise delicate baits (like balao) may swim into a sharp corner and die of suffocation. The best shape of all for a live well is cylindrical.

Not all baitwells are built inside the boat, by the way. Some are fixed to the transom, and others are simply free-standing circular plastic containers up to 48 inches wide that can be removed when not needed. Even a large plastic trash can works, as long as the water in it gets changed often enough. It may be possible to do this with the boat's cockpit raw water washdown system.

INSHORE LIVEBAITING

We won't go into a long list of specific live baits to use in any given part of the coast, because that's easy to find out locally and it would take up too much space here. The information is available for the asking at any tackle shop. For the most part, we'll stick to fishing techniques in this Chapter. See Chapter 18 for bait-rigging details.

Live baits may be fished in any of three obvious zones: on or near the surface; in midwater; and on or near the bottom. Each requires a somewhat different technique.

Many anglers successfully combine live baits with artificial lures. A live shrimp and jig combination is deadly for every fish that eats shrimp, and rare indeed is the inshore species that doesn't. An advantage of this rig is that it can be used to fish the entire water column from surface to bottom—as long as the jig is heavy enough to get to the bottom. It simply can be dropped with the reel in freespool, then retrieved slowly to the surface, with or without any jigging motion. It can be cast long distances and allowed to sink to the bottom before the retrieve starts, or you can start turning the reel handle anytime between the surface and the bottom to cover the midwater zone effectively. The shrimp and jig can also be trolled slowly with deadly results, especially in shallow water with an electric trolling motor. And a small, live baitfish can be substituted for the shrimp.

Fishing a live bait with just one or two hooks is the most common technique. There are many ways the bait can be rigged, but it is important that the hook be only as large as it has to be, and the leader no

Electric trolling motors are very useful to the small-boat saltwater angler. Stick only to those made of corrosion- and rust-resistant materials. This one has been modified for foot steering via a short ¼-inch stainless bolt mounted on top of the control head.

longer or heavier than it has to be, for the bait to look as natural as possible. And that can make all the difference between strikes and no strikes.

The easiest way to fish with a live baitfish is to impale it near the top of the head and toss it in the water, then sit down and wait for a strike. But some baits don't work well that way. And you certainly cannot slow troll or fish a bait thus rigged in any kind of current, because it will spin. It pays to know all of the relatively few basic methods for fishing live baits.

Baits to be fished in a current or trolled slowly must be hooked either through the eyes or the upper lip. Some sardines, for instance, have a soft spot in the bridge of the nose immediately forward of the eye socket, and the hook can be inserted sideways there. Others, like the mullet, do best if the hook is inserted through the upper lip, just forward of the eyes, with the point on top. Splitting the lower lip carefully with a sharp knife allows the mullet to breathe better.

Hooking the bait through the back of the head or even further toward the tail, such as under the dorsal fin, is good for fishing still-water with a float or a kite. Even better yet, sew a "X" of dental floss into the bait's back at the point where you want the hook, then slip the hook through the "X". The bait not only

Live pinfish hooked through back for kite or float fishing.

stays frisky longer this way, there is also much less of a chance that the hook point will be turned back into the bait and thus fouled during the strike.

Small live bait hooked through the nose for drifting or slow trolling.

If a second hook is an absolute must (the bait will look more natural and stay lively longer without it), then use a smaller hook (if possible) for that purpose, kept in place by slipping the point gently through the skin further back toward the tail. The leader for that hook can be attached to the eye of the first hook, and shouldn't be so long that it can become fouled, or so short that it interferes with the bait's natural movements.

Live baits can be fished as deep as necessary by adding weight. The weight can be in the form of an egg sinker on the line above the leader, or a slip-on rubber-cored sinker if you feel it may be necessary to remove it or change the amount of weight. Running a short piece of soft copper wire through the egg sinker and wrapping the ends around the line makes a good automatic release sinker for jumping fish.

Downriggers took a surprising amount of time to gain recognition in saltwater, but they are an excellent way to drift or slowly troll live baits at a precisely known depth with light tackle. The release clip on the ball works just like its counterpart on an outrigger. And the best part of the downrigger system is that the angler has direct control of the bait's depth at all times. If a graph-type depthsounder with a wide beam transducer of 45 degrees is used, it is even possible to track the depth of the weight on the screen.

OFFSHORE LIVEBAITING

The main differences between livebaiting offshore and inshore are the size of the baits and the fish you can catch. Although no one deliberately fishes with baits that large, half-ton marlin have been caught with whole yellowfin tunas in their bellies that weighed well over 50 pounds. And besides the billfishes, every other gamefish in blue water likes live bait. Dolphin (fish), for example, will eagerly attack live shrimp.

All the livebaiting techniques covered for inshore fishing also apply to blue water. But for those anglers deliberately seeking billfish, there are some special considerations.

For one, live baits are most effective wherever billfish are concentrated in a specific area by the presence of natural food, and if there aren't so many sharks in the same area that they quickly become a nuisance. And while this may seem a bit outlandish to someone looking for his or her first billfish, even large sailfish (especially in the Pacific) can be a problem if marlin are your target, because they too will attack marlin-size live baits.

Specific areas where baitfish are likely to concentrate include the waters over seamounts or deep dropoffs; along the edge of a color change, especially offshore from the mouths of rivers, inlets, or harbors that have strong outflowing currents; the vicinity of sargassum weedlines or other flotsam. (In open offshore water, current shear can cause upwelling and/or a sharp temperature gradient.)

Many areas of billfish concentration are already well known, and more are being found every year. They include the Challenger Bank off Bermuda, Hannibal Bank off the island of Coiba in Panama, the La Guaira Bank off Venezuela, Key West's fabled "Wall," the Hump off Islamorada in the Florida Keys, the dropoff north of St. Thomas in the U.S. Virgin Islands, and the Nipple and Elbow south of Pensacola, Florida. There are countless others where baitfish and the trophy predators that feed on them congregate at certain times of the year.

Live baits that do well for marlin include of course the various bonitos and small tunas, mackerel, and dolphin (fish). In fact every year off the Florida Keys in the spring or summer, the word will come over the VHF radio that someone has just lost a small dolphin to a very big marlin that suddenly materialized from beneath a patch of sargassum to inhale the angler's supper as it was being reeled to the boat.

Experienced anglers nearby will usually rush to the area, catch a small dolphin, rig it with a giant hook on a Dacron bridle, and power drift it alongside the line of seaweed. And sometimes a blue marlin will rise to the live bait, an awesome sight suddenly appearing from the depths, and grab it. But this time the angler is ready, and with a little luck the big billfish doesn't get away.

Diving birds show the way to active schools of baitfish and feeding game-fish, such as the large bigeye tuna shown here.

The preferred system for livebaiting marlin is a Dacron bridle. You'll need a heavy monofilament leader (300- to 500-pound test) crimped to a suitable billfish hook, the size of which is dictated by the size of the baits you anticipate using. For bullet bonito-size baits, a 10/0 or 12/0 hook will do. For larger skipjacks, little tunnys, or other large tuna baits, a 13/0 or 14/0 hook is not at all too large. A 5- to 6-inch diameter loop of 20- to 50-pound-test braided Dacron is tied to the bend of the hook, and the other end of the Dacron loop is threaded through the eye of a rigging needle. You can also make a serviceable rigging needle by twisting a small loop into one end of a 5-inch length of #12 wire.

The live bait is brought quickly and gently to the boat—tunas are notoriously delicate and bleed easily from any slight rip in their skin or mouth. The fish is then carefully swung aboard, unhooked gently (single hooks are preferred over trebles for bait-fishing), and cradled in or on a wet towel. Covering the eyes will often calm it down.

The rigging needle, with the end of the Dacron loop through its eye, is passed through the eye socket of the baitfish at the 11 o'clock position (1:00 o'clock if the fish is on its left side). It is this precise location that offers no bony resistance to its penetration. After the needle has drawn the end of the Dacron loop through the eye socket, the hook point is passed through the loop several times, until it comes up tight against the top of the fish's head. This causes the hook to ride point-up against the bait's forehead. With practice, the entire procedure should take no longer than ten seconds, and the bait can be returned to the water in lively condition.

Once the bait has been put back in the water, the boat is kept moving slowly ahead in gear until the strike occurs. Most anglers stay close to the rod, ready to freespool the line for a five- to ten-second dropback before setting the hook.

Sailfish are usually fished with smaller baits and sometimes different techniques. Most anglers use goggle-eyes (a small jack), pinfish, balao (ballyhoo), pilchards, or small blue runners, along with light tackle and small, short-shank hooks.

Baits are drifted or fished from kites or breakaway styrofoam floats over the outer edge of the offshore reefs, usually in between 80 and 180 feet of water, although sometimes out as far as the 300-foot depth contour if you find a current edge, likely looking weedline, or rip. Baits are simply hooked through the lips or back (forward of the dorsal), and fished in freespool. The boat is kicked in and out of gear, or drifts with the wind, with just enough motion to maintain orientation and keep the baits at a suitable distance.

Not wishing to gut-hook the sailfish, most anglers favor little or no dropback. Most fish will be mouth-hooked if the angler is attentive enough.

Yet another billfish livebaiting technique is practiced from Southern California to the tip of the Baja Peninsula. The quarry is the striped marlin. Anglers store live frigate mackerel or mullet in big wells and interrupt their trolling activity to cast these baits whenever tailing striped marlin are spotted.

Some boats have even gone so far as to mount live wells on their foredecks, in order to allow anglers to cast their baits from a better vantage point. It takes considerable skill to cast a mackerel with a conventional reel, placing the bait where the marlin can spot it, but not so close as to spook the fish with the splashdown. About 40 to 50 feet seems to be the right distance.

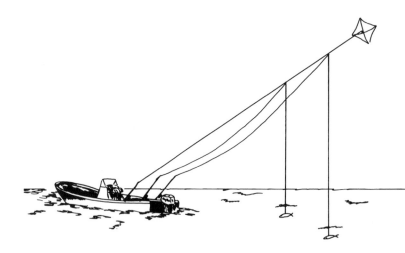

Fishing with a kite. A square kite, especially made for this purpose, is used to suspend one or two baits so that they remain just below the surface with no line or leader showing. Developed for sailfishing on the east coast of Florida, this system is also effective for many other wary game-fish. The fishing lines are held by release clips that allow them to come free at the strike.

The distinctive tail of a striped marlin on the surface is an ideal target for a carefully presented trolled or live bait.

Chapter 20

CHUMMING AND CHUNKING

All gamefish respond to chumming, some more readily than others. We have had sailfish come into our chum slick on a number of occasions, and have even heard of marlin doing the same in other deepwater situations. Chumming has for decades been the traditional way to attract big sharks worldwide. Also reef fish, such as cobia, snappers, and groupers, and the travelers, including bluefish and all of the mackerels. Bonefish rush to chum on the flats, and even the wary permit sticks its nose into the slick at irregular intervals. So do all of the members of the tuna family, which also respond to a variation on the chumming theme known as "chunking."

How well chumming will work for you depends upon how clearly you understand what has to be accomplished. Toss out too much chum, for example, and all the fish will happily chase the floating mass downcurrent so far they might never return. Dispense too little, and the fish you want most may not show up.

Starting with the basics, chumming is accomplished in either of two ways: from a fixed location, where the chum slick is carried away from the source by a current; or from a drifting boat so that the slick is now a trail left by the boat's motion.

The fixed location can be a pier, seawall, jetty, or other spot on shore, or an anchored boat. There *must* be enough current to carry the scent and food particles a good distance, otherwise the probability of success diminishes considerably. Chumming from an unanchored boat obviously requires a source of energy to move the vessel, usually wind, otherwise the results are the same as anchored with no current.

In some situations it takes a lot of "real food" in the slick to bring in the bigger fish, while for others the scent alone is sufficient. Tides and other current play a big role. So does time of year and location.

Many oldtimers consider the process an art, born of experience and understanding.

One of the most interesting and effective chumming and chunking operations we've ever seen is carried out all summer long in the exceptionally clear blue waters surrounding Bermuda. The most prolific spots there are the downcurrent edges of two deep major offshore banks, Challenger and Argus. The boat is anchored on the bank, near the edge,

Chumming with whole small baitfish and cut pieces of larger baitfish is effective, if done properly.

and allowed to hang downcurrent over deep water on a very long anchor rope. The anchor may be in 200 feet or less of water, and the boat may have 400 feet or more under the keel. All species of blue water and reef fish found in those waters may appear in the chum line.

The process begins with just a little bit of ground chum, a "starter," to bring in schools of small bonitos, locally called robins. These fish are caught on a handline or light rod and reel (a lot of fun!) and immediately converted into fresh chum and chunks, further increasing the numbers of baitfish around the boat and before long drawing gamefish from great distances. Deepwater pelagics like yellowfin (Allison) tuna, blackfin tuna, and wahoo are regular attendees. Occasionally a marlin may appear briefly. From the nearby reefs come amberjacks, horseye

Big yellowfin tuna feeding in the chum line.

jacks of unusually large size, snappers, barracuda, and sharks. You never know for sure what species will show up, but it rarely takes long to get good numbers of big fish in the chum line.

The ground chum and slick brings the smaller fish, but it is the chunks, sizable pieces of fresh fish about half the size of a clenched fist, that really get the attention of the bigger tuna. It has never ceased to amaze us that very large yellowfin tuna, some over 150 pounds, which always seem to feed at full throttle when chasing live baitfish in the open sea, can slow down and actually take up feeding stations in the chum slick like freshwater trout during an insect hatch. Before long a definite feeding rhythm is established as they rise repeatedly to chunks of fresh fish, tossed overboard at deliberately spaced intervals. At some point it is simply a matter of substituting a bait with a hook in it, or an artificial that somewhat resembles a chunk of fish.

This is where fly fishing for yellowfin tuna started, because the situation is ideal for a smooth bait-and-switch routine. Anglers have taken this species up to 81 pounds on tarpon-sized fly gear, and hooked much larger. Big reels with 500 or more yards of 30-pound Dacron backing are called for, but sometimes even that isn't enough. We recall hooking one giant, well over 100 pounds, on such tackle. It went down like a safe tossed off the top of a tall building, and never did stop.

Most of the yellowfins in a Bermuda chum slick will range from 30 to 80 pounds, and a 50-pounder on a tarpon weight (12-weight) fly rod or casting rod is tougher than a 100-pound silver king. Even the strike is unreal; the fish rises leisurely to take the fly, then vanishes before your eyes the instant the hook is set, along with hundreds of yards of line, while you pray you won't be spooled before the tuna finally runs out of steam.

Deepwater chumming and chunking for tuna from a drifting boat, where the depth is too great or the current too strong for anchoring, is highly effective in areas where there is evidence of the fish. They might be seen free-jumping or escorted by a flock of hungry birds as they chase baitfish. And even if there is no visible evidence of their presence, just choosing the right area at the right time of year can be sufficient to get the ball rolling.

In this situation, the best chum is often live sardines or other small baitfish, or a mix of ground chum and live sardines, or even a mix of live and dead baitfish. Big dolphin(fish) and wahoo also often join this party, but the primary target is usually

Angler in the foreground has just landed a 50-pound yellowfin tuna on fly tackle; the angler in the background is still fighting a big one.

blackfin, yellowfin, bluefin, or bigeye tuna. The drifting boat covers a lot of ground, eventually creating a chum slick that is several miles in length if the conditions are ideal. Many anglers drift chunks or small, whole baitfish far back in the slick, because on some days the tuna seem to be reluctant to come very close to the boat. Those using artificials, especially heavy jigs, can fish them deep, up to 200 feet down, either "pure" or tipped with a strip of natural bait. There are times when this is by far the most productive method.

Chunk baits, whether fished from an anchored or drifting boat, should be placed both shallow and deep unless it is obvious that all feeding activity is near the surface. And even then the smaller fish may be up high, and the larger deep. A good starting point would be to fish one or two near the surface, without any weight, plus at least one with enough weight to go down at least 50 feet or so, and another

perhaps to 100 feet. If nothing works at any of these depths, try deeper still. it's not unusual to hook tuna at 200 feet or more.

Going deep requires weight. Sometimes a lot of weight. A few ounces fastened directly to the line are seldom a bother, but when more than that is necessary, some sort of release weights are needed. There are a lot of do-it-yourself variations on that theme around, including weights that slide down the line almost to the fish's mouth immediately after hookup, but one we've used successfully is the downrigger. The bait is typically positioned 15 to 20 feet behind the weight. Some anglers even use the weight without the downrigger, tying it to ³⁄₁₆-inch braided line and manipulating it by hand. That's a lot of work, and its effectiveness is reduced if there's a lot of current. Simple manual downriggers aren't expensive; they're also compact, light, and easily portable. We've successfully used C-clamps with them on many boats that aren't equipped with 'rigger plates.

Often any type of chumming and/or chunking is a feast or famine situation, but if you have the patience to stick with it as long as possible, the rewards can be great.

Fishermen seeking yellowtail snapper in the Florida Keys and throughout the Caribbean often mix sand with their ground chum if the currents are running a bit faster than they prefer. The added weight causes it to sink faster. Yellowtails are a reef species, most commonly found near the bottom, and the best fishing for the bigger fish is often in 80 to 120 feet of water. If the chum reaches their depth too far from the boat, they won't follow it upstream far enough to be caught.

On the other hand, anglers and guides fishing the shallows of the Florida flats for bonefish find chumming very productive in those spots where there's current to carry the scent far enough. In this case the prime ingredient is small pieces of very fresh shrimp, but chopped squid also works. Capt. Bill Curtis of Miami uses a hand-operated kitchen vegetable chopper, the kind that has four blades attached to a spring-loaded pushrod housed in a small glass jar, to instantly convert a handful of whole live shrimp into thumbnail-sized chunks. The pieces are scattered over a white spot on the flat just an easy cast downcurrent, and before long fish begin to show.

The prime targets are of course bonefish and permit, but others always appear too. Cowfish, barracuda, sharks, rays, and numerous small scavengers are quick to take advantage of the free buffet. In order to keep the scent going, more chopped shrimp must be added about every twenty minutes.

Live bait makes great chum in many situations, King mackerel, big snappers, bluefish, and many others lose all sense of caution when live sardines or other small baitfish are so used. Obviously this requires a big live well and copious quantities of bait, but the effect is deadly. The best way to get that many sardines, glass minnows, or other suitable small baitfish is by using a cast net, hoop net, or small hand seine. Just be sure to check local regulations before using *any* net; most states at least restrict *where* they can be used, if not also by size and/or seasons.

Chumming can also be used to attract baitfish, especially the type that school, like sardines, balao, pinfish, blue runners, etc. A handy "chum" that you can keep on hand indefinitely without refrigeration is canned sardines or fish-flavored cat food. Buy the cheapest, because it is usually the most odorous. If you choose sardines, get the type packed in water or oil, not in mustard or any other sauce. A small can of sardines can be extended considerably by kneading bread or dry oatmeal with it in a bucket, adding just enough water to make a really moist mix. One loaf of

Freshly cut pieces of live shrimp are excellent chum for many species, especially bonefish, red drum, and yellowtail snapper.

A cast net is a good way to collect your own live bait. Check local regulations before using any net.

bread per can is about right. Even mackerel, blue-fish, and snappers will often respond to this type of chum.

You can use a big can of cat food alone by just punching a few holes in it and letting it hang a foot or two below the surface. This also works with oily sardines, but two or three cans may be needed to get enough of a slick going. The nice thing about this "quickie" chum is that it can be kept aboard indefi-nitely until used—as long as the cans are stored some place where they won't rust through.

One prevalent problem with using chum is that it often tends to be messy. In most areas the accepted practice is to cut the pieces as they are used, right on a transom cutting board. Buckets of water must be used constantly to wash the quickly accumulated gurry overboard, which also adds to the chum slick, otherwise the cockpit soon acquires a strong odor of dead and decomposing fish.

Chum is readily available in many bait shops or marinas, either in large cans, cartons, or frozen blocks. The frozen blocks are usually preferable over

the canned or freeze-dried variety in terms of fresh-ness, but they obviously are more difficult to keep. Some anglers mix the two, placing the block in a net-type laundry bag and hanging it over the side to thaw and dispense slowly. The canned or dried chum can be mixed with water and kept handy in a bucket, to be added by hand as needed.

Still, fresh chum is the most effective of all, except for perhaps live sardines in some instances, but con-stant effort is the price of keeping a good slick going.

A highly favored type of chum in some areas is "net trash" from shrimp boats. This is everything caught during the drags other than the targeted spe-cies of shrimp. It typically consists of small fish, crabs, other types of shrimp with no commercial value, etc. Since commercial shrimping is a night-time operation, the nets and decks are cleaned at dawn. If you're not there at first light to negotiate for the net trash, it's dumped over the side.

Most shrimp boats anchor for the day so the crew can sleep, and sometimes the spot they choose is also a good one for fishing. Especially if a lot of net clean-

A block of frozen ground chum in a mesh bag makes an excellent dispenser. The block will last for several hours.

The net trash from shrimp boats is effective chum.

ing routinely takes place in that general area. Often superb fishing action can be had while tied up to the stern of the anchored shrimper. Some of the best blackfin tuna, king mackerel, snapper, and cobia fishing we've ever enjoyed came about this way.

One of the advantages of chumming is that you can often select your target. Individual fish, especially the larger sizes, frequently adopt specific behavior patterns once they settle down in the free lunch line. Often their reactions to the type of chum and its placement become cyclic and somewhat predictable.

Occasionally, while you're chumming over a wreck or other bottom structure, there will be an exceptionally large fish in the bunch that comes up, such as a big cobia in a school of smaller cobias. As long as there's a lot of chum available, the smaller fish may consistently beat the big one to the baited hook. At such times the answer might be to sharply decrease the flow of chum for a minute or two, then try to direct a cast close to the bigger fish while the others are scattered all over the place wondering where the food disappeared. If your timing is right, it works frequently.

As effective as chumming can be, it won't produce everywhere. It seldom works very well if you simply start dumping chum at random, with little or no thought to where the fish may be or how the currents, if there in fact are any at that location, will disperse the slick. To be most effective, at least the odor must reach the general area where the fish are hanging out, or leave an unbroken scent trail that extends far enough to be crossed by cruising fish. It is quite possible to pour copious quantities of the stuff over a very wide, completely barren area and never attract the first fish.

Chumming carries no guarantees, just a substantially increased potential for angling success. It won't always work, even where there are great numbers of fish. Sometimes they just don't seem to be hungry, no matter how much you dispense and how good the chum may be. Tides can make a difference, too. So if you create a good slick and keep it going for a reasonable length of time, and still get no takers, don't spend the entire day there. Go elsewhere and try again. Usually one or two hours is sufficient to see if it's going to work in any given area.

Chapter 21

HOOKING, LANDING, AND RELEASING GAMEFISH

As it is now more widely recognized that good conservation practices are essential to the future of sportfishing, properly handling and releasing our premium gamefish has become more important. There's really no sense in killing a fish you cannot eat, or bringing home more edible fish at one time than you can practically use. A released fish's chances for survival depend a great deal upon your skill as an angler: how well you can cleanly hook the fish in the mouth (not in the gut!), how quickly you can land it, and whether or not you use the proper techniques to revive and release it. The fate of that fish is truly in your hands.

Gamefish should be considered a recyclable resource. There's no reason why more than one angler cannot have the pleasure of catching and releasing that same fish. And there is also no reason why most fish must be killed to be mounted. The better taxidermists already have precision molds of all species in just about all sizes, and the finished product from a mold mount is usually better than a skin mount. It will certainly last a lot longer, too.

HOOKING FISH

One of the most important items in your tackle bag is some sort of device for sharpening hooks. A file or small stone will do just fine. There are also some pretty good battery-powered sharpeners on the market, but they are bulky, and while you might want to use them for putting a quick point on a lot of hooks in one sitting, the final touch should always be done with a file or flat stone to achieve the most effective point just before the hook goes in the water. Some electromechanical sharpeners create a conical point, certainly far better than no sharp point at all, but with a file or stone you can shape the point precisely as you wish. We're partial to a point that has a diamond shape in cross section and thus provides four cutting edges. Others favor a triangular point with three cutting edges, or a spear point with two. Regardless of which you choose, two to four cutting edges always provides the best penetration.

Many angels prefer a small file, especially the ignition point variety. They're inexpensive and will cut even hard stainless steel quite well. With a little care (i.e. WD-40) they'll last about five or six months. But any small file, or even a stone, will do as long as you have it *readily* available. Hook points need constant attention, more so when fly fishing because they don't get a lot of penetration assistance from the angler during the strike. A long, relatively soft fly rod isn't as good a hook-setting device as a short, stiff baitcasting stick.

Before any hook can penetrate significantly it must first be so sharp that just a little pressure is sufficient to make it hang somewhere inside the fish's mouth. One good definition of sharp means a point that cannot slide across your thumbnail without hanging up. Testing it with your fingertip really doesn't prove a whole lot, except maybe to let you know if it really is dull.

Keeping a good point on the hook means checking it constantly, each time before it goes in the water, if you're fishing for concrete-mouthed biggies like tarpon and sailfish. Just the slightest brush against something hard, like the gunwale of the boat or the bony mouth of the last fish you missed, is often just enough to take the razor edge off the point. Having a file at your fingertips is a must so that you can instantly touch up the point whenever it's needed.

Some fish have very hard mouths. Some have soft, easily torn mouth tissues. Many are more like thick rubber. And thus different fish require somewhat different hook-setting procedures. Among the soft-mouthed fishes are seatrout, lookdowns, and many small panfish. A tarpon or billfish has a mouth like concrete, and a bonefish or cobia is typical of the rubber-lipped variety. In all cases the hook should always be as sharp as possible so that it penetrates easily instead of tearing. But there are some differences in how you should set that hook.

To set the hook in a soft-mouthed fish, simply lift the rod gently to tighten the line. A rubber-lipped fish requires more effort in the form of a more deliberate hook-setting swing of the rod either vertically or horizontally. But when it comes to consistently hooking the hard-mouthed variety, you must be ready to put maximum effort into the task. This means just about all the pressure the line will tolerate without breaking.

Start with the rod pointed directly at the fish, not off to one side so that you have very little arm-swinging room left to strike with. All of the slack should be out of the line at the instant of setting the hook.

Probably the most common mistake most new-comers make in saltwater fishing is striking *too soon!* If you do absolutely *nothing* until you feel the fish pulling hard against the rod, you'll hook more fish by far than the other guy with hair-trigger striking reflexes. If the fish takes the bait with a lot of slack in the line, by all means keep reeling until you feel the line go tight and the weight of the fish on the other end.

Lure fishermen have little time to think about setting the hook after the strike. There's no drop-back involved. It's just a matter of getting a tight line and

Flats guide Capt. Bill Curtis of Miami carefully releases a bonefish so that it will be around to fight another day.

The sideways strike, as shown here by angler Dick Moore, is the most effective way to hook gamefish if you're not sitting in a fighting chair.

applying pressure. Anglers using bait sometimes have to allow a little time for the fish to "chew on it" before setting the hook. But allowing the fish so much time with the bait that it deliberately becomes gut-hooked is poor sportsmanship. So is the use of treble hooks with anything but artificial lures, a practice now thankfully outlawed in some states.

If you know what species you're fishing for, you can program your mental computer in advance for the proper striking sequence. You can hook that seatrout by just getting the line tight with a turn or two of the reel handle. And you can also hook a bonefish on a small fly by just holding the fly line in your hand, squeezing it tightly for just a second or so as it tries to pull away, but not so long there's a risk of breaking the tippet.

You should do the same for a tarpon or sailfish, but in this case you'll rapidly accelerate the pressure on the hook point by sweeping the rod sideways (*not* upwards!) with a sharp, jerking motion. As soon as the sideways sweep is completed, focus *all* of your concentration on keeping the line as drum tight as possible, but of course not quite tight enough to break it. Maintain this hard pressure as long as possible, always ready for the violent reaction that will follow.

A few years ago we conducted some experiments on striking techniques. We compared jabbing the hook with exerting a constant pressure. Repeatedly yanking the rod back hard many times to set the hook is perceived by many anglers to be like trying to drive a nail into a board with a hammer. It seems logical enough, but our experiments with scientific measuring devices clearly proved otherwise.

Jabbing only produces hard pressure on the hook point for a fraction of a second. Most of the time there is little or no pressure on the point at all. And if you happen to yank back just a little too hard while the fish is surging away, the likelihood of breaking the line increases considerably.

In order for any hook—barbed or barbless—to penetrate far enough to hold properly, the point must first "hang" somewhere inside that fish's mouth. If this occurs, the odds increase sharply that the fish will assist the point's penetration through its own frantic efforts to escape. That's important, because some fish have a mouth so hard that you have little chance of completely setting the hook without this assistance.

The advantage in keeping hard, constant pressure on the hook rather than jabbing is that whenever the point slides into some softer place, there will be enough pressure to cause the point to begin to penetrate deeply. To do this you simply swing the rod sharply sideways, add some finger pressure to the reel spool if necessary, and concentrate fiercely on maintaining as much pressure as possible without risk of breaking the line. Once the fish appears to be hooked and surges away, jabbing may now even be of some help in burying the point a little deeper. Strike only against the reel's drag for this maneuver.

A big-game angler with heavy tackle must rely upon the forward motion of the boat to provide the constant pressure, and in that case jabbing may help push the point in a bit. A seasoned skipper will also throttle up quickly to reduce the possibility of slack line occurring during the hooking process.

FIGHTING THE FISH

Most experienced light-tackle anglers don't use a lot of drag with fast fish. A good rule of thumb is about one-quarter of the line's breaking strength for fast, jumping fish, and one-third to one-half for fishing around rocks or other structure. Just because you're using, for example, 20-pound-test line and the fish weighs only 15, that doesn't mean you don't have to let it take any line. Many fish can exert considerably more than their own body weight against the line under certain conditions. Then there is at least some friction between even the smoothest rod guides and the line, which adds to the total resistance of the line as the fish tows it through the water. Water adds yet more resistance, which increases both with the fish's speed and the length of line being dragged. And finally, the resistance of the reel's drag increases as the diameter of the layers of line on it decrease. It doesn't take a physicist to guess what happens if you apply too much pressure at the reel while all of this is going on.

Line drag becomes even more important to the flycaster because of the relatively large diameter of the fly line. In this instance, a good rule of thumb for all fast fish, no matter how big, is to set the drag as light as possible. Just a pound or two, enough to prevent the reel from backlashing when the fish suddenly rockets out of there. With light tackle, you aren't going to make the fish stop until it decides to on its own. When the fish halts and the time comes to apply more drag, use careful finger pressure on the spool or rim for the needed extra resistance.

We constantly hear talk about reducing or eliminating line stretch for better fish hooking and fighting, but our experience doesn't bear this out. You should think of line stretch as an ally, an effective shock absorber, just like the bend of the rod. Even when striking a fish, it allows you to maintain a lot of constant pressure for many seconds while trying to get the hook buried.

Lots of line stretch can even help in fighting a big fish, especially a big *jumping* fish. Some flyrodders even insert 100 feet of monofilament line between the fly line and the no-stretch Dacron backing for this reason. The mono should be the same test strength as the rest of the backing; it acts as a long, soft shock absorber whenever the fish makes any sudden surges or jumps.

Constant hard pressure is the key to beating any big fish on any form of light tackle. The only time you should let up is while the fish is running or jumping. Allowing it to rest, even for only a minute or two so you can take a breather, only prolongs the fight by many times the length of those rest periods. Make the hooked fish work hard for every inch of line it gets, either through speed and acrobatics against light resistance, or by pulling slowly against a lot of manually applied drag at the reel.

While the fish is off in the distance, changing rod angles doesn't effectively change the direction of pull. If switching from straight up to horizontal on one side or the other from time to time is more comfortable, there's no harm in that unless doing so might allow the line to snag something on the boat or in the water. But when the fish gets close, say within less than 100 feet, that's the time to get "down and dirty."

Down and dirty means frequently changing the rod position from an upward angle to horizontal or even a lower angle than that. Even so low that the tip is several feet under the surface at times, if you're wading or in a small boat. During all of this the angler exerts as much pressure on the fish as the line will tolerate, and frequently changes the rod angle from one side to the other. It's not a complicated procedure and with a little practice soon becomes second nature.

Sooner or later, through this sort of change-of-direction pressure, you'll eventually be able to stop the tiring fish from swimming forward at all by deliberately pulling the rod very slowly backward. Once any fish can no longer swim forward under its own power, it is beaten. At that point some of them even give up so easily you get the impression that its spirit (at least its will to fight) is broken. At any rate, stopping that fish from swimming forward with a deliberate backward pull is the control point every angler should strive for.

LANDING AND RELEASING

We'll assume at this point you plan to release the fish alive. The discussion that follows is based upon that assumption. Otherwise a net is sufficient for landing the smaller fish you wish to keep, and a body gaff for others too large for the net.

The way you release the fish will determine its chances for survival. Handle it with great care, especially if you wish to take a photograph as a memento of the event. Always use wet hands with any fish that can be easily lifted clear of the water, but by all means have the camera ready to shoot *before* removing it from the water. Take a few shots of it in the water alongside the boat, then a couple of quickies with it lifted out. Then put it back as quickly as possible.

A big fish may be easily injured by taking it out of the water. Some marine biologists have expressed the opinion that holding it up by the jaw with a release gaff may cause internal damage—not damage done by the gaff itself but rather by the entire body weight hanging unsupported. The same applies to lifting a fish with your fingers inside its gillplates, with the additional risk of doing serious damage to the sensitive gills. If you feel compelled to remove the fish from the water, at least allow as much of its weight as possible to rest upon some smooth surface of the boat, and get it back overboard as soon as possible.

Any fish exhausted after a long fight needs a little TLC to get going again. The easiest way is by pulling or pushing it gently forward through the water, thereby accelerating the flow of oxygenated water across its gills. If it is allowed to sink to the bottom immobile, the odds are great it will not survive.

If possible, always wait until it regains enough strength to try to pull free. Once it can obviously swim, let it go. Many anglers add a gentle knuckle rap right where the tail joins the body; this seems to stimulate its swimming ability noticeably.

How the fish is landed also makes a difference. Smaller fish can be netted, if necessary, but that procedure does carry some risk of eye damage. Better to hold it in the water and gently remove the hook. And best yet is to simply reach down and remove the hook with pliers or a hook remover without ever touching the fish. Even big fish like tarpon can be released this way if thoroughly beaten. If there are no teeth to be dealt with, holding the fish by the lower jaw while reviving it works just fine. Any procedure that does not disturb the body's mucous

coating (and thus make it more susceptible to bacterial infection) improves its survival potential.

A study piece of string makes a handy pocket hook-puller that works if the hook is not too far inside the fish's mouth. A 12-inch piece of ¹⁄₁₆- to ¹⁄₈-inch braided nylon or 80- to 100-pound-test monofilament is perfect. We prefer the mono over the braid, by the way. Tie one end to the middle of a short piece of wood dowel, ³⁄₈ to ½ inch thick, to make a convenient handle. Tie a loop just big enough to slip easily over the dowel in the other end. To use, just pass the "puller" line around the leader and slide the small end loop over the wood handle. Grasp the handle in one hand with the "puller" line between the two middle fingers, and slide the big loop thus formed in it down to the bend of the hook. Now push firmly down and away from you with the hand holding the leader as you yank upward firmly with the hand holding the puller. The combined effect of these two separate hand motions will be to rapidly rotate the hook and yank it out backward in an upward direction.

A small gaff or even a piece of stiff stainless steel wire with a tiny crook in one end will yank the fishhook just as well as the string. It works so well that most of the time you don't even have to touch the fish, regardless of its size.

There is also an excellent stainless-steel hook remover that works with all types of hooks, including trebles, even if the hooks are way down inside the fish's mouth. At one end is a set of serrated jaws for grasping the hook, and a squeeze-type pistol grip at the other end to manipulate the jaws. It comes in two sizes, 9½ and 6 inches long (Hookout Inc., Columbia, PA 17512). We've been using a Hookout for years, and it has successfully extricated many plugs from deep inside the mouths of such toughies as 100-pound tarpon.

A rope gaff can be used to land and release a fish if it's too big to handle any other way, but always use it with care. The small puncture wound it makes in the lower jaw membrane isn't likely to do serious damage, as long as the point doesn't penetrate anything else. *Never* insert the point from the outside; it is best to introduce it gently from inside the mouth. Don't jam the point home with unnecessary force, or yank the fish's head suddenly upward, and its reaction to this restraint will be far less violent.

Most anglers make their own inexpensive rope gaffs out of a large saltwater fishhook with its barb mashed flat and a suitable loop of braided nylon through the eye. The size of the fish you will be dealing with determines the size of the hook. A short

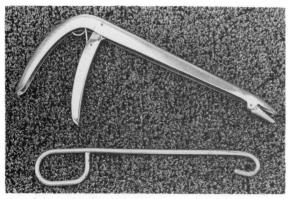

Stainless-steel Baker Hookout at top allows the angler to reach deep into the mouth of a large fish and safely remove the hooks without risk of injury. The homemade hook puller at bottom is of ⅛-inch stainless steel and only works when the hook is in or close to the lips.

piece of vinyl tubing on the rope handle will protect the point from damage, and you from the point.

Many saltwater fish can be quieted by simply rolling them over on their backs and pinning them gently against your leg (if wading) or the side of the boat (if conditions permit).

Even fish with big teeth can be handled by hand if reasonable care is exercised. A barracuda has a thick lower jawbone, sufficient for a good handhold from the outside. The bigger the fish, the larger this "handle." Small-mouthed toothy critters like mackerel can often be tailed, usually by hand. Wear a wet cotton glove for any of this, if you can. It's easier on the fish's protective body coating.

All billfish have a natural handle. Use gloves to protect your own skin from its very abrasive surface. A long gaff can even be used effectively to land billfish without ever penetrating any part of the body. Just reach out and place the hook over the bill, and the fish is easily guided to boatside.

If somehow the fish does get hooked in the gills, it has a better chance of survival if you can manage to cut the barb off before *carefully* removing the hook. Otherwise, just cut the leader and leave it there. Or if it's a bulky lure, cut the hooks off and leave them while removing the lure. You can always put new hooks on it later.

You don't even have to kill a fish to weigh it. There are plenty of good hand scales on the market, suitable for fish up to 50 pounds. You can even weigh it in the landing net and then subtract the weight of the net after you've let it go. If it's too large for a hand scale, use two pieces of line or a tape measure to get its length (from lower jaw to fork of tail, but excluding the bill if its a sail, marlin, or swordfish) and girth at the widest point of the body. The formula below will yield a very close estimate:

$$\text{Weight (lbs)} = \frac{\text{Girth squared} \times \text{Length (inches)}}{800}$$

Some anglers even carry an inexpensive electronic calculator to crunch the numbers.

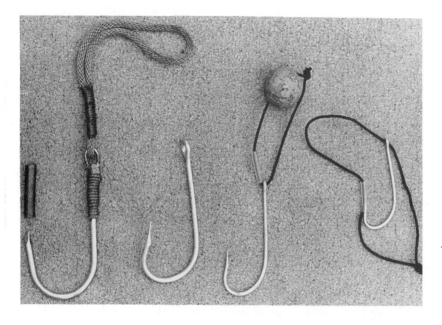

Rope gaffs (from left): a 3-inch stainless gaff hook, a 14/0 long-shank plated saltwater hook that can be adapted as shown by the next two pocket-size "gaffs." With or without a float, the small braided line has a piece of vinyl tubing to protect the user when stowed. Never wrap the rope around the wrist for lip-gaffing large fish; the loop should be large enough to go around the thumb and the back of the hand before crossing the palm.

THE INTERNATIONAL GAME FISH ASSOCIATION

Celebrating its 50th birthday in 1990, the IGFA is today recognized world-wide as the keeper of all gamefish records for fresh and salt water. Actually it does a lot more than just keep records. It has become perhaps *the* most respected spokesman for the recreational angling world. In addition, the facilities at its headquarters in Ft. Lauderdale, Florida, hold the largest collection of data on recreational fishing.

Included are a library with over 8,000 books on fishes and recreational angling, a vast collection of fishing-related photographs, films, and video tapes, and a museum of angling artifacts and memorabilia. If you'd like to see the type of big-game tackle Zane Grey used to capture giant marlin and swordfish, for example, this is the place to go.

Individuals and clubs are invited to become members of the IGFA. For as little as $20 per year, you receive the bimonthly newsletter The International Angler, as well as the annual *World Record Game Fishes*, and more. The annual is over 300 pages long and contains a complete listing of all world records in all line and tackle classes, plus interesting articles by well-known outdoor authors, and a complete list of all angling rules.

The IGFA also maintains a number of very special "clubs," such as the 5-to-1, 10-to-1, 15-to-1, and 20-to-1 clubs. The entry fee is $25, and membership is open to anyone catching a gamefish that weighs 5, 10, 15, or 20 times more than their line's pound test. For example, an angler who caught a 100-pounder on 20-pound test would be eligible for the 5-to-1 club. Then there's the elite Thousand Pound Club, where line test doesn't count, but the fish has to be a marlin, tuna, or qualified species of shark weighing 1,000 pounds or more.

For more information, contact the International Game Fish Association, 3000 East Las Olas Blvd., Ft. Lauderdale, FL 33316–1616. (305) 467–0161.

During the past few years the IGFA has expanded its line and tackle class categories considerably. And new species of fish are being added to the record listings every year, so if you catch something that you feel belongs in the books and isn't already there, fill out an application and submit it. You might get lucky.

FOR FURTHER READING

Since we obviously cannot cover all aspects of modern saltwater angling in a book of this size, for those of you who would like to learn more about specific techniques, we recommend the following books.

BAITS, RIGS, AND TACKLE, *by Vic Dunaway*. Wickstrom Publishers, Inc., 5901 SW 74 Street, Miami, FL 33143. All the fine details of bait and tackle rigging.

COMPLETE SURFCASTER, THE, *by Boyd Pfeiffer*. Nick Lyons Books, 31 West 21 Street, New York, NY 10010. Comprehensive coverage of gear and technique.

DOING IT STAND-UP STYLE, *by Nick Curcione*. Outdoor Ventures, Ltd., 1921 E. Carnegie, Suite N, Santa Ana, CA 92705. A guide to long-range West Coast party-boat fishing and stand-up tackle.

FISHERMAN'S BOATING BOOK, *by Bob Stearns*. Nick Lyons Books, 31 West 21 Street, New York, NY 10010. Detailed practical boating information for the angler.

McCLANE'S FIELD GUIDE TO SALTWATER FISHES OF NORTH AMERICA, *by A. J. McClane*. Henry Holt & Company, 115 W 18 Street, New York, NY 10011. Excellent coverage of saltwater gamefishes with color illustrations.

PAN ANGLING'S WORLD GUIDE TO FLY FISHING, *by Jim C. Chapralis*. Pan Angling Publishing Co., 180 N. Michigan Avenue, Chicago, IL 60601. Great spots worldwide for the fly fisherman.

PRACTICAL FISHING KNOTS, *by Lefty Kreh and Mark Sosin*. Nick Lyons Books, 31 West 21 Street, New York, NY 10010. Most of the important angling knots are explained here.

SALT WATER FLY PATTERNS, *by Lefty Kreh*, Maral, Inc., 2700 West Orangethorpe, Fullerton, CA 92633. An up-to-date listing of productive patterns, with color illustrations and tying information.

ISBN	TITLE	PRICE (U.S./Canadian)	X	QTY	=	TOTAL
42351-9	ADVANCED DEER HUNTER'S BIBLE	$12.00/$15.00		____		_____
42221-0	ARCHER'S AND BOWHUNTER'S BIBLE	$12.00/$15.00		____		_____
15155-1	ARCHER'S BIBLE	$11.00/$14.00		____		_____
24690-0	BASS FISHERMAN'S BIBLE (3rd Ed.)	$11.00/$14.00		____		_____
24578-5	CANOER'S BIBLE	$12.00/$15.00		____		_____
19985-6	DEER HUNTER'S BIBLE	$12.00/$15.00		____		_____
42242-3	FLY FISHERMAN'S BIBLE	$12.00/$15.00		____		_____
26223-X	FRESHWATER FISHERMAN'S BIBLE	$12.00/$15.00		____		_____
42383-7	GAME BIRD HUNTER'S BIBLE	$12.00/$15.00		____		_____
24102-X	GOLFER'S BIBLE	$12.00/$15.00		____		_____
18291-0	GUNNER'S BIBLE	$12.00/$15.00		____		_____
18343-7	HORSEMAN'S BIBLE	$12.00/$15.00		____		_____
17219-2	HUNTER'S BIBLE	$9.95/$12.95		____		_____
42224-5	PANFISHERMAN'S BIBLE	$12.00/$15.00		____		_____
23747-2	RIFLEMAN'S BIBLE	$12.00/$15.00		____		_____
18874-9	RUNNER'S BIBLE	$11.00/$14.00		____		_____
26444-5	SALTWATER FISHERMAN'S BIBLE	$12.00/$15.00		____		_____
23907-6	SHOTGUNNER'S BIBLE	$12.00/$15.00		____		_____
13543-2	SKIN DIVER'S BIBLE	$12.00/$15.00		____		_____
26540-9	SNOW SKIER'S BIBLE	$12.00/$15.00		____		_____
41111-1	TROUT AND SALMON FISHERMAN'S BIBLE	$11.00/$14.00		____		_____
42223-7	TURKEY HUNTER'S BIBLE	$12.00/$15.00		____		_____

Shipping and handling (Add $2.50 per order) _____

TOTAL _____

Please send me the titles I have indicated above. I am enclosing $_____. Send check or money order in U.S. funds only (no COD's or cash, please). Please make check payable to Doubleday Consumer Services. Allow 4-6 weeks for delivery. Prices and availability are subject to change without notice.

Name_____

Address_____

City_____State_____Zip_____

Send completed coupon and payment to:
Doubleday Consumer Services
Dept. OB3
2451 South Wolf Road
Des Plaines, IL 60018

OB3/3-94